THE
MARYKNOLL
BOOK
OF
TREASURES

Maryknoll Publications, Maryknoll, N. Y.

THE MARYKNOLL BOOK OF TREASURES

an anthology
of mission literature

EDITED AND SELECTED BY

ALBERT J. NEVINS, M.M.

*Maryknoll's official symbol is the Chi Rho
(pronounced key row). It is composed
of a circle that represents the world
and the first two letters
of Christ's name in Greek. It signifies
"Christ over the world."*

FOREWORD

Over a decade ago Maryknoll produced what was then the first anthology in English of mission literature. We called it *The Maryknoll Golden Book* and it was a great success. We remarked at that time that what most impressed us was the vast amount of excellent material that had to be left out because of lack of room. Some of that material plus many newly found pieces now appear in this second anthology.

THE MARYKNOLL BOOK OF TREASURES is designed for a general readership. Therefore the esoteric and theoretical has been avoided. What this anthology is designed to do is to give reading pleasure. There are stories of triumph and failure, heroism and humor. It is the hope of the editor that the reader will find inspiration here and moments that will touch the heart. There are stories of martyrdom but these are an integral part of mission history. There are stories of simple people whose lives contain a message for us all. Unlike the first volume there is a sampling of authors from the Orient and Africa.

The editor is deeply grateful to all the authors and publishers who have granted the permissions that make this book possible. It is hoped that these stories and articles will be tidbits that will want to make the reader go back to the full source. It is also our hope that this book will give its readers a greater understanding of the vast mission world and its peoples and the desire to assist in the salvation of all men.

Albert J. Nevins, M.M.
Editor

CONTENTS

Poetry

Short Features

SELECTIONS BY AUTHOR:

THE BRIDGE

by Sister Jeanne Marie

Sister froze in panic until the Bunun man came to her rescue.

It hung there, as improbable as a spider's web, symbol of man's hope and daring and of his transience—a bridge. Far up in the mountains of Formosa where the aboriginal Bununo live, it hung, it swung, it swayed across a canyon. In the evening it was cool and cloud-wrapped; at midday it scintillated under the sun. Below it at all times an ominous grey torrent rushed down through the gorge toward the distant rice fields and the ultimate sea; when the rains were done, the rounded rocks emerged to bask like turtles in the emptied bed. Paved with water or with rocks, the chasm looked menacing from above, from the swinging bridge.

The bridge was swinging now, the side to the east tilted a little. Pouring down over faraway Mongolia the winter winds blew strongly out of the northwest; crossing great China they blew steadily on; tearing unchecked over the fuming Formosa strait they beat against the island's mountains and however checked and subdued and turned aside, finally funneled their cunning way through the passes and now washed against the swinging bridge in bursts and backwashes like the sea.

Fifty years ago the bridge might have been made entirely of vines, of lianas, might have looked so much a part of the mountain that you would have thought that two forests had leaned out to link hands across the abyss. But today, having been made over in modern times and in the modern manner, it is up-to-date. It has two steel cables on which, every six feet or so, bamboo cross-ties are fastened. On the cross-ties are laid, not too neatly, not too securely, wooden planks. Hanging about three and a half or four feet above this catwalk on either side are two single wires, one for the right hand, one for the left — guide lines, psychological supports. At least there had been two . . .

Having travelled two hours out of Changhua by pick-up-truck and having held clinic for several hours in Tamaroo, then walked twenty minutes up the mountain, Sister Antonia Maria, Maryknoll Sister and M.D., stood in her white habit with her little black bag in her hand and looked above and beyond the gorge in the direction of her next destination, Shin I Hsiang, "Believe Righteousness Village." She could not see it but she knew that she would find it and its full complement of three hundred inhabitants hidden behind the trees forty minutes' climb ahead. And many of the three hundred people would want and need medical attention.

She turned her eyes from the mountain and looked at the bridge in front of her for the second time. She had no love for swinging bridges.

Behind her came Julie Wong, her clinic helper, a catechist or native teacher, and two Maryknoll Fathers visiting Tamaroo and Shin I Hsiang to instruct, and examine the catechumens — Bunun folk readying themselves by study and practice for baptism. Besides these, there were several Bunun men carrying clinic medicines and supplies and several other aborigines who had casually joined the party going in their direction.

Now everybody stood back where the path ended and the bridge began and waited for her to cross. Walking a swinging bridge alone is easier than walking it with company. Alone there is not opponent rhythm to contend with; there is just the rippling jounce set up by your own tread and the long slow sideward swing under the hand of the wind.

But a recent typhoon had damaged the bridge. Where there should have been two wire hand-holds now there was only one.

And the typhoon had worked some other injury too so that the bridge sagged somewhat towards its western, its weaker side, the quarter from which the wind blew. It was on that same side that the hand, the eye, the mind lacked the support of that single, that silly, that supremely vital wire.

It did no good to stand and stare. Sister Antonia Maria shifted her little black bag from her right to her left hand, felt like a child hesitating before rushing in to jump rope — "making biscuits" as they used to call it at home. She jogged her little black bag up and down in her left hand, and slid her right along the guide wire. One of the Bunun men, a catechumen who had casually joined the group, came forward, took the bag out of her hand and stepped back again. She had a fleeting glance of the prematurely lined face, the wide shoulders, and the high chest that she had come to associate with these mountain men.

At this stage, she thought, I can never make up my mind whether I am the guest of honor or a guinea pig.

It did no good to stand and stare. She said her usual prayer and started across.

The little swell created by her own pace began to ripple along under her feet. The cables and wires and bamboo cross-ties complained to one another in groans and squeaks and rattles. The vagrant gusts from remote Mongolia leaned against the side of the bridge, withdrew, came back again and leaned a little harder. Her flat-heeled shoes had leather soles. She did not exactly think about these but was aware of how ill-equipped she was to keep her footing on those listing planks.

On her left, uncurtained by a single wire, a single thread, the vertiginous drop opened out. It created a suction for the eye, the mind, the body. She made herself go on, came toward the end of a plank, had to step sideways to continue on to the next and, as she looked to find her footing, saw eternity a step ahead, a step away.

Whether she faltered, whether she stopped she was not sure, but certainly fear spread out from the mind all along the nerves. Her muscles became both rigid and flaccid. She sweated yet felt deathly cold. The hand sliding along the guide wire grew too tense to be of any use. She did not, could not think or pray.

Then suddenly the terrifying panorama was screened off. Walking lightly in his bare feet, his lined face under the twisted head cloth set squarely ahead, the Bunun man moved up and stood between her and the sight that had so unnerved her and then went on carefully, quietly, as she stepped out to keep pace with him. They walked almost abreast of one another, the man a little ahead and on the downside of the listing catwalk. He had nothing to hold on to except the little black bag that he carried in his left hand. If she slipped, if she so much as leaned against him, he could not save himself; but she felt a new courage and they went on together and gained the other side of the ninety-foot span as one.

Standing safely on the footpath, on the solid, the good, the welcome earth, what could she say to him? Even if she had been born of his people, gifted with his mountain speech, she could not have expressed her gratitude. He seemed to understand, smiled and nodded, and trotted easily ahead up the path, the little black bag still in his hand.

FOR THOSE WHO DO NOT YET BELIEVE IN CHRIST

Let us pray also for those who do not yet believe in Christ, that they may be filled with the light of the Holy Spirit and be enabled to enter the way that leads to salvation.

O almighty and eternal God, you have handed over the nations to your beloved Son. Unite to your Church the families of all peoples. May they search for the light of truth and so come to you, the one true God. Through Jesus Christ. Amen.

—GOOD FRIDAY LITURGY

LAND OF PROWESS

by John P. Jordan

Bishop Shanahan was the great apostle to the Ibo people of southern Nigeria.

More powerful than the leopard, and more dangerous, was the bush-cow, a huge animal built on the lines of the buffalo and endowed with most of the characteristics of the rhinoceros. He was the accepted symbol of strength in every Ibo town and it was to indicate strength that the horns of the bush-cow were carved on the head of the *ikenga* (household god). No man ever thought of challenging such an adversary without a rifle capable of knocking out an elephant, and natives hunted them only in groups equipped with guns and spears. Even then fatalities were frequent, because the bush-cow had great speed, combined with a sense of smell more accurate than an Irish setter's, and, when in doubt, always charged.

Father Shanahan unwittingly set up a new record for personal bravery in one area of Iboland by dealing with one of these brutes singlehanded and almost casually. The incident occurred about four miles from the spot where he said his first Mass in the interior. He was striding along behind a line of carriers, when suddenly a horde of terror-stricken natives came tearing down the path in front of him, crying out that a huge bush-cow had appeared from out the tall ikpo grass beside their village, and

*From *Bishop Shanahan of Southern Nigeria,* by John P. Jordan. Clonmore and Reynolds, Ltd., Dublin, used by permission.

was even then charging about in frenzy. Without a moment's delay, he grabbed a hippo rod from someone nearby and set off at the double in the direction of the village. Probably he felt that an Irish farmer's son, who knew how sensitive was a bull's nose, would also know how to handle any variety of African beef.

The bush-cow and the missionary met in a narrow path almost at once. Simultaneously both charged. "Swish" came the hippo rod down on the beast's nose, as the missionary flung himself to one side. There was a terrific snort of surprised anger and a mighty whirl for a second charge. "Swish" — dead on the same tender part of the same tender nose. The animal turned, and fled bellowing toward the bush, with a triumphant and now blood-thirsty Irishman in pursuit. "Oh, I enjoyed that!"

The incident had been observed from the trees round about, where terrified natives had taken refuge. It was not just a nine days' wonder. It was something that had no parallel in the history of the town, something that would be rehearsed in detail for generations. The natives shouted and chattered, and described and pantomimed, and held up their hands and shook their heads in a vain effort to bring home to each other the magnitude of what had happened. No such man had ever been seen in their town before. Henceforth, his word would be law there, for who dared resist him? Actually it did become law, and when he put a church in the place, it remained the only one, because the people would not allow any other. It is so to this day, and it takes a dozen Catholic teachers to look after all the classes in the school there. This was just an incident in Father Shanahan's career, and though he thought nothing of it, he knew how to utilize it.

"Our Divine Lord utilized everything about Him to bring the Jews to the knowledge and love of His Father. He gave them parables from the husbanding of the vineyard and the sowing of the crops; analogies from the flashing of lightning and dancing in the market place; object lessons from the littleness of children and the beauty of flowers. My work was like His. I would imitate Him by observing life and supernaturalizing what I observed."

He admitted finding joy as well as profit in observing exhibitions of native strength and skill, notably at wrestling combats, because the love of contest was in his blood from old Rugby days in Rockwell, and in addition he admired the splendid physique of the contestants. "Magnificent men," he would say, "a shame to see them without the Faith." Magnificent men they certainly were, as they parried and slapped and sparred for openings. They fought within a definite area or ring. First they would advance to the center and touch hands as boxers do in Europe. After that they would retire, and come forward the second time bent low, with long arms fringing the ground, and quick eyes searching for an opening. There would be feints and grabs, and sudden slaps in the face to arouse temper, and finally a lightning dive and a jerk around the knee that lifted an opponent off balance and laid him flat on the ground. Then terrific uproar.

There is no record of Father Shanahan in the wrestler's ring, though there is a perfectly authenticated story of how one of his fellow-missionaries, an Irishman still in Nigeria, made use of the sport to further the Catholic faith! This man had erected a school in a very backward village and found it impossible to get more than a few children into it. He tried every ruse learnt by fifteen years' experience, and failed. Finally, he hit on an ingenious solution of the problem. He sent word to the headmen of the village that as they could not appreciate education but could appreciate wrestling, he would meet them and beat them on their own ground. "Have your champion wrestler outside the school building at five o'clock," he said, "and I shall bring a wrestler who will just make him look like a small pickaninny. And my wrestler will not be a black man either."

The challenge was received with the greatest delight, because the village had the finest wrestler in the area and had nothing to fear. To add spice to the prospective victory, there was the certainty that Father's wrestler would not be a black man. Well, a victory over a white man would be a million times better. The celebrations for victory would go on for days. There would be a feast without equal, and palm wine would course freely and frequently down spacious and thirsty throats. The village enthused.

Punctually at 5 P.M. on the appointed evening, the Father careened into the school compound on a Raleigh bicycle. He had a passenger gripping the handlebars firmly, and balanced neatly on a small saddle on the cross-bar. Not a white man, however, but a large and supercilious chimpanzee. The two were off the bike and marching hand in "hand" up and down the school compound before the hundreds of astonished natives got back their breath. This animal was a new one on them, for chimps did not exist within a hundred miles of their place, and not one of them had ever seen one before. All the normal kinds of wild life they had shot or trapped or speared; the elephant that roamed the swampy Anam country twenty miles to the south; the crocodile that infested their rivers; the leopard which lay on the great arms of trees by day and stalked their village by night in search of dog or goat or unwary child; the small brown monkeys that chattered in the trees and the great red ones which barked like dogs; all these they knew and understood. But this! What was this? After the first shock had passed they began to hazard guesses.

"Hi! he has face like old man."

"His mouth is wide too much."

"His body is black like ours."

"He has the arms of strong *okolobia*."

These and a host of other remarks filled the air as the chimp paraded up and down the playground, one "hand" nonchalantly gripping that of his master, the other tapping the broad deep chest lightly. Quite plainly he was not enamoured of his audience, for as his brown eyes darted up and down the touch line, he scowled unmistakably and finally spat in derision. Then he drew himself up to his full four feet and completely ignored them.

It was no easy matter to calm down the excited natives sufficiently to get the wrestling going, but the Father finally managed it. A great ring was made and the combatants faced each other. "Go on now, Mickey, and do your stuff," he said, tapping the chimp on the back and pointing toward the youthful black Hercules advancing from the opposite corner.

Mickey was into the ring with a bound. Here was action, and action was what he craved for. He frolicked about in sheer joy for a few moments before settling down to grimmer business, but wisely kept out of reach of the young giant opposite. His antics caused terrific excitement. In the end he took his cue from his opponent and circled around in the approved style.

Round and round they moved in ever narrowing circles, until they were within touching distance. Out flashed a long black arm, only to be countered by a sudden slap from a powerful and hairy paw. Step and counter step, feint and parry, push and thrust—but no decisive fall. Then the chimp sprang in as though to grab a leg, and was instantly met with a hand-off that sent him flying. Not a technical knock-out, though, for he landed on all fours. Just enough to bring frenzied cheers from the spectators. Their champion was doing well.

Too well, perhaps, for as the chimp jumped in a second time in apparently the self-same way, the black man's arm lunged forward even more viciously than before. But this time it did not connect. The chimp flattened out with incredible swiftness and the blow passed over his head, while the wrestler lost balance for a fraction of time. Even as he did, a sinewy pair of black paws gripped his ankles and jerked mightily. In a second he was well and truly on the flat of his back, victim to a tackle Basil McLear would have envied.

"Put it there, Mickey, old man!" cried the delighted Father, as he rushed in to congratulate the victor. And Mickey shook hands with the solemnity of an archduke.

This was only the first step toward victory. The second had yet to come. And it came quickly. Even while loud-voiced and excited comment filled the air, the Father raised his hand for silence.

"Now look here, you people," he said, "if I told you last week that I could teach you something about wrestling, you would not have believed me. But you believe now, because you have seen my wrestler beat your champion. Is it not so?"

"It is so!"

"Well, then, you can believe me now when I tell you that school is good for your children. After all, if I knew how to train this (pointing to the chimp) to wrestle, I know how to train your children properly in school. What do you think?"

"The Father is right," they cried, "our children must be trained in his school."

And trained they were.

MARYKNOLL IN SNOW

The snow has fallen in the night:
How beautiful, O wintry sight!
* I stand and look my fill and see*
* Thy witchery.*

Branches and twigs of bush and tree
Outlined in pure winter snow I see,
* Some sorcerer with magic wand*
* Transformed the land!*

Dazzling, the sunrise sets aglow
The myriad traceries of the snow,
* Till rubies sparkle, diamonds, too,*
* And sapphires blue.*

An appletree folds in its prong
What was the robin's theme and song—
* A nest, abandoned months ago,*
* now gemmed in snow.*

Oh, how it minds of many things!
* Homecomings after wanderings!*
* Outpourings of familiar tunes*
*   In coming Junes!*

—ANONYMOUS

NEVER A PRIZE WINNER

by Theodore T. Bache

Father Sweeney devoted his life to victims of leprosy in China and Korea. In death he was praised as a light to the world.

The biting cold of the late November wind whipped around the craggy Korean hillside and pierced the procession as it moved silently over the hard-frozen road to the leper colony where the man they were mourning had worked and lived.

They wore across their shoulders their white robes of mourning, and atop their heads tottered flimsy gauze hats. The only sounds heard were those of a dancing flutist moving ahead of the black and white velvet-draped ambulance in which the casket rested.

They passed through the entrance to the colony and moved by the buildings for which he had labored and begged. They stopped and waited with no words spoken before the small chapel where a month before he had struggled in pain for an hour and a half to offer one of his last Masses for his beloved lepers.

When all were there they began to file inside. Lepers, awkwardly grotesque with missing limbs and misshapen features. Leprous parents and their unafflicted children. Korean and American priests. Soldiers from the American 8th Army. The poor. The poorer. And the rich. They were cold and some rubbed their feet or cupped reddened hands to their mouths.

29

Some did not feel any sensation of cold. They could not, for they were the lepers—his lepers.

The tall, broad-shouldered American priest, whom he had called to his bedside, stood before the casket in the chapel and spoke. He was Father Edward Moffett.

"We are here to bury a man born 71 years ago . . . who was ordained a Maryknoll priest in 1920 and for the past 40 years was the salt of the earth and a light to the world, here in the Orient. Joseph Aloysius Sweeney. Behold a great priest . . . "

Father Moffett spoke with the depth and the meaning he could evoke only for having loved dearly, as a brother and a fellow priest, the man whose weakened and limp body he held in his arms only a few days before. Then the man lay delirious and dying, but now he rested in peace in the simple casket in the drafty chapel.

But Father Joe Sweeney certainly never would have forgiven Father Ed Moffett if the praise had been uttered while he was alive. For he was too humble and, in his Connecticut Yankee ways, too practical a man to have stood still for much of that.

Joseph Aloysius Sweeney was born in New Britain, Connecticut, a quiet New England town, on September 4, 1895. He was the first of six children born to Joseph P. Sweeney and Delia Houlihan Sweeney and the first of four who went into the religious life. Leo, who was ordained at Maryknoll after him and also served in Korea, died in 1944.

"Father Joseph Sweeney was first and last a priest. His life cried out to all the world . . . he offered his credentials to all men even as Christ Himself did—not in words, but in deeds. But who was he?"

He was a big man—big of heart and mind and body and strength—whose love and generosity extended in all directions and never stopped until the day he died. When he first arrived in South China in 1932 he was sickened by the account of the massacre of 100 lepers in a nearby village, the *ma fung lo*—"the numb ones," as they were called.

If any man would have been sickened by this, not every one

would have interceded for another group of lepers who were being threatened with drowning. His was an unusual act in the Orient. Many Chinese and even the lepers themselves were puzzled and suspicious of the big, six-foot-three, foreign priest who acknowledged their presence by saving their lives. Indeed, they even thought his friendly gestures were part of a greater plot to kill them.

"The charity of Christ urged him on . . . and only the good God knows how many he baptized, confirmed on their deathbed, fed the Body and Blood of Christ, and raised his priestly hands over in absolution."

He gave the lepers their first home, for they lived in graveyards where they could dig up the rotting lumber from old caskets to build their simple shacks and be left alone. He lived among them and brought to them modern methods for treatment of their disease. He gave them life and hope and meaning in their drab day-to-day existence.

The odds always seemed to be working against Big Joe, as the priests affectionately called him. A typhoon flattened and battered his expanding leper colony at Gate of Heaven. Not long after he had rebuilt it, the invading Japanese army arrived to take over the strategic fort directly across the Kongmoon River. And there began a deadly matching of wits with bullets for the freedom to move safely about the leper compound and, on moonless nights, run the river in boats for supplies and medicine. Big Joe had his share of narrow escapes.

"Father Sweeney was the Apostle to Lepers, Father of the Poor, but first and above all he was a dispenser of the mysteries of God."

It was a mystery to many how he escaped the night his frail craft, loaded precariously with badly needed supplies and medicine, was almost cut in half by the patrol boat which sliced through the dark waters spewing bullets. But he stayed alive six hours in the water drifting and swimming toward a distant, deserted island.

When the day of his inevitable expulsion from China came he

was, in a way, a man without a country. Deep down inside he felt he would never see his lepers again. But he survived the war in better condition than did the Gate of Heaven leper colony. It was in shambles when he finally was able to return.

Soon the word spread that Big Joe was back in business. In no time he was able to write home that he had "a shortage of everything but lepers." The Japanese were gone but the Chinese Communists were at hand. Again, in 1953, he was forced to leave the country. He said almost tearfully that it was the saddest day of his life.

He returned to the United States. Korea was ahead of him, but first he was to be the recipient of the Damien-Dutton Award, named after the famous missionaries of the Molokai Leprosarium.

The Press Club of his hometown of New Britain chose to honor him too, as Man of the Year. It was an early May evening. More than 300 people, including the Connecticut hierarchy and the state's governor, John Lodge, were present for the ceremonies. They gave the tall, now somewhat gaunt missioner thunderous applause. One by one the speakers took their place at the podium and directed words of admiration toward Father Joe Sweeney.

When the scroll was presented to him, he held it for an emotion-filled minute before speaking. He was deeply moved and grateful.

"This seems like some sort of a dream," he said quietly, his eyes lowering to the scroll he held. "I can claim no distinction except being associated with the most despised of all, those in the great country of China." It was an allusion, the audience knew, to the hatred flung upon foreign missionaries like himself by the Communist Chinese. They gave no love to these men.

"Actually I am a very ordinary person," he continued. "I never won a prize in school. I never won a letter in athletics. I can't sing or dance or preach except in a very ordinary way."

In Rome, he said, where he had stopped on his return from the Orient and received an audience with Pope Pius XII, he visited the catacombs and saw those places where Christians had been persecuted nearly two thousand years before. And he thought of the China he knew.

"At the leprosarium it was the same thing. The Reds came to the people with wiles and guile . . . and terror. I find out today that the people still practice their religion — stronger and better than ever."

He paused and lowered his head. As he did there were three hundred people in the room who felt with him the lump in his throat. And thousands of miles away in China were countless numbers of Chinese, lepers and nonafflicted alike, who, just like the people honoring Father Joe Sweeney that night, thought of him as a giant, a symbol of hope and a man for all men.

"In the name of all those people," he continued, a moist twinkle in his eyes turning into a proud smile, "and in the name of the rest of us ordinary people here in New Britain, I would like to accept this award."

"We stand at his graveside, down next to the lepers' graves. Let us also pray for ourselves, pray that we might stir up the grace within ourselves . . . For we must carry on the heritage of this great priest — Father Joseph Aloysius Sweeney."

The Korean armistice was barely three years old when he arrived in Korea to begin work anew with victims of leprosy at An Yang in the southern half of the divided country. There he worked for eleven years with relentless determination. He introduced more modern methods of treatment, including the Marianum Antigen serum and the use of mobile clinics. Many doctors and nurses helped him full-time, especially in the later years.

In 1962, when he was 67, the people and the government of South Korea thanked him warmly by awarding him their Order of Cultural Merit national medal. It was a big day for Father Joe but, as always, he was back behind the wheel of his ambulance early the next morning. He made the rounds of the five leprosy treatment centers he had established through the generosity of others. He never neglected his own well-being and health — at least not intentionally — but in his last summer he knew that he must begin to slow down. He had cancer of the stomach. He died peacefully, anointed by his regional superior, in the arms of Father Moffett whom he asked to continue his work.

Five hundred priests and religious and more than eight hundred laity filled the cathedral in Seoul for his funeral. After Mass came the procession to his leper colony, 20 miles to the south. His people were waiting at the gate. It was dusk in Korea.

"We mourn today not for Father Sweeney, but for ourselves. We have lost a great priest. Pray for his soul. May he rest in peace."

A DISTANT THOUGHT

The moonlight that penetrates the grove
  is more gentle.
The wind discreetly
  does not disturb the sleeping waves of the lake.
I recall a distant thought
  listening to the voice of my dead husband.
He is already gone
  and here I remain alone.
The stars are asleep
  in the far, far off sky.
I recall a distant thought
  dreaming day-dreams in my heart.

—CHUNG IN-BO

MUSHROOM TALE

by Edward A. McGurkin

It's usually a good idea to get all the facts.

A story Africans in Maswa enjoy, goes like this:

Two British colonial agents liked mushrooms very much but they could never be sure which were poisonous and which were not. Once they gathered a good mess of mushrooms and cooked them, reasoning they could try them on the dog first. If he survived, then they would give the mushrooms a go.

This they did and after a reasonable time called in the dog to give him the once over. They checked his pulse, made him stick out his tongue, and thumped him on the back. To all this the dog responded with cheerful wagging of his tail. Convinced, the two British gentlemen settled down to enjoy their favorite dish.

Just as they finished the last tasty morsels, the houseboy came in, exclaiming: "Bwana, your dog is dead."

Both agents turned pale. One began taking his pulse while the other promptly called for a doctor.

"Right from the start I knew they had a queer taste," complained one agent. A cold sweat formed on his brow.

The doctor came, listened to their tale and started to prepare an emetic. But first he called in the houseboy and said, "Tell me exactly how the dog acted as he was dying."

"Acted?" asked the boy. "He didn't act. He was killed instantly when that truck hit him."

PASSER-BY

I walk the winding paddy paths,
*   That cross the valley floors,*
And climb the stony mountain trails
*   Past all the staring doors*
Of little mud-brick villages,
*   With streets of cobble-stone,*
Where Christ has never entered in
*   And God is not yet known.*
Of all the trials of mission life,
*   This is the hardest part:*
To walk thru many villages, indifferent
*   little villages,*
*   That break the priestly heart.*

The cities are but transient things,
*   Where men are not at home;*
(Their population shifts with trade,
*   For traders ever roam.)*
Small hope for winning these for Christ,
*   For gain is all their goal;*
They have not time to squander
*   On the interests of the soul.*
But should He find no harvest
*   Where men are used to toil,*
In all the little villages, hard working
*   little villages,*
Deep-rooted in the soil?

The poor have ever been His own,
*   And where may men be found*
Poorer than those who toil for rice
*   On China's crowded ground?*
They are His own but know Him not;
*   They do not heed His voice.*
And so I fain must pass their doors;
*   I have no other choice.*
Of all the trials of mission life,
*   This is the hardest part:*
To walk thru many villages, indifferent
*   little villages,*
*   That break the priestly heart.*

— M. A. CHURCHILL

A PLEA FOR THE FREEDOM OF MONKEYS

by Alan Paton

A distinguished author takes a satirical view of South Africa's policy of separate development.

The City of Durban has taken very calmly the decision of the Minister of Railways and Harbours to employ forty Indian shunters on the South African Railways. It is only the Nationalists that are perturbed. Yet they need not be, because shunting is not really a traditional white occupation. Van Riebeck (leader of the first Cape settlement, 1652) knew nothing about shunting. In fact, railways are not really South African. They are only one hundred years old, about the same age as the first British settlers would now be, and though their locomotives may blow and whistle, they are not really part of the South African scene.

A much more serious crisis is the book embargo. Here are all these books lying about, and no one to censor them. The solution is simple. Hand over the South African Railways to the Indians, and transfer all the railwaymen to the Publications Board, so that they can read the backlog of books, so that we can read them too. Indians however will not be allowed to drive the White Train,† and rightly too, because this is quite outside their tradition.

* From *Contact* VII, No. 13.

† South Africa has dual capitals, Cape Town and Pretoria. The White Train moves the executive arm of the Government between them twice annually.

Another crisis will soon arise in the nursing profession. Soon there will be no white girls available, because they are needed in managerial capacities. Here again there is a solution to hand. Let white people be nursed by Coloured nurses, Coloured people by Indian nurses, Indian people by African nurses. This sews the whole thing up.

Flogging may have to be abolished. It is a white occupation, but it is getting harder and harder to get white floggers. One cannot obviously apply the nursing solution to flogging, because it leaves the question wide open, who will flog the Bantu? Furthermore one somehow cannot quite get used to the idea of Coloured floggers for white people; it is not in the tradition of either of these proud people.

The business of postmen is very tricky. Here, at Kloof, we first had African postmen, but now we have Indian postmen. I must confess I don't like it. I would rather see Coloured postmen here, and send all the Indian postmen to Coloured areas, and all the African postmen to Indian areas. That would again sew the whole thing up nicely, and would show, I think, the immense adaptability of the theory of separate development.

Is it not fascinating to see how adaptable the policy of Job Reservation is also? There is no fear that it will collapse. Heaven will collapse just as soon. That is because Christianity and Job Reservation are really the same thing. There is only one possible justification for kicking a man out of his job, and that is if it is done in a Christian spirit. The same is true about kicking a man out of his home under the Group Areas Act. I apologise for appearing to bring religion into politics, but I am not really doing so. Here, by a miracle, they are one and the same thing.

Some people say Job Reservation is finished. They say it is impossible for white South Africa to supply the engineers, architects, telephonists, clerks, barmen, for the entire country. This is only Communist propaganda. In fact there is still a great source of labour untapped. I refer to our monkeys and baboons. Surely many of us have heard Oscar Wolheim's (a founder of the Liberal Party) famous story of the farmer who trained baboons for agriculture. They were highly efficient and would do anything except the most menial labour.

It is not pleasant to speak disparagingly of our monkeys and baboons, because they are truly South African. But the fact is that they have done too little for their country. They eat the fruit, and leave the pips for white South Africa. In the Kruger National Park they are degenerating, and sit on the roadside begging food from those endeavouring to enjoy their hard-earned holidays.

If these animals could be trained—and a problem like that should be child's play for those who in sixteen years have solved the racial problems of South Africa—many more white South Africans would be freed for managerial positions. It would not surprise me if our monkeys became the best-fed and happiest monkeys in all Africa. The tide of Communism would be halted, and the world would come to see the excellence of our policies.

One thing would have to be made quite clear however. Monkeys would not become part of the nation. They could work in our industries and on our farms, but they would remain citizens of the *kloofs* and *krantzes*.* No true South African would wish to disturb the freedom of their care-free lives. Nor, I am sure, would our monkeys wish it otherwise.

*Literally, ravines and hills. Actually, a reference to Verwoerd's "homelands" plan.

T H E   B L O O M

The flower blooms petal by petal,
  a whole universe blooms.
It is the moment
  when the last bud is trembling to unfold.
The wind calms. The sun stops breathing,
  and so I close my eyes quietly.

—SO WOL KIM

THE HANDS OF GOD

And may the gracious care
of the Lord our God be ours;
prosper the work of our hands for us!
Psalm 89:17

He who numbers the fish of the deepest seas
and charts the course of undiscovered stars,
fashions human hands in the image of His love.

For what is more beautiful than the hands of
an infant reaching for its mother, or the
hands of a husband clasped in prayer?

Because human hands are the extension of divine
hands, each man bears the burden of healing,
comforting, and transforming God's family.

God's family, speaking many tongues and flourishing
many colors, is more precious than swift fish
or burning stars. God's family lives forever.

For, although He is lord, creator, mentor, and
cause of all creatures, when He speaks to man
He calls Himself father.

Upon every human heart, He leaves His fingerprint.
We walk, like small children, on the palm of
His hand.

THE FAMINE

by Pearl Buck

Any farmer will devote all of his energy to possess the
piece of land over which he toils so unceasingly. This is
the story of a farmer in China and his acquisition of
land.

It seemed as though once the gods turned against a man they
will not consider him again. The rains, which should have come
in early summer, withheld themselves, and day after day the
skies shone with fresh and careless brilliance. The parched and
starving earth was nothing to them. From dawn to dawn there
was not a cloud, and at night the stars hung out of the sky,
golden and cruel in their beauty.

The fields, although Wang Lung cultivated them desperately,
dried and cracked, and the young wheat stalks, which had sprung
up courageously with the coming of spring and had prepared
their heads for the grain, when they found nothing coming from
the soil or the sky for them, ceased their growing and stood
motionless at first under the sun and at last dwindled and yellowed into a barren harvest. The young rice beds which Wang
Lung sowed at first were squares of jade upon the brown earth.
He carried water to them day after day after he had given up
the wheat, the heavy wooden buckets slung upon a bamboo
pole across his shoulders. But though a furrow grew upon his

*From *The Good Earth,* by Pearl Buck. Copyright 1931 by Pearl Buck, renewed. Reprinted by the permission of The Viking Press, Inc.

flesh and a callous formed there as large as a bowl, no rain came.

At last the water in the pond dried into a cake of clay and the water even in the well sunk so low that O-lan said to him,

"If the children must drink and the old man have his hot water the plants must go dry."

Wang Lung answered with anger that broke into a sob.

"Well, and they must all starve if the plants starve." It was true that all their lives depended upon the earth.

Only the piece of land by the moat bore harvest, and, this because at last when summer wore away without rain, Wang Lung abandoned all his other fields and stayed the day out at this one, dipping water from the moat to pour upon the greedy soil. This year for the first time he sold his grain as soon as it was harvested, and when he felt the silver upon his palm he gripped it hard in defiance. He would, he told himself, in spite of gods and drought, do that which he had determined. His body he had broken and his sweat he had spilled for this handful of silver and he would do what he would with it. And he hurried to the House of Hwang and he met the land agent there and he said without ceremony.

"I have that with which to buy the land adjoining mine by the moat."

Now Wang Lung had heard here and there that for the House of Hwang it had been a year verging upon poverty. The old lady had not had her dole of opium to the full for many days and she was like an old tigress in her hunger so that each day she sent for the agent and she cursed him and struck his face with her fan, screaming at him.

"And are there not acres of land left, yet?" until he was beside himself.

He had even given up the moneys which ordinarily he held back from the family transactions for his own use, so beside himself had he been. And as if this were not enough the Old Lord took yet another concubine, a slave who was the child of a slave who had been his creature in her youth, but who was now wed to a man servant in the house, because the Old Lord's desire for her failed before he took her into his room as concubine. This child of the slave, who was not more than sixteen, he now saw with fresh lust, for as he grew old and infirm and heavy with flesh he seemed to desire more and more women who were slight and young, even to childhood so that there was no slaking his lust. As the Old Mistress with her opium, so he with his lusts, and there was no making him understand there was not money for jade earrings for his favorites and not gold for their pretty hands. He could not comprehend the words "no money," who all his life had but to reach out his hand and fill it as often as he would.

And seeing their parents thus, the young lords shrugged their shoulders and said there must still be enough for their lifetime. They united in only one thing and this was to berate the agent for his ill management of the estates, so that he who had once been oily and unctuous, a man of plenty and of ease, was now become anxious and harried and his flesh gone so that his skin hung upon him like an old garment.

Neither had Heaven sent rain upon the fields of the House of Hwang, and there, too, there were no harvests, and so when Wang Lung came to the agent crying, "I have silver," it was as though one came saying to the hungry, "I have food."

The agent grasped at it, and where before there had been dickering and tea-drinking, now the two men spoke in eager whispers, and more quickly than they could speak whole words, the money passed from one hand to the other and papers were signed and sealed and the land was Wang Lung's.

And once again Wang Lung did not count the passing of silver, which was his flesh and his blood, a hard thing. He bought with it the desire of his heart. He had now a vast field of good land, for the new field was twice as large as the first. But more to him than its dark fertility was the fact that it had belonged once to the family of a prince. And this time he told no one, not even O-lan, what he had done.

Month passed into month and still no rain fell. As autumn approached the clouds gathered unwillingly in the sky, small, light clouds, and in the village street one could see men standing about, idle and anxious, their faces upturned to the sky, judging closely of this cloud and that, discussing together as to whether any held rain in it. But before sufficient cloud could gather for promise, a bitter wind rose out of the northwest, the acrid wind of the distant desert, and blew the clouds from the sky as one gathers dust from a floor with a broom. And the sky was empty and barren, and the stately sun rose each morning and made its march and set solitary each night. And the moon in its time shone like a lesser sun for clearness.

From his fields Wang Lung reaped scanty harvest of hardy beans, and from his corn field, which he had planted in despair when the rice beds had yellowed and died before ever the plants had been set into the watered field, he plucked short stubby ears with the grains scattered here and there. There was not a bean lost in the threshing. He set the two little boys to sifting the dust of the threshing floor between their fingers after he and the woman had flailed the bean vines, and he shelled the corn upon the floor in the middle room, watching sharply every grain that flew wide. When he would have put the cobs away for fuel, his wife spoke out,

"No — do not waste them in burning. I remember when I was a child in Shantung when years like this came, even the cobs we ground and ate. It is better than grass."

When she had spoken they all fell silent, even the children. There was foreboding in these strange brilliant days when the land was failing them. Only the girl child knew no fear. For her there were the mother's two great breasts as yet filled for her needs. But O-lan, giving her suck, muttered,

"Eat, poor fool — eat, while there is yet that which can be eaten."

And then, as though there were not enough evil, O-lan was again with child, and her milk dried up, and the frightened house was filled with the sound of a child continually crying for food.

If one had asked Wang Lung,

"And how are you fed through the autumn?" he would have answered, "I do not know — a little food here and there."

But there was none to ask him that. None asked of any other

in the whole countryside, "How are you fed?" None asked anything except of himself, "How shall I be fed this day?" And parents said, "How shall we be fed, we and our children?"

Now Wang Lung's ox he had cared for as long as he could. He had given the beast a bit of straw and a handful of vines as long as these lasted and then he had gone out and torn leaves from the trees for it until winter came and these were gone. Then since there was no land to plough, since seed, if it were planted only dried in the earth, and since they had eaten all their seed, he turned the ox out to hunt for itself, sending the eldest boy to sit upon its back all day and hold the rope passed through its nostrils so that it would not be stolen. But latterly he had not dared even to do this, lest men from the village, even his neighbors, might overcome the lad and seize the ox for food, and kill it. So he kept the ox on the threshold until it grew lean as its skeleton.

But there came a day when there was no rice left and no wheat left and there were only a few beans and a meager store of corn, and the ox lowed with its hunger and the old man said,

"We will eat the ox, next."

Then Wang Lung cried out, for it was to him as though one said, "We will eat a man next." The ox was his companion in the fields and he had walked behind and praised it and cursed it as his mood was, and from his youth he had known the beast, when they had bought it a small calf. And he said,

"How can we eat the ox? How shall we plough again?"

But the old man answered, tranquil enough,

"Well, and it is your life or the beast's and your son's life or the beast's and a man can buy an ox again more easily than his own life."

But Wang Lung would not that day kill it. And the next day passed and the next and the children cried out for food and they would not be comforted and O-lan looked at Wang Lung, beseeching him for the children, and he saw at last that the thing was to be done. So he said roughly,

"Let it be killed then, but I cannot do it."

He went into the room where he slept and he laid himself upon the bed and he wrapped the quilt about his head that he might not hear the beast's bellowing when it died.

Then O-lan crept out and she took a great iron knife she had in the kitchen and she cut a great gash in the beast's neck, and thus she severed its life. And she took a bowl and caught its blood to cook for them to eat in a pudding, and she skinned and hacked to pieces the great carcass, and Wang Lung would not come out until the thing was wholly done and the flesh was cooked and upon the table. But when he tried to eat the flesh of his ox his gorge rose and he could not swallow it and he drank only a little of the soup. And O-lan said to him,

"An ox is but an ox and this one grew old. Eat, for there will be another one day and far better than this one."

Wang Lung was a little comforted then and he ate a morsel and then more, and they all ate. But the ox was eaten at last and the bones cracked for the marrow, and it was all too quickly gone, and there was nothing left of it except the skin, dried and hard and stretched upon the rack of bamboo O-lan had made to hold it spread.

At first there had been hostility in the village against Wang Lung because it was supposed that he had silver which he was hiding and food stored away. His uncle, who was among the first to be hungry, came importuning to his door, and indeed the man and his wife and his seven children had nothing to eat. Wang Lung measured unwillingly into the skirt of his uncle's robe a small heap of beans and a precious handful of corn. Then he said with firmness,

"It is all I can spare and I have first my old father to consider, even if I had no children."

When his uncle came again Wang Lung cried out,

"Even filial piety will not feed my house!" and he sent his uncle empty away.

From that day his uncle turned against him like a dog that has been kicked, and he whispered about the village in this house and in that.

"My nephew there, he has silver and he has food, but he will give none of it to us, not even to me, and to my children, who are his own bones and flesh. We can do nothing but starve."

And as family after family finished its store in the small village and spent its last coin in the scanty markets of the town, and the winds of winter came down from the desert, cold as a knife of steel and dry and barren, the hearts of the villagers grew distraught with their own hunger and with the hunger of their pinched wives and crying children, and when Wang Lung's uncle shivered about the streets like a lean dog and whispered from his famished lips, "There is one who has food — there is one whose children are fat, still," the men took up poles and went one night to the house of Wang Lung and beat upon the door. And when he had opened to the voices of his neighbors, they fell upon and pushed him out of the doorway and threw out of the house his frightened children, and they fell upon every corner, and they scrabbled every surface with their hands to find where he had hidden his food. Then when they found his wretched store of a few dried beans and a bowlful of dried corn they gave a great howl of disappointment and despair, and they seized his bits of furniture, the table and the benches and the bed where the old man lay, frightened and weeping.

Then O-lan came forward and spoke, and her plain, slow voice rose above the men.

"Not that — not that yet," she called out. "It is not yet time to take out table and the benches and the bed from our house. You have all our food. But out of your own houses you have not sold yet your table and your benches. Leave us ours. We are even. We have not a bean or a grain of corn more than you — no, you have more than we, now, for you have all of ours. Heaven will strike you if you take more. Now, we will go out together and hunt for grass to eat and bark from the trees, you for your children, and we for our three children, and for this fourth who is to be born in such times." She pressed her hand to her belly as she spoke, and the men were ashamed before her and went out one by one, for they were not evil men except when they starved.

One lingered, that one called Ching, a small, silent yellow man with a face like an ape's in the best of times, and now hollowed and anxious. He would have spoken some good word of shame, for he was an honest man and only his crying child had forced him to evil. But in his bosom was a handful of beans he had snatched when the store was found and he was fearful lest he must return them if he spoke at all, and so he only looked at Wang Lung with haggard, speechless eyes and he went out.

Wang Lung stood there in his dooryard where year after year he had threshed his good harvests, and which had lain now for many months idle and useless. There was nothing left in the house to feed his father and his children—nothing to feed this woman of his who besides the nourishment of her own body had this other one to feed into growth, this other one who would, with the cruelty of new and ardent life, steal from the very flesh and blood of its mother. He had an instant of extreme fear. Then into his blood like soothing wine flowed this comfort. He said in his heart,

"They cannot take the land from me. The labor of my body and the fruit of the fields I have put into that which cannot be taken away. If I had the silver, they would have taken it. If I had bought something with the silver to store it, they would have taken it all. I have the land still, and it is mine."

PRAYER FOR THE CHILDREN OF CHINA

O Lord of Heaven, who had compassion on the multitude, pity the children of China who are without food and without shelter, homeless in the land of their birth, and dying before they have lived to love you. Let the evils that have come upon them be softened by your everlasting mercy, and let the dark years of their cruel suffering be soon ended.

Lord of Heaven, once a little Child in the care of a tender Mother, remember now these children of China, and give them, dear Lord, we pray, the protection of your divine might, so that they, too, may grow in wisdom, age, and grace—for of such is your Kingdom of Heaven.

—REV. JAMES M. DROUGHT, M.M.

SITTING BULL CONCLUDES A TREATY

by E. Laveille

> The Indians referred to Father De Smet as the white man who did not speak with "the double tongue." Here is the story of his mediation with the Sioux.

Father De Smet returned to St. Louis in the month of August and suffered from the intense heat, as in the preceding year. "More and more I feel the weight of years. My strength is failing and I am getting thin. I still hope to spend a year or two with the Indians, especially those who are at enmity with the whites. A large number of chiefs have invited me to visit them and seem disposed to make peace, but the winter is too far advanced and I am too weak to undertake the journey of over three thousand miles. I must put it off until next spring." When spring came he was able to carry out his intentions, however.

Generals Sully and Parker were of the opinion that an understanding could be arrived at with the hostile tribes. On the other hand, the complete submission of the Indians, if obtained by force of arms, would cost the country five hundred million dollars. It was deemed wiser to continue negotiations.

A new commission was empowered to conclude a lasting peace; it was composed of the most distinguished officers of

---

*From *The Life of Father De Smet,* by E. Laveille, S. J. Copyright 1915 by P. J. Kenedy & Sons.

the United States Army: Generals Sherman, Harney, Sanborn, Terry, and Sheridan. It is noteworthy that these men, who had just brought the Civil War to a close, now asked the aid of a missionary to induce a few thousand Indians to lay down their arms.

Father De Smet gladly placed his services at the disposal of the commission. He had full confidence in their integrity and wrote of them: "I do not hesitate to say that the gentlemen composing the commission are all animated with the best of feelings toward the Indian tribes and want to provide for their future welfare. Resistance on the part of the Indians will finally be overcome and would bring great misery among them."

On March 30, 1868, the missionary left St. Louis in his sixty-eighth year and in broken health, to embark on the most perilous undertaking of his life. He joined the commission, which traveled by way of Chicago and Omaha. The first council with the Indians was held on the borders of the Platte River; the results were satisfactory, but news was brought that certain tribes, notably the Hunkpapas and Ogallalas, had refused to treat with the whites. So long as these tribes, two of the most powerful in the plains, refused to disarm, peace could not be assured.

It was evident that Father De Smet alone could triumph over their fierce animosity, so he offered to go in person to invite them to a conference that would take place three months later at Fort Rice. Deeming it wiser to advance ahead of the commission, he traveled up the Missouri alone. A Black Robe in the midst of military uniforms would be unseemly to the Indians and far from agreeable.

After thirty-three days of difficult navigation he reached the fort situated near the mouth of the Cannonball River, where hundreds of Indians were gathered to attend "the great peace council." Learning that he had arrived, they rushed to the river and gave him a warm ovation; then they conducted him to the lodge that had been prepared for him, where the great chiefs were anxiously waiting to learn the Government's intentions toward them. He assured them of the Government's peaceful attitude, but declared he could not conclude any negotiations before the arrival of the commissioners. The following days he devoted to instructing the Indians, and six hundred children received baptism. He also prepared the soldiers in the garrison to receive the sacraments on the day of Pentecost.

On June 1 the missionary announced that he was going to seek the hostile tribes, in order to induce the chiefs to attend the conference. The Indians were astounded at such audacity, and wished to dissuade him. "Black Robe," they said, "it will cost you your scalp." But the missionary replied: "Before a picture of the Blessed Virgin, Mother and Protector of all nations, six lamps are burning day and night during my absence, and before these lamps more than a thousand children implore heaven's protection for me." Then the Indians lifted their hands to heaven, exclaiming: "How wonderful! How splendid! We want to accompany you. When will you start?" "Tomorrow at sunrise."

The missionary accepted, however, only an escort of twenty-four men, and for interpreter chose an old trapper named Galpin, who had lived for thirty years among the Sioux.

The moment of his departure was a solemn one. Surrounded by the Indian chiefs and soldiers from the fort, the Father placed his journey under the protection of the Great Spirit, and recommended himself to the prayers of his friends, many of whom never expected to see him again.

The Indians whom he wished to reconcile with the whites were nursing their hatred on the far side of the Bad Lands, an immense, sterile plain, furrowed with deep undulations. Numbering over five thousand, they roamed about with the uneasiness and restlessness of wild beasts. They were pagans, and knew of the Catholic religion only through the prestige attached to the Black Robe.

Taking a westerly course, the missionary's caravan traveled for days without coming upon any traces of the white man, and only now and then encountered the remains of some Indian warrior, supported on four poles. The Indians would then halt, smoke the calumet, and celebrate in song the bravery of the dead.

"Thou hast preceded us to the land of souls;
Today at thy tomb we admire thy lofty deeds.
Thy death has been avenged by thy brothers in arms.
Repose in peace, illustrious warrior!"

As they advanced vegetation became sparse; they had only stagnant, greenish water to drink, and even game was becoming scarce. Despite these hardships, Father De Smet's cheerfulness kept up the courage of his companions.

One evening one of the men of his escort, who had formerly been a great enemy to the whites, entered his tent. "Black Robe" said the Indian, extending his hand, "ever since our departure I have observed you and am more than ever convinced you are a great and brave man. As I have always admired the brave, it rejoices my heart to see you." He then conversed at length with the missionary upon the means to bring about peace.

On June 9, Father De Smet dispatched four men to seek the enemy's camp and provisioned each with a quantity of tobacco. "The gift of tobacco is equivalent to an invitation or signifies the desire for a conference upon an important affair. If the tobacco is accepted, you can present yourself; if not, access to the camp is forbidden you."

Six days later a band of Indians appeared upon the horizon. These were scouts, and were followed by a deputation of eighteen warriors, who had come to shake hands with the missionary and smoke the calumet of peace. "Black Robe," they said, "your tobacco has been accepted. The chiefs and warriors are eager to know the object of your visit; but entrance to our camp is accorded to you alone; no other white man could come out of it with his scalp."

The camp was three days' journey away, in the valley of the Yellowstone near the confluence of the Powder River. On June 19 they reached the hills that overlook the river, and from there Father De Smet beheld a detachment of five hundred warriors coming across the plain to meet him. "I immediately unfurled my standard of peace, which was a banner with the holy name of Jesus on one side, and on the other a picture of the Blessed Virgin surrounded with a halo of stars. Believing it the United States flag, the Indians halted, and appeared to be holding a consultation. The four chiefs rode up at full gallop and hovered about the banner. But as soon as they learned what it represented, they shook hands with me and signaled to their warriors to approach. They all drew themselves up in a single line and we did the same. Then the two lines approached each other. On both sides rose cries and shouts of joy. I was moved to tears by the reception these pagan sons of the desert gave me."

Then followed, according to their custom, the exchange of presents; afterward they started, with the banner at their head, for the camp only a few miles distant. There Father De Smet found the Hunkpapas, the Ogallalas, the Blackfeet, the Miniconjous, and others. The great chief, Four Horns, shared his authority with Black Moon, No Neck, and Sitting Bull. The last name was soon to become famous. His courage, his eloquence, and his prestige made him the most formidable of the redskins. Eight years later he was to successfully lead the final resistance of his expiring people. It was this fierce chief who received Father De Smet; he had prepared for him a large lodge in the center of the camp, where a guard of his faithful warriors stood watch day and night.

Exhausted by his sixteen days' march, the missionary asked that he might be allowed to rest, and although surrounded by four thousand Indians, sworn enemies of the whites, he tranquilly fell asleep in the full assurance of the good faith of Indian hospitality; until he awakened, his guard kept watch over the venerable white man, wrapped in his Jesuit cloak.

When he opened his eyes the four chiefs were standing before him, and, in the name of his tribe, Sitting Bull addressed him:

"Black Robe, I hardly sustain myself beneath the weight of white men's blood I have shed. The whites provoked the war; their injustices, their indignities to our families, the cruel, unheard-of, and wholly unprovoked massacre at Fort Lyon (where Chivington commanded) of six or seven hundred

women, children, and old men, shook all the veins which bind
and support me. I rose, tomahawk in hand, and I have done all
the hurt to the whites that I could. Today thou art among us,
and in thy presence my hands fall to the ground as if dead. I
will listen to thy good words, and as bad as I have been to the
whites just so good am I ready to become toward them."

Complying with Father De Smet's request, the chiefs con-
voked a great council for the next day, when the Black Robe
would inform them of the Government's proposals, and the
warriors would decide if they should send a deputation to Fort
Rice to treat for peace with the commissioners.

Early on the morning of June 20, men and women began
preparing the place for the conference; this space covered nearly
a half acre, and was surrounded by a series of tepees or Indian
lodges, composed of twenty-four buffalo skins each, which were
suspended on long pine poles. The banner of the Holy Virgin
rose from the center, and on one side a seat covered with fine
buffalo skins was prepared for the Black Robe. When all the
Indians, at the appointed hour, had taken their places, ranged in
a circle, Father De Smet was solemnly introduced by the two
head chiefs, Four Horns and Black Moon. The council was
opened with songs and dances, noisy and joyful, in which the
warriors alone took part. Then Four Horns lighted his calumet
of peace; he presented it first solemnly to the Great Spirit,
imploring His light and favor, and then to the four cardinal
points, and to the sun and earth, as witnesses to the action of
the council. Then he himself passed the calumet from mouth to
mouth, commencing with Father De Smet. When the ceremony
of the calumet was finished, the head chief addressed the missionary, saying:

"Speak, Black Robe, my ears are open to hear your words."

All this was done with the greatest gravity and amid a profound silence.

Then the Father rose to his feet and raising his hands to
heaven implored guidance from on high. For almost an hour
he laid before them the disinterested motives that had brought
him among them, which could only tend to their happiness. He

spoke especially of the dangers with which they were surrounded, and of their weakness beside the great strength of the
whites, if the Great Father were forced to use it against them.
The harm done by the war had been terrible, and the crimes
committed on both sides atrocious. The Great Father desired
that all should be forgotten and buried. Today his hand was
ready to aid them, to give them agricultural implements, domes-
tic animals, men to teach them field-work, and teachers of both
sexes to instruct their children, and all this was offered them
without the least remuneration or cession of lands on their part.

"And now," said Father De Smet in conclusion, "in the name
of the Great Spirit, and in the presence of your chiefs and braves
here assembled, I conjure you to bury all resentment and accept
the hand that is generously offered to you. The banner before you
is the sacred emblem of peace, and never before has it been
carried such a distance. I will leave it with your chiefs as a
guarantee of my sincerity, and as a continual reminder of my
wishes for the happiness of the Sioux tribes."

No one interrupted the orator, and when he was done, Black
Moon arose.

"Black Robe, your words are plain and good, and filled with
truth. I shall lay them up in my memory. Still, our hearts are
sore. They have received deep wounds. These wounds are yet to
be healed. A cruel war has desolated and impoverished our
country; the desolating torch of war was not kindled by us; it
was the Sioux east of us and the Cheyennes south of us who
raised the war first, to revenge themselves for the white man's
cruelties and injustice. We have been forced to take part, for
we are victims of their rapacity and wrongdoing. Today, when
we ride over our plains, we find them spotted here and there
with blood; these are not the bloodstains of buffalo and deer
killed in the chase, but those of our own comrades or of white
men, sacrificed to vengeance. The buffalo, the elk, the antelope,
the bighorn, and the deer have quitted our immense plains; we
hardly find them any more, except at intervals, and always less
numerous. May it not be the odor of human blood that puts them
to flight?

"I will say further—against our will, the whites are cutting up our country with their highways; they build forts and arm them with thunderers. They kill our animals, and more than they need. They cut down our forests without paying us their value. Not content with ruining us, they maltreat and massacre our people.

"We are opposed to having these big roads, which drive the buffalo away from our country. The soil is ours, and we are determined not to yield an inch of it. Here our fathers were born and buried. We desire, like them, to live here, and to be buried in this same soil. We have been forced to hate the whites. Let them treat us like brothers and the war will cease. Let them stay at home; we will never go to trouble them. To see them come in and build their cabins revolts us, and we are determined to resist or die. Thou, Messenger of Peace, thou hast given us a glimpse of a better future. Very well; so be it; let us hope. Let us throw a veil over the past, and let it be forgotten. I have only a word more to say; in the presence of all my people, I express to you here my thanks for the good news that you have announced and for all your good counsel and advice. We accept your tobacco. Some of our warriors will go with you to Fort Rice to hear the words and propositions of the Great Father's commissioners. If their words are acceptable, peace shall be made." Then he took his seat.

All applauded the words of Black Moon. The other chiefs followed and touched on the same matters and pronounced in favor of peace. Sitting Bull named only three conditions for the peace; the whites should abandon their forts; no more land should be ceded to them; lastly, they must respect the trees, especially the oaks, which the Indians almost worshiped. "They have resisted the storms of winter and the heat of summer," he said, "and like ourselves, they seem to draw from them new vigor."

A standard-bearer was chosen for the sacred banner. The honor fell to a warrior covered with scars and distinguished for his exploits. "I expressed the wish," writes Father De Smet, "that this banner on which were embroidered the name of Jesus and the image of the Blessed Virgin might be for all a pledge of happiness and safety. For a last time I recommended the tribe to the protection of Mary, *auxilium et refugium Indianorum,* as she was anciently in Paraguay, in Canada, everywhere and forevermore."

The council lasted four hours. It ended with a song that roused the echoes of the hills, and a dance that made the ground tremble. Upon his return to his lodge, the missionary found it invaded by a clamoring crowd of mothers with their babies in their arms, and followed by their other children. He at once came forth to them and they crowded around him with a rare trustfulness, very unusual among Indian children, to offer him their little hands. The mothers were not satisfied until he laid his hands upon the heads of all the babies and little ones, when they withdrew contented and happy. To contemplate the reflection of pure souls in the innocent glance of these children was a solace and repose after his arduous labors.

The next morning before daybreak, Father De Smet set off on his return journey to the fort, where the commissioners were anxiously awaiting the result of his interview. Repeating the ceremony of his arrival, the chiefs escorted him, and did not leave him until he had crossed the Powder River. Eight deputies chosen by the council and several warriors accompanied him back, among them a venerable old man, a worthy emulator of the virtues of Pananniapapi, who had come to the camp to shake the missionary's hand and to express his happiness at seeing him again. On his breast he wore a copper cross, old and worn. This was the only religious token Father De Smet had seen in all the camp, and it filled him with joy and emotion. He questioned the old man to know from whom he had received this cross. "It was you, Black Robe, who gave me this cross. I have not laid it aside for twenty-six snows. The cross has raised me to the clouds among my people. If I still walk the earth, it is to the cross that I owe it, and the Great Spirit has blessed my numerous family."

The Father asked him to explain further, and he continued:

"When I was younger, I loved whiskey to madness, and at every chance I would get drunk and commit excesses. It is now twenty-six snows since my last wild orgy. I was stupid and sick from it. Just then I had the good fortune to meet you, and you made known to me that my behavior was against the will of the Master of life and offended Him grievously. Since then I have often had opportunities; my friends have sometimes sought to induce me to join them in their illicit enjoyments, but each time this cross has come to my help. I would take it between my hands and would recall your words and invoke the Great Spirit. Ever since we first met I have renounced drink, and have never touched a drop."

Struck by this heroic perseverance, Father De Smet wanted to baptize the old man, but there was not time to instruct him. The intrepid neophyte at once proposed to join the caravan, happy in the thought that when they camped he could receive instructions from the Black Robe. At the end of eight days he was made a Christian, and with a soul overflowing with joy, returned to his tribe.

Two days later Father De Smet arrived at Fort Rice. News of his success had reached the officers and soldiers, who had prepared a triumphal reception for him. Hundreds of Indians, proudly wrapped in their mantles, their heads ornamented with feathers and ribbons, and their faces daubed with vermilion, came to meet him. The air rang with cries of joy, in which the deputies from the Hunkpapas took part. "The warriors formed a long file and marched with true military precision. It was a really remarkable spectacle, though little in accord with the tastes of the good Father, who does not love the sound of trumpets and the glare of parades," an eyewitness reported.

On July 2 the great peace council was held, in which fifty thousand Indians were represented. Not in half a century had there been such an assembly on the Missouri. The presiding generals made solemn promises to the Indians that if they would lay aside their arms, the Government would respect their rights, provide for their livelihood, and treat them as friends. Then the representatives of the tribes spoke in turn, beginning with the standard-bearer of the Hunkpapas, whose discourse was a faithful repetition of the speeches Black Moon and Sitting Bull had made to Father De Smet. When the Hunkpapas consented to make peace, the assent of the other tribes was assured. On condition of an adequate indemnity, the Sioux were to cede to the United States their reservations in Kansas and Nebraska, but they were to demand the exclusive possession of the lands north of the Niobrara.

Upon these conditions the treaty was signed. The commissioners distributed presents to the Indians, who then dispersed, each one rejoicing over a reconciliation which he believed to be lasting.

"I am persuaded," writes Major General Stanley, "that this is the most complete and the wisest of all the treaties thus far concluded with the Indians of this country. Without doubt the fulfillment of the provisions of this treaty will assure peace with the Sioux. But whatever may be the result, we can never forget nor shall we ever cease to admire the disinterested devotion of the Reverend Father De Smet, who, at the age of sixty-eight years, did not hesitate, in the midst of the heat of summer, to undertake a long and perilous journey across the burning plains, destitute of trees and even of grass; having none but corrupted and unwholesome water, constantly exposed to scalping by the Indians, and this without seeking either honors or remuneration of any sort; but solely to arrest the shedding of blood, to save, if it might be, some lives, and preserve some habitations to these savage children of the desert."

The generals who negotiated the peace wished at once to acknowledge their debt of gratitude, and immediately after the signing of the treaty they presented an address to Father De Smet, enumerating the eminent services he had rendered the United States. "We are satisfied that but for your long and painful journey into the heart of the hostile country, and but for the influence over even the most hostile of the tribes which your years of labor among them have given you, the results which we have reached here could not have been accomplished. We are well aware that our thanks can be but of little worth to you, and that you will find true reward for your labors and for the dangers and privations which you have encountered in the consciousness that you have done much to promote peace on earth and good will to men; but we should do injustice to our own feelings were we not to render to you our thanks and express our deep sense of the obligations under which you have laid us."

The humble missionary did not tarry long to listen to such praise. On July 4 he started for St. Louis. He also believed that peace was assured, and so it would have been had not the cupidity of the whites overruled the good faith of the treaty.

THE HARVEST

From the valleys of purple mountains, from the windy high plateaus,
From the heat of deep green jungles and the silver of arctic snows,
From the fields of temperate climate and the stretches
of sun-bleached sand,
One cry swells up in chorus: "Help us to understand!"

Out of the glorious beauty that swells on the restless sea,
Throbs the universal yearning of all humanity.
Souls in the prison of darkness reach for some fragments of light,
To bear hope of the morning and shatter the curtains of night.
Somewhere in the alleys of blackness, somewhere in the caverns of fear,
Lies the secret, anguished yearning for some beacon bright and clear.

Plant the seed in the valleys, the mountains, the high plateaus;
Sow in the fertile jungles, the arctic's shifting snows;
Plant in the temperate fields and the golden, burning sand—
For the Word will flower and flourish in the thirstiest of land!

Under the spell of grandeur that is the jeweled sky,
One faith, one hope, will answer mankind's unceasing cry.
Reaching to grasp the sunlight, the seeds break from the sod
And stretch in full ripe beauty to the bosom of their God.

—CASSIE EUGENIA DIXON

THIS IS A VOCATION

by Robert J. Ledogar

A vocation is a mystery.
They call it,
In official language,
"An attraction for the life."
How did it start?
A book, a friend of yours,
Some "real good guy" you knew.
Maybe it was that fifth-grade hero worship for the priest
That all boys have,
But yours stayed on.

> You try to give some reasons for it
> But it's really hard to just say why
> You made the choice you did.
> And that's because God made the choice,
> Not you.

It isn't that He tells you in a blinding vision,
As with St. Paul.
He doesn't even whisper softly to your heart
(As we were told when we were very young) —
Not really anyway.
He takes you as you are, in love with yourself,
Mostly,
And Him very little.
He gives you dreams of great accomplishments
For yourself mostly,
And Him very little.
And it doesn't matter really;

God uses every earthly way:
The great romance, escape, most anything,
As long as it can be outgrown.
There is adventure in a vocation,
Not the adventure of a midnight sick-call in
    the jungle,
Or a journey over mountain trails on horseback.
It is the adventure of losing yourself in the
    will of God;
Of discovering God's plan for the future, of
    the world,
Not yours.
His plan is never just what you expected.
But it's always new,
Always exciting,
And it's His.
This is the adventure:
The leap into the dark,
The readiness for anything—
Anything He wills that you should do,
When,
Where,
With whom,
Because and in the way
He wants it.
    That's a vocation.

KINGDOM WITHOUT GUNPOWDER

by Adolph J. Paschang

His original gift suddenly seemed inappropriate.

Chow Kung, personal geomancer, astronomer, expounder of dreams, and general wise man for the Han emperor, was alone in his gloomy study, preparing an important experiment. He put certain proportions of saltpeter, sulphur, and charcoal dust in the crockery jar, filled the jar with pebbles, and inserted a rice-straw fuse. Then he touched a flame to the fuse and ran to cover behind a wooden cabinet in a far corner of the room.

There was a shocking blast. Shards of the wine jar scarred the walls, and pebbles crashed against the roof tiles. The experimenter fanned the acrid smoke from his face and smirked with satisfaction.

"It can do," he muttered. "It is as I thought. It is good!"

After the smoke had cleared away, Chow Kung carefully inscribed the measures of the ingredients of his explosive mixture on a little plaque of bamboo and hid it inside his robes.

"Now," he said, "my theory has proved itself. It is time I was on my way."

The wise man walked through a series of courtyards and halls, to the private apartments of his master and patron, the emperor of China. (Because of his position on the palace staff, he had the privilege of audience with the ruler at any hour.) He knelt before the lounging emperor and tapped the brick floor with his forehead.

"Great Man," Chow Kung said, "this unworthy one craves

leave to remove himself for a time from the radiance of Your Presence."

"For what reason?" asked the emperor, languidly sipping tea.

"To travel far under the sky in search of wisdom, and to bring it back for the glory of the Great Man's realm."

The "Great Man" grunted assent and lazily motioned with his long-nailed fingers for the petitioner to depart.

Chow Kung went from the royal presence gladly. He felt no compunction for not having stated the true reason for the intended journey. He knew that no good, and perhaps some harm, would result if he were rash enough to tell his dissipated master that he was going to join a caravan of wise men from countries ouside the Middle Kingdom—wise men who were following a strange, new star. The shallow-minded emperor had no interest in the Sacred Books of the Jews or the tradition, much discussed among scholars of distant nations, which held that a Prince would be born who would conquer all within the four seas. The Chinese wise man certainly could not tell his royal master about the secret discovery that would give the new Prince a new power, a new weapon, an explosive that would make his armies invincible. The Han emperor would want this weapon for himself and would use it for wicked purposes. But the expected Prince, the tradition said, would do only good to mankind. Chow Kung intended to put his newly invented weapon in the newborn Prince's hands, and to offer himself to be his wise man.

"What shall I take on my journey?" the Chinese wise man considered. "Gold or silver I need little of. There are sick people everywhere; my knowledge of healing herbs will secure from them, in return, the simple food I need. Ah, but I must take my sleeping-mat—that excellent, thick mat of fine grass, soft as hair, which I myself wove and which can be folded into a small package."

The caravan followed the star, whiling away the days in earnest discussion of wisdom. When they entered the stable, the sight of the Child, lying in the manger, reassured them. They knelt and performed acts of worship, each one according to the customs of his own nation. They offered their gifts to the Child, and they understood then the symbolical meaning of what they had been inspired to bring.

Chow Kung tapped the earth three times with his forehead, then gazed long upon the face of the Child. At last he spoke to his companions:

"Among my people I am said to be wise in the reading of faces, and in the foretelling of human destinies. This Infant is, indeed, a Prince who will conquer the world. But he will not do it by means of the weapon that was to be my gift for him." The Chinese wise man then drew from within his garments the bamboo plaque inscribed with the secret formula of the explosive. With no hesitation, he took the plaque to the fire that was smoldering in a corner of the stable, and dropped his former treasure into the flames.

"But I have a better present for this newborn Prince—a present that is fitting for the kind of life that he will lead. Many a night this will ease his weary body."

Chow Kung unfolded the sleeping-mat, soft as hair, which his own hands had woven, and gently spread it over the straw on which lay the smiling Prince of all mankind.

MARYKNOLL DEPARTURE ECHOES

God guard you, Christian messengers, while on the boundless sea,
And keep you safe from shipwreck, from ills and dangers free;
And may He guide you through strange lands, where none have heard
  His Name,
That unto them who dwell in gloom, you may His grace proclaim.
God and our Lady shield you, and keep you on your way,
And apostolic gift of tongues lend you in far Cathay.

—ANONYMOUS

SAINT FRANCIS XAVIER ON
SANCIAN ISLAND

He walked enrapt this golden strand,
These very sands in ardor trod,
Whence eager eyes roved to command
The last redoubt unwon to God;
While now the wave of summer sea,
Plashing its cadence at his feet,
Creator praised more ceaselessly
Than his heart's beat.

And on the wave-girt hillock yon
The mighty Firebrand dimmed and fell,
Angelic hosts attending on
The sweet but almost loth farewell
Of envied peer, Cross-smitten till,
Scarce heaven oped, is victory won—
With one dark world to conquer still
For Mary's Son.

O lovely little isle, thy rugged shore
By lealest love in memory hallowed kept
Shall pilgrim prayer bedew forevermore,
Where Xavier slept.

—BISHOP JAMES E. WALSH

THE MISSIONER

by Graham P. McDonnell

> God is glorified best when men manifest and communicate to each other the blessings He has bestowed upon them.

Spring is a delightful season in central Japan. It does not last very long, but to people who live in Mie Prefecture on the Pacific Ocean coast, the fleeting weeks of spring are an air-conditioned prelude to the hot, stifling summer troubled by frequent typhoons.

These raging storms from the not-so-peaceful Pacific buffet the area every year, making life difficult at times for all, including Maryknoll missioners in the eleven parishes that dot the prefecture like a string of cultured pearls. Mie Prefecture is the home of these pearls, but its economic strength is based more on large factories that are moving into the rich rice-producing coastlands.

At the northern tip of the prefecture near the large seaport of Nagoya lies the sprawling flatland city of Kuwana, lapped by the sea and backed by a rear guard of high mountains. Here live one hundred thousand persons who either commute to Nagoya or find work in local industries to earn a living.

If spring is the favorite season of the year to people in Kuwana, Sunday is the day to enjoy it with excursions to the seashore or hikes in the nearby mountains. To the several hundred

Christians in the city, Sunday also means a pleasant trip to church, where they have a choice of two morning Masses and one in the evening. One Sunday morning in spring not long ago, these Christians were somewhat surprised during Mass when two priests went to the pulpit together.

Father Robert J. Reiley, their acting pastor, spoke first in Japanese.

"This morning we have a visitor from the United States," he said.

"He is Father Thomas Sadler, director of the Propagation of the Faith in Alabama. He wants to speak to you."

As the guest looked around, he began to tell them why he had come to Japan. His work, he explained, was to make the worldwide work of the Church better known in America, and to collect funds for missioners who work in different parts of the world to bring Christ's message to as many persons as possible.

Immediately the Christians in the small, ultramodern church donated by American Catholics thought of their pastor, Father Mark Tennien, and of Father Reiley, who was taking Father Tennien's place while he was home on a visit. Their heads nodded in agreement as Father Reiley translated the message line by line. Yes, they understood the importance of a missioner, for without him they would not have received the Faith they treasured.

"I am going to visit a leper colony in India when I leave Japan," the priest from Alabama continued. "They have little, so I am asking you Christians in Kuwana to help them. If you do, I am sure that God will bless you and this parish."

Less than ten minutes ticked away during the unusual bilingual plea for help, but it was long enough to convince the people of their obligation. They responded enthusiastically with a gift three times the regular Sunday offering. In cash it was not much, but the sacrifice entailed marked a growing maturity among them, all new Christians. When Father Sadler packed his bags and left Kuwana that Sunday afternoon, he had the pleasure of knowing he was the first Propagation director to take up a collection for the missions in the area of Kuwana.

It did not take Father Reiley long to experience the benefits of his parishioners' generosity. That afternoon, the young people had planned to help a local farmer get his land ready for planting. He had been sick for a few weeks and without them it would be too late. Soon after Mass, three of them crammed into the back seat of Father Reiley's minicar for the hour's ride to the farm. I went along to record the good deed on film, and to lend a hand.

"The farmer's father-in-law is dying," he remarked as we bumped along the country road. "I've asked him several times about baptism, but he hasn't shown any interest yet."

"At least we can stop in and visit him," I suggested. The tiny car with five passengers bounced uncomfortably low on the road until one deep rut stopped the two-cylinder car with a knockout punch, delaying the trip for nearly an hour. It was early afternoon before we reached the farm. After the teen-agers pulled themselves out of the back seat and wandered off, the two of us remained in the car for a few minutes.

"You know, Bob," I said, "the Gospel for last Sunday promised us anything in Christ's name, if we ask for it. Let's ask God to encourage this old man to accept baptism." After saying one fervent "Our Father," we unwound from our seats and walked toward the farmhouse.

Gomen kudasai! We tried again, "Anyone home?" There was no answer, so we slipped off our shoes at the door and stepped up on the cool *tatami* (straw mat) floor. Father Reiley led the way to the sick man's room and silently opened the sliding door. A Japanese bed and a low table were the only furniture in the small room that opened out to the garden. The old man was sleeping soundly, but he awoke when we approached and was alert to the situation.

"Go ahead and take some pictures if you like," said Father Reiley.

"That's just the thing I wanted. I need a good photograph for my funeral, you know."

"You won't need that picture for awhile yet, *ojiisan*," said the priest with a smile. The old man beamed when he heard the

Japanese word *ojiisan,* or grandfather. After all, at seventy-three, he was old enough to be the priest's grandfather. "You should think about baptism first," continued Father Reiley. "You want to go to heaven, don't you?"

Yes, he wanted to go to heaven, nodded the old man in agreement. He knew about God and believed in His Son, but at the moment he was more interested in a good portrait for his funeral. At all Japanese funerals, a photograph of the deceased person is prominently displayed. Moving in for a close-up, I asked:

"*Ojiisan,* do you have your ticket to get into heaven?"

"A ticket to get into heaven? What do you mean?" he answered with a puzzled frown.

"It's like this," explained Father Reiley, picking up the cue. "You know about Christ, how He came to save all men, and help them find happiness forever."

"I like that idea of happiness," he admitted cautiously.

"Baptism is the *nyujoken,* your entrance ticket to heaven," said Father Reiley who knew how important such tickets are in Japan, where admission to any gathering is by ticket only. "With baptism, *ojiisan,* you are sure of getting into heaven. Without it, you're taking a chance."

"If that's the case, the sooner the better, young man. You can baptize me right now."

Father Reiley began preparing for the ceremony. As he poured the baptismal water, I took the pictures. Confirmation and anointing of the sick followed immediately.

With the baptism of *ojiisan* the generosity of the teen-agers at the farm and of the parishioners at Mass had already reaped an early harvest for the Church in Kuwana. It had been a good day. Throughout Japan there were other reasons for joy during the hour we spent with the old man. More than one hundred babies were born, and the total for that day was about twenty-seven hundred. Perhaps nine of those newly born persons will someday be Catholic. No more than twenty will be Christian if the present rate of progress stays the same.

Conversions in Japan number around ten thousand per year at the present time. The total number of Catholics is slowly increasing, but at a slower rate than the population. In 1966, the number of Catholics reached three hundred thirty-three thousand. If all the Christians in Japan are counted, the total is not yet a million, or less than one per cent of the population.

How does the missioner build a Church against those odds? Should he pack up his trunks and go back home where there is a shortage of priests and a heavy work load to keep him busy and happy? In short, what is the meaning of a missioner in twentieth-century Japan, or in any one of the so-called "mission" countries around the world?

The answer to these questions and to many others can be found in decrees on mission activity and other subjects treated in the sessions of Vatican II. The Church is aware that there still remains a gigantic missionary task for her to accomplish, for the message of Christ has not yet been heard, or scarcely so, by two billion human beings.

Guide lines drawn up at the Council plead with the Church to become a part of all different groups of people for the same motive that led Christ to bind Himself in virtue of His Incarnation to the definite social and cultural conditions of Palestine nearly two thousand years ago.

If missioners go into "mission" lands simply to plant the cross as triumphal spiritual victors, they will fail. But if they go as co-operators, with a message of service and love for all, many persons will welcome them, and some will choose to follow.

Kuwana is a case in point. In September 1958, Father Tennien, exiled from Red China, began living in Kuwana on a small plot of land between a Buddhist temple and a Shinto shrine. In 1959, he built a modern, functional church, where he was able to gather a few Christians and some "yet-to-be" Christians. Before the walls were up a ferocious typhoon lashed central Japan with the worst storm that anyone could remember. Hundreds were killed and thousands were driven out of their homes. At the church, one of the higher spots of land in the city, two feet of water covered the freshly-poured foundations.

Reports from outlying villages began to filter in with pleas for food and clothing. The Christians, eager to help, used boats to reach areas of the greatest need. Money for the unfinished church was commandeered to buy rice and relief goods shipped by trucks from Kyoto. As the waters subsided, the church became a center of hope and aid for a thousand persons a day until the area struggled back to normalcy nearly two months later. The work, dubbed "Operation Mercy" by Father Tennien, earned much goodwill for the Church in Kuwana, and it led some persons to learn more about the teachings of Christ.

Little by little, the number of Christians grew, and Father Tennien was able to spend more time with other needs which were as pressing as the aftermath of the typhoon, but not quite as apparent. He soon realized that one thing the people wanted was a kindergarten for their children to get a good start in life. There were other such schools in the city, but with the number of young families moving into the area, this opportunity for service became more demanding.

After months of planning, he was able to obtain the land, permits, and donations for the project. With a Japanese architect, Father Tennien worked out his ideas that soon materialized as one of the finest kindergartens in Japan. Some Catholics and many others not yet in the fold enjoy the fruits of his labor and vision. By offering their children a chance to get the best in preschool education, he was effectively bringing the Church to Kuwana. To help him with the additional duties imposed by the kindergarten, Father Tennien needed an assistant. That is how Father Reiley of Pottsville, Pennsylvania, happened to come to Kuwana.

Together the two missioners worked to discover and meet the needs of the people in Kuwana. As the only foreigners there, they both realized that a class in English conversation was a definite possibility. Some of Father Tennien's students had won English speech contests and many more wanted to study. Since the end of World War II most students in Japan have been taught to read and write English. In middle school and in high school they study grammar and develop a basic vocabulary that helps them in college, where science and economics textbooks are often in English. But speaking English is something they cannot learn in school.

With the help of a college professor in the parish, Father Reiley started a panel-discussion group that met after the regular English classes for adults. Short talks were given about various aspects of the Faith. Questions in either English or Japanese by the students helped them learn something about the Church, and enabled them to practice their English too.

In some cases this type of work does lead some to the Church, but the missioner who expects those results and waits for them is bound to be disappointed. The student who comes for conversation does not want to study the Bible in English. At a Catholic school, he expects a good education, and in a hostel, he wants a place to live and study. If the missioner can offer these things without strings attached, both he and his service will be accepted.

The Church in Japan has built and staffed old folks' homes, schools and homes for handicapped children, hospitals and schools. Youth centers and hostels are other contributions. These projects on an institutional level show that the Church is interested in the people, not as potential converts, but as fellow human beings. On the private level of personal contacts, missioners have found needs on all sides that have often developed into lasting friendships.

One day Father Reiley and another priest, both still unsure of the Japanese they had learned in school, were lost in Tokyo. They asked a young man for directions. He was a newspaper reporter who was extremely helpful, as he guided them to their destination. When they were parting, he asked if he might visit them sometime. A few days later he and Father Reiley met and talked about many things—baseball, politics, and life in the United States. Two hours later, just before leaving, he asked Father Reiley to help him with an English problem. The two hours had been a "warming up" period so necessary in Japanese etiquette.

Soon the two became good friends. On one occasion they

were talking about the value of the human person. Their views differed, and as their voices rose, the conversation became quite heated. Then, abruptly, the young man changed the subject to Japanese history, and for thirty minutes he fascinated his missionary friend with some little-known facts about an early emperor of Japan.

"We couldn't argue about Japanese history—at least I couldn't," recalls Father Reiley. The young man told him later that he had changed the conversation deliberately, so that they could part with a good feeling, or *kimochi*. To Father Reiley, still new in Japan, it was a lesson worth remembering.

The work of the Church and her missioners in a country like Japan, or in any country, should always be that of service. There will be many opportunities to explain why we are doing our work, and some persons will be attracted to learn more. These are the persons who will carry on this Christian witness. In the meantime, the role of the missioner is that of continued service with only a few of the consolations of the harvest. He is a guest, a friendly outsider who is willing to help, whatever the need. He can do nothing about being an outsider, but he should be friendly, sympathetic, and helpful. Only then will his message have any chance of acceptance.

One question that bothers missioners is not so much "When will Japan be ready for Christianity," but, "When will Christianity be ready for Japan, for that matter, for the Orient?" The message that Francis Xavier brought to Japan four hundred years ago had, naturally, a strong European stamp. This might have developed into a genuine Oriental Christianity if it had not been suppressed by persecution. The message that missioners today are presenting to Japan has a similar Western stamp which hopefully will gradually disappear as a result of the Second Vatican Council and a greater understanding of different cultures in the Church.

The missioner who can adapt to the ways of the people he works among will do much to prepare Christianity for Japan. But only the Japanese, the Korean, the Chinese, or the Indian can make the subtle distinctions to fit their own religious aspirations. Without the wise missioner to find and train those men, encourage and lead them, this problem will remain unsolved. One of the challenges to the missioner is to live as a guest, to serve, to lead, and to encourage the Church to develop to that point where Christians of his adopted country can make the vital adaptations.

There is another problem that Francis Xavier did not have to face. The average person in Japan is puzzled by the multiplicity of Christian sects. When the historical causes are explained to them, they nod, "I see, it's just like Buddhism in Japan." The missioner who can cooperate with other Christian missionaries, and treat them as brothers, is needed in Japan to help heal this wound.

Soon after the first session of Vatican II closed, one of the Protestant ministers in central Japan asked a Catholic friend if the bishop of Kyoto would give them a talk. At the gathering an American Protestant missionary remarked to Father Reiley, "There's one thing about you Catholics. You are very willing to invite others to your church, but you never come to see us or join in our services."

"I decided then and there to visit him," recalls Father Reiley. Together they discovered many profitable insights in their work to bring Christ to the Japanese.

In Japan, as in many "mission" countries, a missioner is struck by the number of naturally good individuals he meets. This impression is vividly described by Father Reiley in these words: "If these people are so good without Christianity, what would they be as Christians, as persons who had received the fullness of Christ's teachings? But then you soon realize that among the Japanese, as among every other nation of human beings, there are some wonderful people, and there are others who aren't so nice."

Missioners can learn by sincere and patient dialogue what treasures a bountiful God has distributed among the nations of the earth. At the same time he tries to illumine these treasures with the light of the gospel, to set them free. This dialogue, this constant search to find the goodness and the needs of the people among whom he lives takes time and demands humility. It is a challenging life simply because there are no blueprints. Of course there are routine tasks, but in so many areas the paths are not marked. The missioner must take those paths to establish the Church. He must seek out those who are ready for the gospel, and he must be kind and patient to those who are not, always remembering that he is their guest.

Missionary activity among the nations, says Vatican II, differs from pastoral activity exercised among the faithful, as well as from undertakings aimed at restoring unity among Christians. This may not be apparent to the casual observer, who will find parishes in almost every city in Japan. In these eight hundred centers of Christian life he will find activities similar to parishes all over the world.

But these parish activities do not take up all of the missioner's time. His daily schedule will be filled with other tasks, such as teaching at a nearby university, or calling on the mayor to seek government help for crippled children. He will be busy studying the language and the customs of his people, always alert to ways and means of helping the entire community. For a person who has a sense of adventure and a sincere interest in others, it is a happy life with countless opportunities for service.

THE BODY

Obviously this body is a garment
that sits here vacantly.
A piece of drifting cloud
that stops in a corner of the sky.
This body is a garment
the soul wears but temporarily.

— "BLUEBIRD"

PRIEST IN A SEAL HOUSE

by Gontran de Poncins

For six years he had been living on nothing but frozen
fish and he was none the worse for it.

I am going to say to you that a human being can live without
complaint in an ice-house built for seals at a temperature of
fifty-five degrees below zero, and you are going to doubt my
word. Yet what I say is true, for this was how Father Henry
lived; and when I say "ice-house for seals" I am not using
metaphorical language. Father Henry lived in a hole dug out
by the Eskimos in the side of a hill as a place in which to store
seal-meat in summer. The earth of this hill is frozen a hundred
feet down, and it is so cold that you can hardly hold your bare
hand to its surface.

An Eskimo would not have lived in this hole. An igloo is a
thousand times warmer, especially one built out on the sea
over the water warm beneath the coat of ice. I asked Father
Henry why he lived thus. He said merely that it was more con-
venient, and pushed me ahead of him into his cavern.

If I were to describe the interior, draw it for you inch by
inch, I should still be unable to convey the reality to you. There
was a wooden door framed in the side of the slope. You stooped
to enter the doorway and found yourself in a passage. On the
right, standing as usual on end, were a half dozen frozen seal

* From *Kabloona*, by Gontran de Poncins. Copyright by Reynal & Hitchcock,
used by permission.

powdered with snow. On the left lay a bitch, suckled by a puppy. Ahead was a second door and behind it a second passage about ten feet deep and so narrow that you went through it sidewise, so low that your hood scraped the snow that had drifted in and sent it down into your neck. At the end of this passage was the hermit's cave.

Two seal-oil lamps were burning as I went in. These lamps light up an igloo, because an igloo is circular and more or less white: here they gave off only a faint gleam and the corners of the cave were hidden in darkness. The lamps stood on an empty barrel at the left of the door. Above them hung the drying rack, a sort of net suspended from three nails in which, if you looked hard enough, you could see a glove, a boot, but surely not a pair. At the right a shelf had been nailed up, and on it stood a queerly shaped kerosene lamp, the lid of a pot, a circular Eskimo knife, a rag, an empty tobacco tin, and a box of salt. Straight ahead, facing the door, was a couch.

Compared with this hole, an igloo was a palace. From the door to the couch opposite measured four and one half feet. Two people could not stand comfortably here, and when Father Henry said Mass I used to kneel on the couch. "If you didn't, you would be in my way," was how he put it. It was so small that when I came in from outdoors I never contrived to shake the snow off my coat without shaking it all over the couch.

The couch was a rickety wooden surface supported in the middle by a strut, over which two caribou hides had been spread. On these three planks forming a slightly tilted surface, Father Henry slept. To the right was a hole in the ground, which we blocked in part by the packing case containing my effects.

"The box will be your couch," said Father Henry; "and if you remember to keep out of that hole, you'll be perfectly comfortable."

Father Henry has no table knife, and I doubt that he has ever had a fork. His spoon disappeared a few days before my arrival, and he thought it might have fallen into the hole. I pushed the box aside and began to hunt for the spoon. After I had pulled up a dozen frozen fish-heads, an old parka, a sack with a bit of flour still in it, and five Arctic-hare hides, I found the spoon.

No white man has anything to boast of in the Arctic, but Father Henry no longer had the little with which he had started. Whatever he had possessed on first coming out here was to him part of a forgotten past, and he referred to it as "all those things." It had helped in the beginning, but now "all that" was superfluous. What, for example, did he want with a plate when his only meal of the day was a lump of frozen fish, eaten on waking in the morning? What good was that lamp to him, since he had no kerosene? How could he have used a pen here where ink froze? A napkin, which would have stiffened like a board in this cold? The only thing to do was to lick one's fingers, and indeed the gesture had become automatic with him. But since he knew that I was what Frenchy Chartrand at Coppermine had called a "cream puff," he gave me a ptarmigan skin to wipe my fingers on. This is the classic towel of the Arctic. It lasts the whole winter through without washing, and if you really mean to honor your guest, it is with this ptarmigan skin that you wipe his plate.

Father Henry lacked every object known to the civilization of the white man. "Those things make no sense here," — and with that phrase he disposed of the subject. When I unpacked my gifts for him, rejoicing in advance over the delight they would give him, he stood by shaking his head. No, he can no longer eat white man's food: not even rice. He cannot digest the stuff. "That sort of food doesn't keep a man warm. Frozen fish, now . . . " He loves frozen fish. There is nothing like it, he says, to warm you inside. Doctors tell you that you ought to vary your diet. Well . . . For six years he had been living on nothing but frozen fish, and he was none the worse off for it. When he awoke he groped on the ground, picked up a great chunk of fish frozen so hard that he had to thaw it out a little with his lips and breath before he could bite into it, and with this he regaled himself. It was succulent, it warmed you up, it sated your hunger, and you felt fine. As for eating in the evening, no: it would have kept him awake all night.

Despite this discouragement I continued to unpack. The cheese: I should finish it myself. The cigars (Gibson's gift): there was a Belgian priest at Repulse Bay who loved cigars, and they were put aside for him. The pipe: poor Father Henry! He had had a pipe. Smoking it from time to time had been his only luxury. But my Lord Bishop had asked all his missionaries to make one supplementary sacrifice, and Father Henry had sacrificed his pipe. I protested; but I do not believe I quite got him to promise to smoke again. As for the rest of the gifts, he took them and put them to one side, saying absentmindedly, "Very kind, very kind." His thanks were an acknowledgement of the intention: the gifts themselves had no meaning for him, no value.

His possessions were limited to lamps, dogs, sealing nets, and clothes. He spent a great deal of time looking to his lamps, and the Eskimos teased him about it. "You do it better than we do," they would say with their smile; and it is a fact that nothing wants so much attention as a seal-oil lamp. You can spend hours trimming the improvised wick, shortening or lengthening it, adding more seal-oil — or rather blubber which, melting, becomes oil — when you hear it splutter. It used to make me smile to see Father Henry, in the midst of his Mass, between the syllables of an *Introibo ad altare*, turn from the plank on the right that was his altar and trim the wick while he continued his service.

It was six o'clock next morning when I awoke. I had slept badly on my box, unable to stretch my legs and half fallen into the hole. Father Henry had long been up and tended to his lamps, and now he was sitting on the couch. He had slept in his clothes: one could not do otherwise in this terrible cold that rose from the earth, and he was sitting motionless, fearing to wake me, murmuring his prayers to himself. Now that I was awake he prepared his altar by shoving to one side the kerosene lamp and empty tobacco tin, and the Mass began. I "served," squatting on the couch.

"Dominus," said Father Henry; and then ducking beneath a beam overhead he appeared round the other side:

"*Vobiscum.*"

And I, from the couch: "*Et cum spiritu tuo.*" . . .

When he heard confession from one of the natives, his box was the outer passage and the scene took place under the vitreous eyes of the frozen seal. In this virtual darkness, at fifty degrees below, the two men would kneel and murmur together.

All day long I was weary, unable to get warm. I lay in my sleeping-bag and drank tea, and as Father Henry drank with me we chatted. I tore the paper off a packet of biscuits and said as I threw the wrapper away:

"An Eskimo would pick up a bit of paper like that as soon as you threw it down."

"So would I," Father Henry said calmly, and he picked up what I had thrown away and put it on a shelf. He told me how he had been informed of my coming. Nothing could better display the mentality of these natives.

An Eskimo had come running into the cavern and had stood breathless before him. He was the bearer of astounding news and proud to be bringing it. But he did not speak. It is ill-bred to be in haste, and it is ill-bred also to attack any subject directly. So, shaking the snow from his clothes, he had taken a mug of tea from the unsuspecting priest and had drunk it in silence. Then, having cut himself a slice of fish, he had eaten, and smoked a cigarette. Time passed, and Father Henry went about his household tasks.

Eventually Father Henry asked him a question.

"*Kis-si-wi?*" (Are you alone?)

"*Nak-ka.*" (No.)

"*Oo-shu-tik-sak,*" said the Eskimo, giving Shongili's true name and refraining from mentioning me.

"*Sug-mat?*" (How does that happen?)

The Eskimo looked at Father Henry and smiled. Now he was heavy with his news, electrically charged, bursting to speak, proud of his mission of annunciation. And yet he was silent again for a time. Finally he exploded:

"*Kabloona-ralu!*"

Father Henry stopped short and turned round with a start. "What is his name?"

"Ma-i-ke."

All this meant nothing to Father Henry, for he knew nothing about me, not even this nickname by which I was known among the Eskimos. (Of themselves, the Eskimos might have called me "He of the Long Ears" or something equally flattering.) He hunted round in his mind. Who could it be?

"What does he do?"

"*Nu-nang-juar-le-rie.*" (He draws the image of the earth.) The Eskimos had seen me sketching.

"Is it Learmonth?"

"That is not his name."

"Is it a policeman?"

"I believe not. He went into the igloos. He saw the Cross. He 'follows' as we do."

"Does he speak Eskimo?"

At this point Father Henry said to me: "Observe the delicacy of these men. He might have said, 'Badly.' Instead, in order not to hurt any one, he said, 'All that he has said to us, we have clearly understood.'

"Then," Father Henry went on, "they brought you gradually into Pelly Bay. I was at work shovelling the snow away from my door while one of them on the watch called out to me: 'He is in sight. He is turning the point. He will be here in a moment.' And I, hunting feverishly for my gloves! 'He is very near.' And then, just as I started out of the door: '*A-ood-lar-mat,*' — He has arrived!"

We talked of many things and among others of dogs, for Father Henry had a superb team of which in his selfless way he was proud.

"The more I see of the dogs," he said, "the better I understand the men. The same defects; the same qualities. And how different they are from our dogs at home! What hypocrisy there is in them at times, and with what pleasure they play tricks on you, turning round each time to give you the same jeering look.

On the other hand I have known them to go a week without food, trotting along at a steady pace with no single whimper of complaint. To go three or four days hungry is their frequent lot, and when night falls and the sled is stopped, they will lie down and go to sleep unfed, as if they expected nothing better."

I expressed my regret that I should never know the Eskimo language well enough to grasp its inner essence, and should therefore never know the men who spoke it, seeing that language is the faithful mirror of a people's spirit.

"If you knew what condensation there is in their language!" Father Henry exclaimed. "Their phrases are as sober as their faces. A gleam in an Eskimo's eye tells you more than a half dozen of our sentences concerning desire, repugnance, or another emotion. Each Eskimo word is like that gleam: it suggests at once what has happened and what is to come, and it contains that touch of the unexpressed which makes this people so mysterious and attractive.

"Their shades of expression are infinite," he went on. "They are Asiatic, and perhaps for that reason imperceptible to us. We are so habituated to our simple yes and no that we ignore the existence of a scale of gradations between affirmation and negation. It took me a long time to understand what was going on in their minds, and many things had to be revealed to me before I knew where I stood with these men. They would explain: 'He did not refuse to do as you asked; he merely told you that there were obstacles in the way.' Or: 'He did not deceive you, he did not lie to you; he merely omitted to affirm the thing to you.' It was hard for me to grasp the care they took not to commit themselves. Each time that they speak they leave themselves a back door through which to retreat. For example:

"An Eskimo comes in from trapping. There are several visitors in his igloo. He picks up the snow-beater, and when his clothes are free of snow he takes them off. All this without a word. Then, as he knows that the others are waiting for him to speak, he says: 'Those foxes! There is no way to get them.' Silence 'And besides, I'm not good for much any more. An old man.' Again silence. Finally, still as if he were speaking to himself: 'But I got three to-day.' "

I told Father Henry of my trouble getting to Pelly Bay. He was astonished.

"How could it possibly have taken so long?"

"I can't say. And yet, heaven knows I told those men often enough that I was in a hurry to get here."

Father Henry laughed. "That's it then," he said. "That explains it. You deserved to be led round and round in a circle to teach you a lesson."

And he told me how he went about getting a sled up to Repulse Bay in double time.

He would send for an Eskimo and say to him: "I want you to go to Repulse Bay. It will take you a good bit of time. You are young; probably you do not know the way very well; your dogs are not worth much. Still, nobody else is available, so go along."

Times passes, and the Eskimo is back from the trip.

"Well?" says Father Henry to him.

The man looks crestfallen. Things went badly. The weather was worse than he had expected. Then one of the dogs fell sick. And there were other difficulties, each of which he lists with scrupulous care. But he had gone and come in twelve days, just the same, and he knew that Father Henry knew that was fast travelling.

When we spoke of Eskimo murder, Father Henry told me about a man now at Committee Bay who had come to him one day, and, after the usual tea and silence, had said to him suddenly:

"I took the old woman out on the ice today."

It was his own mother that he had driven out and set down at sea to freeze to death. He was fond of her, he explained. He had always been kind to her. But she was too old, she was no longer good for anything; so blind, she couldn't even find the porch to crawl into the igloo. So, on a day of blizzard, the whole family agreeing, he had taken her out, and they had struck camp and gone off, leaving her to die.

"With God's help I hope in time to change these things, to soften some of their ways," said Father Henry; "but it is difficult. They live a hard life, and it is in all respects a material life. They would say, if they knew our words, that they had to 'face facts.' That man had indeed been a good son. You must have seen yourself how they look after the aged on the trail, running back so often to the sled to see if the old people are warm enough, if they are comfortable, if they are not perhaps hungry and want a bit of fish. And the old people are a burden on the trail, a cause of delay and of complication. But the day comes when, after years with no word of complaint, the young people deem the thing no longer possible, and they leave the old man or the old woman on the ice. The old people are told in advance what their end is to be, and they submit peacefully without a word of recrimination. Sometimes, indeed, they are the first to suggest this end for themselves."

There are violent murders, however, that are harder to explain. The murder, for example, that results purely from the instinct of the hunter. One of Father Henry's stories I had already been told at King.

Three men were on the trail together. Evening came and they built an igloo. They sat talking and smoking. The igloo had been hastily put up and a wide hole appeared overhead which one of the men went out to patch up. As the two others continued to sit and smoke, one of them chanced to raise his eyes. Overhead the third was patching the hole. His loose clothing had parted, and his great brown belly was bare and visible as he worked.

"A fine belly," said the first Eskimo.

The other raised his head. *"Eh-eh-eh!"* he affirmed with appreciation, "a very fine belly."

They continued to stare at it. The first man spoke again: "I could stick my knife into a belly like that."

The second man said nothing. He stood up and planted his snow-knife into that belly. It was irresistible: the belly was too fine.

Father Henry and I took to each other from the beginning.

A seal ice-house brings people together more quickly than a hotel room, and a good deal more intimately. Conversation in such a place is frank and honest, untrammelled by the reticences of society.

I said to him one day: "Don't you find this life too hard for you, living alone like this?"

"Oh, no," he said; "I am really very happy here. My life is simple, I have no worries, I have everything I need." (He had nothing at all!) "Only one thing preys on my mind now and then: it is — what will become of me when I am old?"

He said this with such an air of confessing a secret weakness that my heart swelled with sudden emotion, and I tried clumsily to comfort him.

"When you are old," I said, "you will go back among the white men. You will be given a mission at Chesterfield, or at Churchill."

"No, no, no!" he protested, "not that."

What could I say? I had no right to press the point. But at that moment I wished with all my heart that every man who had a warm house and assurance of a comfortable old age might see this lone priest in the Arctic.

Another time I expostulated with him. "You cannot live like this," I said, "devoid of everything. You are not responsible to yourself alone. You have a mission to fulfill, and you must equip yourself for it, must have those things that will ensure your health and well-being so that you may fulfill it properly. Let me take back those foxes of yours" — offerings brought by the natives — "and trade them for you at the Post. I'll send you back the things you need."

He refused categorically. "No, no. I have not the right to dispose of the foxes. They belong to my bishop."

"Never mind your bishop!" I said. "Let me have those five foxes."

But he was unshakable. "No," he said, wagging his head; "impossible."

"Very well," said I crossly. "You need harness, nets, rope —

not for yourself, but for your mission, and I am going to send them to you. You will force me to pay for them out of my own pocket."

Ah, the poor man! I had faced him with a case of conscience, and he was upset. "All right, all right," he agreed. "But it is very bad of you to put me in this position. I'll let you have the foxes."

He didn't though. When time came for me to leave, his scruples had returned. "I've thought it over," he said, "and I find you are wrong. There is nothing I need."

I had been with him several days when I began to see that something was gnawing at him. Something was on his mind, and he was going round and round in a circle.

"Come," I said. "What is it? You have something on your mind."

It must really have been preying on him for he made no attempt to evade me.

"Ah, well," he said. "You see for yourself how it is. Here you are, a layman, enduring these privations, travelling 'tough' " — another locution of the North — "depriving yourself of your only cheese for me. Well, if you do these things what should I, a religious, be doing?"

I stared at him. His eyes were hollow, brilliant, strangely brilliant. A religious, indeed! What a distance that one word suddenly placed between him and me! This man was animated and kept alive by something other than the power of nature. Life had in a sense withdrawn from him, and a thing more subtle, more mysterious, had taken its place. He was doubly superior to me, by his humility and by his mystical essence as priest. "I am of the most humble extraction," he had said to me. He was a Norman peasant, and it came to me suddenly that if he had chosen to live in this seal-hole instead of an igloo, his choice had been motivated in part by the peasant instinct to build his own sort of farmstead, even here in the Arctic. He took no particular pride from his origin, nor is it because he referred to it that I speak of his humility, which was Christian, not worldly. He was a direct, simple, naked soul dressed only in the seamless garment of his Christianity.

By grace of that garment, his flesh was as if it were not. When I said, for example, "It is not warm this morning," he would answer mechanically, "No, it is not warm"; but he did not feel the cold. "Cold" was to him merely a word; and if he stopped up the door, or livened up the lamp, it was for my sake he did it. He had nothing to do with "those things," and this struggle was not his struggle: he was somewhere else, living another life, fighting with other weapons. He was right and I was wrong in those moments when I rebelled against his existence and insisted rashly that he "could not live like this." I was stupid not to see, then, that he truly had no need of anything. He lived, he sustained himself, by prayer. Had he been dependent only upon human strength he would have lived in despair, been driven mad. But he called upon other forces, and they preserved him. Incredible as it would seem to the incredulous, when the blizzard was too intense to be borne, he prayed, and the wind dropped. When, one day, he was about to die of hunger—he and the single Eskimo who accompanied him—he prayed; and that night there were two seals in their net. It was childish of me to attempt to win him back to reality: he could not live with reality.

I, the "scientist," was non-existent beside this peasant mystic. He towered over me. My resources were as nothing compared to his, which were inexhaustible. His mystical vestment was shelter enough against hunger, against cold, against every assault of the physical world from which he lived apart. Once again I had been taught that the spirit was immune and irresistible, and matter corruptible and weak. There is something more than cannon in war, and something more than grub and shelter in the existence of this conqueror of the Arctic. If, seeing what I have seen, a man still refused to believe this, he would do better to stay at home, for he had proved himself no traveller.

For three days, sleds had been running between the different camps of the Arviligjuarmiut to arrange in advance for some one to drive me back to King William Land. I had said to Father Henry that I should wait until he found an Eskimo who had an errand at the Post, and that I hoped the man would not be a worthless fellow like Shongili. Father Henry had taken a mental census of the clan, very conscientiously, and then declared that the best man for the job was Ittimangnerk.

This was the start of a series of complicated manoeuvres. First, someone had to be sent to Ittimangnerk to let him know that Father Henry wanted to see him. Off went a sled to the camp where he was thought to be.

The sled came back with Ittimangnerk's brother, Manilak. It appeared that Ittimangnerk was far to the north, hunting the seal in the open waters.

With a note from the priest, Manilak started for the north. Either he would bring back his brother, or he would bring an answer from his brother. We should have to wait several days, meanwhile, for Ittimangnerk was sixty miles off. By the time we had his answer there would have been done one hundred and sixty miles of travelling on my account.

Five days later, Manilak came back, bringing with him, written in syllabic Eskimo, a letter from Ittimangnerk so beautiful that I must transcribe it:

"Since the white man has no companion for his journey, I shall go with him. I greet the white man. I go now to hunt seal for the journey. What shall I do? I will be so shy with the white man. Write to me. Encourage me. Ittimangnerk greets the Priest."

We decided as follows. When time came for me to leave, Manilak would fetch me and would drive me as far as a camp situated half way between Pelly Bay and the open water. There I should be met by his brother, and we would proceed together to King William Land. Manilak should have done two hundred miles of trail for me out of pure goodness of heart.

This was the coldest season of the year, when the thermometer was never higher than fifty degrees below zero. The trail back was bound to be hard, and though I hoped for much from these true Eskimos, I could not look forward to the journey with entire ease of mind.

Father Henry gave me a walrus tusk, and I left him divers little gifts—among them a half sack of flour, five candles, a knife, a half bottle of rum (from Gibson). Probably he would never make use of any of these things.

As I was about to be driven off he took both my hands. "Your visit has done me a great deal of good," he said. "I believe that I shall be a better man for your having been here." I have wandered pretty much everywhere; nowhere have I heard words more beautiful.

JUST FOR ME

For me? You say it was for me
  The Son of God came down to earth,
Born just as any Indian babe,
  Then, bundled up, was laid upon the hay—
How could it be? How could it be?

Where is He now? Does He live far away?
  Show me the trail! Please tell me more of Him.
How I should like to see Him! Yet I'm old:
  I cannot walk the trails as once I could
And mountain paths are steep.
  So, if I went, I'd have to travel slow.
Would you go with me, if I were to go?

"Come unto me!" Those words included me?
  He calls for me*? You're* sure *He calls for me?*
Would He receive me*, if I came to Him?*
  He cares *for me? You say He cares for* me*!*
Ah, then, I'll come—my heart cries out for Him!
  Oh, that I might have known Him long ago, when I was wee.
To think I almost missed Him! And He came for me*!*

—WALTER S. MILLER

SAVAGE NEW GUINEA

by Jens Bjerre

The author finds a world far removed from the twentieth century in which strange diseases and unexplained quarrels take place.

Having completed my collection amongst the Engas, I chartered a plane by radio to fly the collection and me to Headquarters in Mount Hagen; from there I intended to continue to the Southern Highlands district immediately, for that area also sends patrols into relatively unexplored areas.

I waited three days for the plane to come to Laiagam; but every morning I was told over the wireless that the plane had started but had had to turn back because clouds were closing in over the mountains and hindering visibility.

New Guinea's pilots are the most capable in the world—and they need to be, for they fly in the world's most dangerous flying area. In small machines such as Cessna, Dragon and Norseman they wind their way in and out between the mountains and the clouds, bringing supplies to lonely patrol stations which are often hidden under a layer of cloud in deep valleys. They fly guided less by map and instruments than by landmarks such as mountain peaks, rivers, lakes, waterfalls, valleys, and villages. Often the clouds suddenly close in and hide these landmarks from the pilot. Then he has to fly by memory and good judgment as well as compass and altimeter.

Without these daring pilots the major part of New Guinea

would still be unexplored countryside. Several flying accidents happen in New Guinea every year—but even so, astonishingly few considering the dangerous conditions under which flying takes place. A few years ago no company would take out insurance for flying men or materials in New Guinea.

The pilot who flew me in the chartered Cessna plane from Laiagam to the Southern Highlands district entertained me with accounts of emergency landings and precarious situations while we flew between clouds and mountain tops. He told me how, the previous week, he ran into a thunder cloud and lost his way in the clouds during a trip late in the afternoon from Goroka, in the Eastern Highlands, to Mount Hagen. For over an hour he circled round in the clouds without knowing where he was. In the end it grew dark and he gave up all hope of rescue. An emergency landing in the dark in the mountains was tantamount to certain death. Meanwhile the Mount Hagen station, which had been told of his take-off and was expecting him, had alarmed the flying authorities in the coastal town of Madang. From there messages were sent by radio to all patrol stations in the highlands to listen for the machine and report immediately if they heard it.

"And the miracle happened," he said with a smile. "A patrol officer in the Bismarck Mountains—a long way off my normal course—heard the plane circling high up, after he had stood listening for half an hour. He immediately sent a message to the flying authorities in Madang who then informed me of my position. As soon as I knew where I was I could set course for Madang. When they heard me there, they sent up a DC-3 with all its lights blazing. I tailed it closely and landed safely. But that hour while I was circling between the mountain peaks in the absolute dark was worse than all my experiences in the Royal Air Force during the war."

After a couple of hours' flying, we landed in Mendi, the Headquarters of the Southern Highlands district, where I had to wait a few days before I could go further on patrol westwards into the uncontrolled areas. Here in Mendi a modern hospital has been built from materials which were brought up from the coast by air. The district commissioner, Mr. J. R. White, with whom I stayed, introduced me to the hospital's doctor, Dr. Vincent Zigas, who is an emigrant from Estonia and who for some years has worked amongst the natives of New Guinea.

A few years ago one read in the press all over the world about a mysterious illness, Kuru, also called the "laughing death" that had afflicted a particular tribe in New Guinea. It was Dr. Zigas who first discovered the disease, which was completely unknown to medical science and about which we are still in the dark. He organized the fight against it.

"It is misleading to call the phenomenon the laughing death," Dr. Zigas said, when I spoke to him about the phenomenon. "There is no question of the sufferer going laughing to death. The whole thing is horribly tragic. The first symptoms of the illness are that the victims suffer attacks of cramp with violent shaking in all the limbs. They lose control of their voices, and sound as if they are giggling or laughing when they try to articulate. Gradually the victim is completely paralyzed and unable to move, eat, or talk. Six to ten months after they are first attacked they die in a terrible condition of starvation, festering bed-sores and inflammation of the lungs. None has so far been cured. It is the nervous system which is attacked. In laboratories in America and Australia experts are investigating the cause of the disease — but up until now without success.

"The illness is so much the more mysterious because it occurs only in a limited area, where the Forei tribe live. There are about 10,000 people in the area. The illness attacks women especially; over half the tribe's women and about ten percent of the men die of this ghastly disease. In many of the villages there are two and a half times as many men as women.

"The men want to move away, but are not allowed to in case the disease spreads to the surrounding tribes. How long the illness has been in existence is not known, because Europeans have been in contact with the tribe for only a few years.

"The natives themselves believe the illness is due to one who wishes them dead having practiced sorcery. They believe it can happen that a man steals something or other belonging to the one he wants to kill — perhaps a bit of hair or an item of clothing — then wraps it in some leaves and hides it in some secret place, perhaps by a stream. Each day he goes there, unobserved, and takes it out and shakes it violently while he recites some incantations. He repeats this every day until the owner begins to tremble with the Kuru illness. Even though doctors and missionaries have now worked amongst the Forei tribe for several years, the majority of the tribe are still convinced that this is the explanation. Nor have we any other explanation to give them.

"When someone who has been attacked by Kuru dies, the family try to find out who has brought the illness on him by magic. If they suspect someone they carry out a horrible ritual murder called *tukavu*. They waylay the suspect, attack him, and paralyze him by sticking pointed sticks in his armpits. After this they bite through his throat. It is only a few months since a man from the Forei tribe was found with his throat bitten in two. None of the Foreis go out alone in the evening for fear of *tukavu*."

Dr. Zigas also told me of another mysterious illness called Lulu, which is found amongst the Huri and Duna tribes, further west, where we were going on patrol. The symptoms of this disease are sudden hysterical attacks of cramp and mental disturbances, but it isn't fatal like the Kuru.

It happened that some days later, after I had been flown some thirty miles further west to the patrol station Tari and visited Dr. Roger Roderigue here in the hospital for the natives, I chanced to witness such an attack.

One of Dr. Roderigue's patients, a hefty man of quite normal appearance, suddenly fell on his back and began to kick violently, fighting with his arms and hissing and grinding his teeth the meanwhile. Dr. Roderigue put a thick stick under his neck so that he couldn't hit his head on the floor, then pressed a stick between his teeth so that he wouldn't bite his tongue. The attack lasted only a few minutes, after which the native slowly got up and dazedly looked around.

"Some patients run completely amok and destroy everything

they can get hold of belonging to the Europeans, so they can be a danger," said Dr. Roderigue. "But usually they just have an attack of cramp. We don't know the cause of the disease but it is likely that the mental disturbances have a connection with all the new ideas and things which the Europeans bring with them and which they do not understand. We would probably also become a bit unbalanced if a crowd of strange space men from Mars suddenly popped up and revolutionized our lives."

Tari and another patrol station, Koroba, a day's march from it, are the last outposts before the partly unexplored territory around the Strickland River's upper reaches. The natives round about and between the stations are under control, but further out they are only partly so. Patrols must often be sent out to make peace between conflicting tribes. Admittedly organized tribal warfare is stopping but many assassinations still take place.

"In the course of the last month four revenge murders have been reported during conflicts between two tribes south of the Tagari River," said one of the Tari station's three patrol officers, Bob Hoad, the day before we set out on a two weeks' patrol. He explained that the object of the patrol was to make peace between the two clans, the Pureinis and the Komas. They live beside one another so it is difficult to keep watch on them. Previously they have often fought and burnt down each other's huts. But because of the risk of mass arrest they now confine themselves to individual attacks. Only last week a woman came into the station with her husband's cut-off hand, in order to prove that he had been killed.

We set off from Tari in the morning with the usual assortment of police-boys, doctor-boys, interpreter, cook, and bearers. We didn't see many of the natives' huts here where the Huris live; they lie hidden in the jungle, away from the main footpaths, and around their gardens they have dug deep ditches as a defensive measure. The way across these ditches is often barred with a wooden fence which has sharp points on top.

The first two nights we spent in patrol huts, and as usual we bought sweet potatoes for the bearers from the natives and paid with salt, beads, or red colouring powder which is much sought after and used as decoration. The majority of the natives we met were reserved; there was no spontaneous welcome in their greeting. Some lined up and watched us with blank expressions, while others turned away when they saw us.

Shortly after setting out on the third day we passed a strange enclosure of thick bushes and fencing round a big cleared area in the jungle. "That's a sort of bachelor club," explained Bob; "a cross between a barracks and a college. All young men must spend three months in school here, before they marry. It is called Harrobi. They receive instruction here from a couple of slightly older unmarried men on how they must behave. They learn the secret rituals, ceremonies, and taboos, and they also learn how to make good weapons and proper adornments. In short, correct behavior according to tribal traditions. They mustn't come in contact with women and must eat only the food they themselves grow in the enclosure. No married man may go in there."

I kept my status as a married man secret and with the help of the interpreter I got admission to the bachelor club. Here six young men were in the middle of being instructed by a couple of older bachelors in how they should decorate themselves for a particular ceremony. Their faces were painted with imaginative patterns and looked quite fantastic.

Late in the afternoon of the same day we crossed the Tagari River on a raft which took four men at a time. Immediately we reached the other side, the Pureinis' country, we sensed a change in the bearers' attitude. They were clearly nervous because now they were outside their own territory; we also noticed that there was a more tense atmosphere in other ways. For instance, when we passed some gardens where the women were working with their sticks, they fled away with all possible speed. We didn't see any men at all.

"It's a bad sign," said Bob. "There is something in the air here. We should really have changed the bearers and sent these back across the river before dark. Now we'll have to keep them

here till the morning, until we can persuade some of the Pureinis
to work for us."

The interpreter called out many times, whenever we came to
an inhabited part, for the men to come out so that we could
trade with them. But only once did any men come forward—
all armed with bows and arrows. But they made no sign of a
friendly approach. On the contrary, they took up threatening
positions and disappeared at a trot when we began to advance
toward them.

So we decided to pitch camp near some gardens and wait to
see what would happen. When the tents were pitched a few
older men and a couple of adolescent boys came over to us,
after the interpreter had shouted to them several times. They
were naked apart from a little apron of bark strips. We gave
them some barter goods in exchange for sweet potatoes and
drinking water. In the end they became eager to trade with us
and promised to go with us as bearers the next day.

For safety's sake we had the police-boys on guard the whole
night, in shifts. But everything continued peaceful.

In the morning I discovered what a revolting place we had
chosen for a camp. Only a few yards away from us behind the
hedge there was a burial place with a half-decomposed corpse
in an open coffin. It was placed on some poles that raised it off
the ground and was decorated with earth and a little roof. There
was a swarm of flies all round it.

We paid off the bearers we had brought with us from Tari and
they took themselves off homewards as quickly as possible,
obviously relieved at being able to return to their own territory.
We were in the neighbourhood of the Koma clan, but Bob wanted
to be rather nearer to them, so that he could make contact with
both the Komas and the Pureinis and arbitrate between them.

When we had walked a couple of hours with the new bearers
we came to a deserted settlement which showed signs of having
been fought in recently; the gardens were trampled and several
broken spears and arrows were lying around. Shortly after that
we heard excited shouts from about twenty armed warriors who

had appeared on a hill in front of us. It was clear they meant to block the way—they made signs to us to turn back and threatened us with their weapons.

"These are the ones we have to become good friends with," Bob said. "Don't frighten them too much; let's wait a little while."

For half an hour we stood at the foot of the hill and waited while at intervals the interpreter shouted up to the warriors to encourage them. But clearly they interpreted our hesitation as a sign of weakness and it spurred them on still more. Suddenly some of them began to run down the hill and two arrows were shot at us, although without hitting anyone. Immediately we fired a gun off over their heads. All of them at once turned and fled in panic.

We went up the hill and pitched camp on the top, and from there we had an uninterrupted view and could ourselves be seen from all sides. We waited.

Towards afternoon, five or six of the same warriors who a few hours before had begun to attack us quite cheerfully walked into the camp. They were ready to trade with us. They explained to the interpreter that the day before they had been attacked by the Pureinis, which had alarmed them. Gradually more and more of them came to us unarmed.

The rest of the day and night passed uneventfully. But in the morning, just as we were about to get up, two men came running into the camp. They told us excitedly that a murdered man had been found down by the river in the direction we had come from. We took two police-boys and followed the two men; when we had walked for half an hour along the same path we had come along the day before, they turned off and walked a few yards into the jungle. There lay a man whom our police-boys recognized as one of the Huris who had followed behind us the day before. His head was crushed in and his chest ripped open. His heart was missing.

The two natives who had given us the alarm explained that they had come across the dead man by accident early that morning, but they denied any knowledge of who had committed the crime. Gradually several natives gathered round. They were alarmed and all denied knowledge of the murder. It was clearly a personal revenge murder.

We laid the dead man on a stretcher and sent him down to the river bank, while a message was sent over to his clan for them to come and fetch him.

Despite many official enquiries later, the murder was never solved.

CHILDREN OF THE WORLD

Children of the world
we know, you face an age
of exploration into the unknown —
a future greater than we dream,
when man will lose his littleness
as Love illumines him.

Children of the world
we know, already here,
bring your playthings, your boomerangs,
your wicker balls. Play together,
not needing many words,
until drowsiness draws you home,
to slumber tranquilly
upon your common mother earth.
And when you waken with clear eyes,
the world we know will slowly pass,
as you, the future, climb the stars.

—ALICE MOORE REGAN

EVEN ON CHRISTMAS DAY...

Sleep, my darling, sleep and dream,
For you are warm and you have light,
But oh, those hungry ones, tonight
Who have no place to sleep.

Hunger rocks them in her arms,
The cold creeps in, the night winds shake
Their restless sleep and they will wake
And shiver in the dark alone.

Sleep, darling, lullaby.
I cannot tell you, now, my sweet,
Nor frighten you whose little feet
Are clean and warmly shod.

Once on Judea's wintry plain
A Child was cradled in the hay,
A great star shone to light His way,
His mother held Him in her arms.

Sleep, darling, lullaby.
You cannot know who are not told
That children hunger in the cold,
Even on Christmas Day.

—EDNA L.S. BARKER

ECUMENICAL LITANY

"May they all be one, Father, may they be one in us, as you are in me and I am in you" (John 17:21).

For the many times we have looked at the specks in the eyes of our non-Catholic brothers and sisters, rather than at their sincere faith and perseverance and good will, *Lord, forgive us.*

For our sarcasm, narrow-mindedness, and exaggerations in controversy, and our hardness and severe judgments in their regard, *Lord, forgive us.*

For the bad example that we give in our lives — thereby discouraging, lessening, or even destroying the effect of your grace in their souls — *Lord, forgive us.*

For our forgetfulness to pray for them often, warmly, and with brotherly love, *Lord, forgive us.*

In spite of differences of language, color, and nationality, *Jesus make us one.*

In spite of our ignorance of one another, of our prejudices and our dislikes, *Jesus, make us one.*

In spite of all spiritual and intellectual barriers, *Jesus, make us one.*

O God, for your own greater glory, *bring together us separated Christians.*

O God, for the triumph of goodness and truth, *bring together us separated Christians.*

O God, that there may be one sheepfold for the one Shepherd, *bring together us separated Christians.*

O God, that peace may reign in the world, *bring together us separated Christians.*

O God, to fill the heart of your Son with joy, *bring together us separated Christians.*

POPE PAUL'S LETTER TO

BISHOP WALSH

To Our Beloved Brother, James Edward Walsh, Titular Bishop of Sata.

As the fiftieth anniversary of your ordination approaches, we wish, beloved Brother, to send you our heartfelt felicitations.

You have given a splendid example of true priestly fidelity and you have been verily a loyal "steward of the Gospel" as St. Paul is wont to call priests. A half-century of dedicated and selfless service of Christ the priest, the greater part of which was spent in bringing the message of Christ to those who knew Him not, is a stirring example not only to the members of your own Maryknoll Missionary Society, but also to those young men who aspire to this lofty vocation.

You have not stinted in giving of yourself for the people you have loved so much, and even today, as you give further vivid manifestation of your dedication in suffering for Christ, you continue to encourage and inspire others to a similar service. For your love of the Church and for your self-sacrifice we are most grateful. Would that we were able to offer you in person words of comfort and consolation!

We invoke upon you, beloved Brother, an abundance of heavenly graces of consolation and strength, and we lovingly impart to you from a heart filled with gratitude and admiration our paternal apostolic benediction.

From the Vatican, December 7, 1965. Paulus P. P. VI.

QUEEN IN A MUD HUT

by Henry Van Brucht

The beautiful Adogo was a queen who was loved. Then she decided to leave the king.

Up in the sun-bleached plains of Tanganyika, only a few miles from the historic big-game country of Africa, I found a small, thatched roof mud house. Before it, children were playing and laughing in the dust. In the doorway to welcome me stood a middle-aged woman, tall and erect of carriage, her dark face, handsomely molded, reflecting the beauty that passing years had hardly marked. Barefooted, she was clad in a simple white dress, which set off a colored, beaded necklace, the only adornment she wore. Her name was Magdalena Ooko.

I had come to call on Magdalena and her husband, Sylvanus, because of a story I had heard from a Maryknoll Father in Kowak, a story that had all the enchantment of fiction. Smiling, Magdalena invited me into her humble home, apologizing for the fact that her husband, Sylvanus, was not there to welcome me. He was out tending his small herd of cattle, and she called one of the children and told him to fetch his father.

Inside the dark hut, Magdalena offered me a chair, and then with the courtesy so typical of these people, presented me a cup of milk to refresh me after my dusty walk. Before I had finished the milk, Sylvanus entered the hut. He greeted me with warmth, although he had never seen me before. Then after polite preliminaries, I began checking the facts of the story that had been told me in Kowak.

103

When I took my leave hours later, Sylvanus urged me to return again. He sent one of his sons, a lithe, sturdy boy, whose friendliness and sturdiness were impressive, to escort me on the first part of my journey back to Kowak. As the lad trotted alongside me, I thought of the future that might have been his, and as his voice rose and fell in modulated, soft tones, I fancied that I heard the voice of the heir apparent of the Kingdom of Shirati.

Magdalena Ooko, the boy's mother, was not always named Magdalena, nor was she always the wife of a simple African farmer. Once she was known as Adogo, Queen of the land of Shirati. Men looked at her and admired her beauty; women respected her position and envied her wisdom.

Adogo was born to a well-to-do farmer, wealth being measured by native standards here. A bright child, she learned the many lessons taught to her by her mother, and was very adept in picking up the numerous native dialects of this region. As she grew into womanhood, her beauty became more and more evident.

One day, Nyatega, the King of Shirati, was passing through her village and saw Adogo. He was instantly smitten by her beauty, and commanded one of the members of his court to find out who she was.

"She is a jewel worthy of a king's household," Nyatega declared.

It was not long afterwards that an emissary of the King approached the father of Adogo.

"My master would have your daughter, Adogo, in marriage," said the ambassador. "He asks that you accept twenty cows as his dowry."

And so it came to pass that Adogo was given to King Nyatega in marriage. The elders of the land of Shirati still talk of the wedding feast Nyatega gave in honor of his new bride — never was a greater banquet held in Shirati. After the wedding feast, Adogo was taken to the King's house.

Nyatega already had two wives, but it became evident in the weeks that followed that Adogo was his favorite wife. Since the custom of the land decreed that only the favorite wife should be called Queen, it was thus that Adogo became known.

If she was loved by the King, she was equally loved by the King's court, and by the people of the land of Shirati. Her beauty became a byword, but it was not this alone that endeared her to the people. She took charge of the King's household and conducted its affairs in an efficient and tactful manner. She had the gift of bringing happiness into the lives of the people around her. Because of her knowledge of native dialects, she was often called upon to translate for the King. The people of Shirati were proud to have her for a queen.

One of Adogo's duties was to supervise the buying of food for the King's household. To do this, she would go each day to the market. One day she heard a man speaking in the marketplace about a religion that was strange to her. Upon investigating, she discovered that the man's name was Francis, and that he was a catechist for the foreign priests who had come to her land. Each day, thereafter, she paused to listen to Francis.

At the end of two years of listening, she asked to be baptized and received into the Catholic Church. The priest who was visiting her village told her that she was not ready for baptism. The next year, she asked again. Once more she was refused. The following year she again asked. For the third time she was told that she was not ready.

Adogo became very sad at these refusals. Of all the people who had been taught by Francis, she alone remained unbaptized.

Early one morning while the King's household was yet asleep, Adogo arose and slipped away into the darkness. She walked all that day, arriving in Kowak, twenty-eight miles away from her home, long after dark. She went immediately to the Catholic mission and because the Fathers there were asleep, she did not wish to disturb them. That night the Queen of Shirati slept in the open, on the ground.

The next morning as one of the priests was leaving the mission he heard a voice call him.

"Misawa," said the voice.

The priest turned and was surprised to see the Queen of Shirati standing beside the mission gate.

"Father," said Adogo, "all who have studied with Francis,

the catechist of Shirati, have been baptized. That is, all but one, Adogo. I think, Father, that I have not been baptized because I am not the first wife of Nyatega, the King. Is that true, Father?"

"Yes, Adogo, that is true."

"Then, Father, I shall no longer be Queen of Shirati. I will leave the King."

Adogo kept her word. She did not return home. Instead she went to live with an old widow who had a house near the Kowak mission. The widow was glad to have company in her house, and Adogo appreciated the shelter which was now hers.

It was not long before Nyatega learned of Adogo's whereabouts. Roaring imprecations and threats, he arrived in Kowak and went to the mission. The Fathers called Adogo before the King.

"Never again will I return to Shirati," Adogo declared. "I can no longer live as third wife to you."

With a curse, Nyatega leaped from his chair to catch Adogo. "You will come home or I shall . . . "

Nyatega never finished the sentence. For as he was about to seize Adogo, she escaped his clutching hands and fled from the room.

Each time Adogo would hide during the ensuing months, Nyatega would search her out and attempt to apprehend her. But each time Adogo would narrowly escape. The people who once loved Adogo now began to turn against her. In the eyes of the people, she was still the Queen. Adogo had been given to Nyatega in return for twenty cows. Nyatega had celebrated the marriage feast with her. Even now, because of the ardor of his pursuit, it was evident that she was still his favorite wife.

The Fathers at the mission, however, thought differently. They realized that Adogo was sincere in her desire for baptism. One Sunday afternoon in the mission church at Kowak, Adogo was baptized and given the new name of Magdalena.

As a member of the Christian community of Kowak, Magdalena soon came to know her fellow Christians. One of them, a young man named Sylvanus Ooko, seemed especially pleasing to her. Her liking for Sylvanus was soon reciprocated, and it was not long before the two young people were in love. Sylvanus wished to marry Magdalena, but the elders and chiefs of Sylvanus' tribe ruled against the marriage because they feared the wrath of the King of Shirati.

Sylvanus and Magdalena were very unhappy that they could not be married. Sylvanus went to Mwanza hoping to find employment and make enough money which he could offer to the King of Shirati in an effort to gain release for Magdalena. But even in Mwanza the people were afraid of the King and would have nothing to do with Sylvanus. Empty-handed, he returned to Kowak.

The father of Sylvanus, distressed by his son's despondency, went to Shirati to see the King. To his surprise, he found that Nyatega's anger had cooled.

"I no longer have any hope that Adogo will return to me," the King said. "She thinks that it is wrong to be my third wife, and she will not do anything she thinks wrong. If she wishes to marry your son, I shall not prevent this. However, before I release her, I must have a dowry."

Nyatega said this because he was a shrewd man. He realized the situation was hopeless and that he might as well recoup what he could.

"And what dowry is asked?" inquired the father of Sylvanus.

"Twenty cows. That is what I paid for her," answered the King.

The father of Sylvanus agreed to the dowry and within a few days he delivered twenty cows to the King.

Shortly afterwards, Sylvanus and Magdalena were married in the church at Kowak. Each Sunday, now, husband and wife, and their children, come into Kowak for Mass. Magdalena is once again loved by the people for her wisdom and this time, her Christian charity. She hopes that someday one of her sons will become a priest.

"Then he will be even greater than the King of Shirati, or any king in the world," she said.

I asked her if she ever regretted giving up her position as Queen. She answered my question by asking another.

"Should I regret giving up an earthly kingdom for a greater one that has no end?"

I knew from that question why people respected the wisdom of Magdalena, once the popular Queen of Shirati.

IN THE FURROW

Two of us
Are sitting in a furrow, in a field of green barley.
Enjoying the short break after work,
We fill the air with our chatter.

Bright is the sun up above,
And merry the songs of the birds.
The blessings of God abound,
Filling our hearts with gratitude.

Where is the end of the world?
With gracious heaven above,
Two of us work under the sky.
Two of us live on, working the same land, day after day,
Creating joys that never cloy.

Exploding with laughter,
Two of us return to the rows of barley,
Gripping the handles of weeding hoes.
Oh, the joy of walking together
In this field, this path of life.

—SO WOL KIM

MY ORDEAL WITH THE IROQUOIS

by Isaac Jogues

A martyr and saint describes his experiences at the hands
of Indians in what is now New York State.

When desiring to write to Your Reverence, the first doubt that
I had was in which language I ought to do so — Latin or French;
then, having almost forgotten them both, I found equal difficulty in each. Two reasons have moved me to use Latin. The
first, for the sake of being able sometimes to employ certain
sentences from Sacred Scripture, from which I have received
great consolation in my adversities. The second, because I
desire that this letter may not be too common.

Your Reverence's great charity will excuse, as it has done at
other times, my failings: especially since for eight years now I
have been living among barbarians, not only in usages, but also
in a costume similar to theirs. First, then, I beg you, if this letter
shall come into your hands, to aid me with your holy sacrifices,
and prayers by the whole Province — as being among people no
less barbarous by birth than in manners. And I hope you will do
this gladly, when you shall have seen by this letter the obligations under which I am to God, and my need of spiritual help.

We started from the Hurons on the 13th of June, 1642, with
four canoes and 23 persons — 18 barbarians, and five Frenchmen.
The journey — besides the difficulties, especially of portages —
was dangerous by reason of the enemies, who, seizing every

*From *The Jesuit Relations and Allied Documents,* Vol. 39, Hurons 1653.

year the highways, take many prisoners; and I know not how
Father Jean de Brébeuf escaped them last year. They, being incensed against the French, had shortly before declared that, if
they should capture any one of them, they would, besides the
other torments, burn him alive by a slow fire.

The Superiors, aware of the dangers of this journey—necessary, however, for the glory of God—spoke to me of them,
adding that they did not oblige me thereto. But I did not gainsay
them. I embraced with good courage that which obedience put
before me for the glory of God; and if I had excused myself,
someone else, of greater ability, would have been substituted in
my place, with more detriment to the mission. We made the
journey not without fear, dangers, losses, and shipwrecks, and,
35 days after our departure, we arrived safe and sound at the
residence of Three Rivers; due thanks being there rendered to
God, we spent 25 days partly there, partly at Kebek, according
to necessity.

Having finished our business, and celebrated the feast of our
Holy Father Ignatius, we embarked again on the first of August
for the Hurons. On the second day of our journey, some of our
men discovered on the shore fresh tracks of people who had
passed there—without knowing whether or not they were enemies. Eustache Ahatsistari, famous and experienced in war,
believes them enemies. "But, however strong they may be
deemed," he says, "they are not more than three canoes; and
therefore we have nothing to fear." We then continue the journey. But, a mile beyond, we meet them to the number of 70, in
12 canoes, concealed in the grass and woods. They suddenly
surround us, and fire their arquebuses, but without wounding us.
The Hurons, terrified, abandon the canoes, and many flee to the
deepest part of the woods; we were left alone, we four Frenchmen, with a few others, Christians and catechumens, to the
number of twelve or fourteen. Having commended themselves
to God, they stand on the defensive; but, being quickly overwhelmed by numbers, and a Frenchman named René Goupil,
who was fighting among the first, being captured with some
Hurons, they ceased from defense.

I, who was barefoot, would not and could not flee—not willing, moreover, to forsake a Frenchman and the Hurons, who were partly captured without baptism, partly near being the prey of the enemies, who were seeking them in the woods. I therefore stayed alone at the place where the skirmish had occurred, and surrendered myself to the man who was guarding the prisoners, that I might be made their companion in their perils, as I had been on the journey. He was amazed at what I did, and approached, not without fear, to place me with them. I forthwith rejoiced with the Frenchman over the grace which the Lord was showing us: I roused him to constancy, and heard him in confession. After the Hurons had been instructed in the Faith, I baptized them; and as the number increased, my occupation of instructing and baptizing them also increased. There was finally led in among the captives the valiant Eustache Ahatsistari, a Christian; who seeing me, said: "I praise God that he has granted me what I so much desired—to live and die with thee." I knew not what to answer, being oppressed with compassion, when Guillaume Cousture also came up, who had come with me from the Hurons. This man, seeing the impossibility of longer defending himself, had fled with the others into the forests; and as he was a young man not only of courageous disposition, but strong in body, and fleet in running, he was already out of the grasp of the one who was pursuing him. But, having turned back, and seeing that I was not with him, "I will not forsake," he said to himself, "my dear Father alone in the hands of enemies"; and immediately returning to the barbarians, he had of his own accord become a prisoner. Oh, that he had never taken such a resolution! It is no consolation in such cases to have companions of one's misfortunes. But who can prevent the sentiment of charity? Such is the feeling toward us of those laymen who, without any worldly interest, serve God and aid us in our ministrations among the Hurons. This one had slain, in the fight, one of the most prominent among the enemies; he was therefore treated most cruelly. They stripped him naked and, like mad dogs, tore off his nails with their teeth, bit his fingers, and pierced his right hand with a javelin; but he suffered it all with invincible patience—remembering the nails of the Savior, as he told me afterward. I embraced him with great affection, and exhorted him to offer to God those pains, for himself, and for those who tormented him. But those executioners, although admiring me at the beginning, soon afterward grew fierce, and, assailing me with their fists and with knotty sticks, left me half dead on the ground; and a little later, having carried me back to where I was, they also tore off my nails and bit with their teeth my two forefingers, causing me incredible pain. They did the same to René Goupil—leaving unharmed the Hurons, who were now made slaves. Then, having brought us all together again, they made us cross the river, where they divided among themselves the spoil—that is, the riches of the poor Hurons, and what they carried, which was Church utensils, books, etc., things very precious to us.

Meanwhile I baptized some who had not yet received that rite—and among others, an old man of eighty years, who having had orders to embark with the others, said: "How shall I, who am already decrepit, go into a distant and foreign country?" Refusing, then, to do so, he was slain at the same place where he had been baptized—losing the life of the body where he had received that of the soul. Thence, with shouts proper to conquerors, they depart, to conduct us into their countries, to the number of 22 captives, besides three of our men already killed. We suffered many hardships on the journey, wherein we spent 38 days amid hunger, excessive heat, threats, and blows—in addition to the cruel pains of our wounds, not healed, which had putrefied, so that worms dropped from them. They, besides, even went so far—a savage act—as in cold blood to tear out our hair and beards, wounding us with their nails, which are extremely sharp, in the most tender and sensitive parts of the body. I do not mention the inward pains caused at the sight of that funeral pomp of the oldest and most excellent Christians of the new Church of the Hurons, who often drew the tears from my eyes, in the fear lest these cruelties might impede the progress of the Faith, still incipient there.

On the eighth day of our journey, we met two hundred bar-

barians, who were going to attack the French at the fort which
they were building at Richelieu; these, after their fashion, thinking to exercise themselves in cruelty, and thus to derive prosperous results from their wars, wished to travel with us. Thanks
being then rendered to the Sun, which they believe to preside
in wars, and their muskets being fired as a token of rejoicing,
they made us disembark, in order to receive us with heavy blows
of sticks. I, who was the last, and therefore more exposed to
these beatings, fell, midway in the journey which we were obliged
to make to a hill, on which they had erected a stage; and I thought
that I must die there, because I neither could, nor cared to, arise.
What I suffered, is known to one for whose love and cause it
is a pleasant and glorious thing to suffer. Finally, moved by a
cruel mercy—wishing to conduct me alive to their country—
they ceased beating me, and conducted me, half dead, to the
stage—all bleeding from the blows which they had given me,
especially in the face. Having come down from it, they loaded
me with a thousand insults, and with new blows on the neck
and on the rest of the body. They burned one of my fingers, and
crushed another with their teeth; and the others, already bruised
and their sinews torn, they so twisted that even at present,
although partly healed, they are crippled and deformed. A barbarian twice took me by the nose, to cut it off; but this was never
allowed him by that Lord who willed that I should still live—for
the savages are not wont to give life to persons enormously
mutilated. We spent there much of the night, and the rest of it
passed not without great pain, and without food, which even for
many days we had hardly tasted. Our pains were increased by
the cruelties which they practiced upon our Christians—especially upon Eustache, both of whose thumbs they cut off; and
through the midst of the wound made on his left hand they
thrust a sharp skewer, even to the elbow, with unspeakable
pain; but he suffered it with the same—that is, invincible—
constancy. The day following, we encountered other canoes,
which were likewise going to war; those people then cut off
some fingers from our companions; not without our own fear.

On the tenth day, in the afternoon, we left the canoes, in

order to make the remainder of the four days' journey on foot. To the customary severities was added a new toil, to carry their goods, although herein they treated me better than I expected — whether because I could not or whether because I retained in captivity itself, and near to death, a spirit haply too proud. Hunger accompanied us always; we passed three days without any food, but on the fourth we found some wild fruits. I had not provided myself sufficiently when we abandoned the canoes, for fear lest my body should be too robust and vigorous in the fire. On the second day, they put a kettle on the fire, as if to prepare something to eat; but there was nothing in it but warm water, which each one was allowed to drink at his pleasure. Finally, on the 18th day, the eve of the Assumption of the Most Blessed Virgin, we arrived at the first village of the Iroquois. I thanked the Lord, that on the day on which the Christians celebrate so solemn a feast, he had called us to share his pains. We had anticipated that day as truly bitter and calamitous; and it had been easy for René Goupil and for me to avoid it, because often, when unbound about midnight, we were able to flee — with the hope, if not of returning to ours, at least of dying more easily in the woods. But he refused to do so, and I would rather suffer every pain than abandon my French and Huron Christians to death, and deprive them of the consolation which they could receive from a priest at that time.

So, on the eve of the Assumption about the twentieth hour, we arrived at the river which flows past their village. Here were awaiting us, on both banks of the river, the old Huron slaves and the Iroquois, the former to warn us that we should flee, for that otherwise we would be burned; the latter to beat us with sticks, fists, and stones, as before — especially my head, because they hate shaven or short hair. Two nails had been left me; they tore these out with their teeth, and tore off that flesh which is under them, with their very sharp nails, even to the bone. We remained there, exposed to their taunts a few moments; then they led us to the village situated on another hill. Before arriving, we met the young men of the country, in a line, armed with sticks, as before; but we, who knew that, if we had separated ourselves from the number of those who are scourged, we would be separated from the number of the sons, offered ourselves with ready will to our God, who became paternally cruel to the end that he might take pleasure in us, as in his sons. We went one by one. First there walked a Frenchman, altogether naked; René was in the middle; I was last, in shirt and trousers. The Iroquois had placed themselves between us and the Hurons, in order to moderate our pace, for the sake of giving time to anyone who struck us. A long time, and cruelly, not only with sticks, but also with iron rods, which they have from the Dutch; and one of the first, with a piece of iron thick as a fist, attached to a rope, gave us each a blow so fierce that I would have fallen half dead, if the fear of another like blow had not given me strength to pass on. We hardly had strength to reach the stage erected in the middle of the village. René, who was not very nimble, received so many blows, especially in the face, that nothing was seen of him but the whites of his eyes. Hardly did we breathe upon the stage when, with a great rod, we were three times struck on the bare shoulders; and they began to unsheathe knives, in order to cut off the rest of our fingers. Because they esteemed me the most, they began with me, whom they saw respected by the French and the Hurons. There approach me then an old man and a woman, whom he orders to cut off my thumb; at first she refuses, but being, as it were, compelled three or four times by the old man, she finally does so. This woman was an Algonquin, a Christian slave, captured a few months before, and her name was Jeanne. What consolation to suffer at the hands of those for whom one dies rather than abandon them to visible and invisible enemies. Then I, taking with my other hand the amputated thumb, offered it to thee, O my living and true God, mindful of the sacrifices which I had offered thee in thy Church, until, admonished by one of my companions, I let it fall, for fear that they might put it in my mouth, in order to make me swallow it, as they often do, As for René, they cut off his right thumb at the first joint. I thank God that they left me the one on my right hand, so that by this letter I may pray my Fathers and brethren to offer prayers for us in the holy Church of God.

The following day, the feast of the Blessed Virgin, after having kept us till noon on the stage, they conducted us to another village, 5 or 6 miles distant from the first; and the barbarian who was leading me took away my shirt, leaving me nothing, except a rag, which he could not deny to decency, but a piece of sacking, which I myself asked from him, in order to cover my shoulders. But these, bent with so many beatings, refused to sustain that rough and rude weight, especially after a burning sun roasted my skin as in an oven—on account of which, shortly afterward, that of the neck, the shoulders, and the arms, being burned, fell off. At the entrance to this village, they did not omit—although contrary to their custom—to beat us once again, with blows the more atrocious in proportion as the multitude did not hinder them from measuring them; they struck us especially on the bones of the legs, with what pain may be imagined. The rest of the day we remained upon the stage; at night, in a cabin, naked on the bare ground, bound with chains, exposed to the revilings of each sex and of every age. They threw coals and live ashes on our bare flesh, which, for us who were bound, it was difficult to throw off.

We remained there two days and two nights, almost without eating or sleeping—tormented further by the sight of the torments which they inflicted upon our Huron companions, whose wrists they bound so tightly with cords that they fainted therefrom. I regarded these as my spiritual sons, shortly before regenerated to God by holy baptism—that is to say, with the bowels of a Father, to whom love serves as Executioner. I consoled them, however, with the words of the Apostle. . . .
The stages of the barbarians had not yet seen either Frenchmen or Christian Hurons; to satisfy then, the curiosity of all, we were led everywhere. At the third village, we entered with great peace, but not without pain, since we met there four other Hurons freshly captured, and mutilated like us. I found means of instructing in the Faith and baptizing these prisoners, two upon the stage itself, with the dew, which I found quite abundant in the great leaves of turkish corn, the stalks of which they gave us to chew; the other two on the journey to another village, at

a brook which we encountered by the way. Here the rain and the cold made our nakedness more keenly felt; therefore, trembling with cold, I sometimes went down from the stage in order to warm myself in some cabin, but I was forthwith led back to it.

To cut off Guillaume's right forefinger, a barbarian used, not a knife, but a shell, like a saw; which could not cut the tough and slippery sinews; and therefore he tore it off by sheer force, which caused the sufferer's arm to swell even to the elbow. A certain person, out of pity, received him into a hut during those two days that we stayed there, not without anxiety on my side, as I knew not where he was. At night, they led us into a cabin, where they commanded us to sing, as was their wont. It is necessary to obey and to sing. From singing they came to torments, especially in the case of René and me; they burned me with coals and live ashes, especially on the breast; and they bound me upright between two stakes, set between the shoulders and the elbow, with two pieces of bark, wherewith they often bind those whom they burn, so that I thought that I was to be burned. And—that you may know that, if I endured the rest with strength and with patience, it was not my own courage, but that of Him in that torture, being almost left to myself alone. I wept; and on account of the great pain, I begged that they would not tie me so tightly. But it so happened that the Lord permitted that, the more I besought him, the more they bound me. They kept me thus about a quarter of an hour, then they loosed me; otherwise, I would have swooned. I thank thee, O good Jesus, because I have learned with some little experience what thou didst condescend to suffer for me on the Cross, where thy most holy body was not even sustained with cords, but hung by thy hands and feet, transfixed with hardest nails. For spending the rest of the night, they bound us on the earth to several stakes; and what did they not do to us, or try to do? But again I thank you, O Lord, that you kept me pure from the impure hands of the barbarians.

Two days later, they led us to the second village, in order to take final counsel concerning us. Now for seven days they had been leading us from village to village, from stage to stage—being made a spectacle to God and to the angels, the contempt and sport of the barbarians—when finally we were notified of death by fire—news assuredly full of horror, but softened by the thought of the divine will, and by the hope of a better life. I spoke for the last time, as I believed, to the French and the Hurons, to animate them by reminding them of the sufferings of that One, of the brevity of the torments, and the eternity of the glory, etc. I also admonished them, especially Eustache, that in the torments they should look at me, and make some sign, so that I might bestow on them the last absolution, as I did in his case, repeatedly; but the French and almost all the other Hurons were granted life. The fortitude of this man was marvelous; he, with Christian spirit, entreated the Hurons present, that the thought of his death should never prejudice the peace with the Iroquois. They also killed Paul Onnonhoaraton, a young man of about 25 years, of great courage, who laughed at death—being animated with the hope of a better life, as he publicly declared. This man, on the journey, when the Iroquois were coming to torment me, offered himself for me, begging them that they should rather exercise cruelty toward him. God will have rewarded him for that notable charity.

Guillaume was given to an Iroquois family. When they spare the life of any slave, they usually receive him into some family in the place of some dead kinsman, whom the slave is said to bring to life again, by taking the name and the same degree of relationship; so that they call him, like the dead man, "father," "brother," "son," etc. But, in the case of René and myself, because we were not so strong, the final decision was not taken, but they left us together, as it were, in a free slavery. Therein, as being half idle, we began to feel more keenly the pains of unhealed wounds, irritated by a thousand annoying little creatures, from which our mutilated fingers did not permit us to defend ourselves. Meanwhile, those 200 returned, whom we had encountered on the journey—overcome by the French in lesser number, who were commanded by the Chevalier de Montmagni, Governor of the country, whom they were intending to surprise. On this account, it again began to be a question of killing us; but we know not how God prevented the execution of this threat.

On the day of the Nativity of the Blessed Virgin, one of the principal persons among the Dutch, who have a colony about 40 miles distant from the barbarians, came to treat for our ransom. He spent several days there, and offered much, but obtained nothing—the barbarians, in order not to offend him, feigning, by way of excuse, that they would conduct us back to the French. Perhaps the leaders had some such intention; but at the final council which assembled for this affair, the crowd, and those who were most turbulent, prevented its accomplishment. Indeed, if by special providence of God we had not been outside the village when the council was ended, they would have killed us; but, having sought us awhile in vain, they finally returned each one to his own village. René and I having gone back, and been warned of the danger, we withdrew without, toward a hill, in order to perform our devotions with more liberty; we offered our lives to God, and began the Rosary of the Blessed Virgin. We were at the fourth decade when we met two young men, who commanded us to return to the village. "This encounter," I said to René, "is not auspicious, especially in these circumstances. Let us commend ourselves to God and to the Blessed Virgin." In fact, at the gate of the village, one of these two draws a hatchet, which he has kept concealed, and strikes René's head with it. He fell, half dead, but remembered according to the agreement made between us, to invoke the most holy name of Jesus, in order to obtain indulgence. I, expecting a like blow, uncover myself, and cast myself on my knees; but the barbarian, having left me a little time thus, commanded me to rise, saying he had not permission to kill me, as I was under the protection of another family. I then arise, and give the last absolution to my dear companion, who still breathed, but whose life the barbarian finally took away with two more blows. He was not more than 35 years of age; he was a man of unusual simplicity and innocence of life, of invincible patience, and very conformable to the divine will. He was worthy to be acknowledged by Your Reverence as yours, not only because he had been, with credit, for several months in our novitiate, but also because here he had consecrated himself, under obedience to the Superiors of the Society, in the service of our neophytes and catechumens, to whom with the art of surgery he was of great assistance; and finally, because, a few days before, he had consecrated himself with the vows. The long prayers that he made had rendered him odious to the barbarians, who for this reason esteemed him a sorcerer; but the sign of the cross, which he often made on the brows of children, was the last and true cause of his death — an old man, grandfather of one of them, having ordered the murderer to chastise with death the Frenchman's superstition, as practiced on the person of one of his descendants; and I learned this from the child's mother, and from many others of the country.

But I was given to another master, who hated us mortally: in consequence, they believed so surely that he would kill me, that he who had lent me that wherewith to cover myself, asked it from me again, in order not to lose it at my death. I did not fail, however, on the following day, to seek, even at the peril of my life, the body of the deceased, for the sake of burying it. They had tied a rope to his neck, and dragged him naked through the whole village, and had then thrown him into the river, at some distance away. My first master warned me to withdraw, if I did not wish to be killed like him; but I, who was weary of that manner of living, would have reckoned it great gain to die in the exercise of a work of mercy. I then pursued my journey, and with the guidance and aid of a man of the country — furnished me for escort by the same person who, out of friendship, was dissuading me from going thither— I found him by the bank of the river, half eaten by dogs; and there, at the bottom of a dry torrent, I cover him with stones, intending to return thither the following day alone, with a pickaxe, in order to bury him securely.

I found, at my return, two armed young men, who were awaiting me to conduct me, as they said, to another village — but really, to kill me in some retired place. I told them I could not follow them without orders from my master, who would not consent. It was necessary to hinder, on the following day, another, who had come for this purpose, from seeking me in a field; I go again, I seek everywhere, and I myself go into the river up to my waist—although it was swollen by the night's rains, and cold, since it was the month of October. I seek him with my hands and with my feet; they tell me that the high water has removed him elsewhere. I hold obsequies for him as best I can, singing the psalms and prayers thereto appointed by the Church; I mingle my tears with the water of the torrent; I groan and sigh. I can gain no news of him before the following spring, when, the snows being melted, the young men of the country notify me that they have seen his bones on the same bank of the river; these, together with the head, having reverently kissed, I then finally buried as best I could. I know not how many dangers to life I incurred in those two months. They sought a part of that which clothed me—which was half a blanket, seven handbreadths wide. At another time, I was destined as a sacrifice to the shade of a little innocent, who had died in our cabin; I hoped in you, I prayed to you, but my sins were not yet purged. Therefore the slayer, changing his mind, thwarted me in my hope, and the women, who for this purpose were leading me abroad—laden with presents for the murderer—put themselves as it were to flight, and abandoned me there alone. But not so indeed my God; I consoled myself by reading the Epistle to the Hebrews, expounded by Godelli; I also possessed an image, with the indulgence, and a little cross of wood, which I always carried with me as my treasures.

At the middle of October began the stag hunt, a time for them of sports and feasts, but, for me, of outrages and persecutions—because, when I began to announce to them a God, a Paradise, and a Hell, although indeed they listened to me at the start, and admired, yet, weary with the continuation thereof, and because the chase was not successful, they began to accuse and persecute me. They have recourse in their necessities to a demon whom they call Aireskoi, to whom they offer, as it were, the first-fruits of everything. When, for instance, a stag has been taken, they call the eldest of the hut or of the village, to the end that he may bless it or sacrifice it. This man, standing opposite the one who holds some of the flesh, says with a loud voice: "Oh, Demon Aireskoi, we offer thee this flesh, and prepare for thee a feast with it, that thou mayst eat of it, and show us where are the stags, and send them into our snares — or, at least, that we may see them again in the winter," etc.; or, in sickness, "to the end that we may recover health." They do the same in fishing, war, etc. Having heard this ceremony, I was horrified, and I was always careful to abstain from this flesh offered to the demon — toward whom they interpreted this action as manifest contempt, and a cause of their lack of success in hunting. Nor would they longer hear me speak of God, or answer me the questions that I put to them about the language, wherewith they saw that I was attacking their superstitions.

I therefore went out every morning from a cabin where the demon and the dreams were almost always adored — and escaped to a neighboring hill, where, in a large tree, I had made a great cross; and there, now meditating, now reading, I conversed with my God, whom I alone in those vast wilds adored. The barbarians did not perceive this till somewhat later, when they found me kneeling, as usual, before that cross, which they hated, and said that it was hated by the Dutch; they began, on this account, to treat me worse than before — without, however, being able to hinder me from continuing elsewhere my prayers. I suffered there great hunger, while our Egyptians were feasting. The snows having increased, the cold was added thereto, as I had only a rag for clothing and bed, and they would not allow me the use of any of those skins which they had in great abundance; I suffered, besides the pain of my wounds, not yet perfectly healed, fears and inward pangs, I know not whether I should be alive. I had recourse to my wonted asylum of Sacred Scripture. I thus passed two months "in the school of the beech-trees," as once said Saint Bernard — until, being unable to endure me longer, they sent me away, carrying a load of meat, to the place whence I had started — there to be put to death, as was commonly said.

Meanwhile I saw the barbarians well covered with the clothes which they had taken from us, and, which vexed me, with the sacred robes, which they profaned. It is true that, toward the middle of January, when the chase was done, they gave me some other skins with which to cover myself; and a man from Lorraine who lived among the neighboring Dutch, sent me, by way of alms, a blanket. Moreover, an Iroquois woman—one of their principal personages, whose only son had died not long before— began to take some care of me, and then I gave myself wholly to the study of the language; and because I was in a place where all the councils were held—not only of our village, but of all the country—I had opportunity to instruct the chief persons of the nation in our holy mysteries, and to preach to them the Faith. They gave me opportunity for this by the sun and the moon; the size of the earth; the vastness of the ocean, and its flood and ebb tides; of the limits of the world; whether the earth did not somewhere touch the sky, etc.; and, because I contented them in some manner, they admired me, and said that they would have made a great mistake in killing me, as they had so many times resolved. But, when I passed from creatures to the Creator, they mocked me with the fables which they relate of the creation of the world—which originated, by their saying, from a tortoise. But I told them of the true God—their Aireskoi being no other than a lying demon, who, driven out by virtue of the cross from the rest of the world, had taken refuge among them, in order to receive from them some particle of that honor which was now everywhere denied him. I did not uselessly lose time there; for I baptized not only many children, but many sick people, and adult captives, who I think are now in heaven. But not all who heard me—and, by a sort of courtesy common among them, applauded me—believed me and were converted, even among the sick.

I journeyed, from time to time, to the other villages, in order to visit our captive neophytes; to console them, and to administer to them the holy sacrament of penance; to assist the dying, and baptize them—especially the children, five of whom, in a neighboring village, were no sooner baptized than they flew to heaven. But this period did not last more than two months longer—that is, until the middle of the month of March, when here the snows melt, and then they go fishing; I, too, went in company with an old man and an old woman, together with a little child. The journey was one of four days; the goal, a lake where a few little fish are caught, which they smoke in order to preserve them, and carry them back to their country—meanwhile living on the entrails alone. I was already used to these, also to the intestines of deer, which they cook and eat thus stinking, without opening or emptying them, with mushrooms cooked in water, and frogs entire, without skinning or opening them. How often in these journeys the woods and mountains for the first time echoed the praises of their Creator, altogether unwonted there. On how many oaks did I carve the most holy name of Jesus, to expel from them the terrified demons! On how many the most holy cross. And it was precisely at the time when the Church commemorates the bitter passion of the Savior, upon which I had sufficient time to meditate at the foot of a tall pine, at some distance in the woods, where I had carved a great cross.

But this peace did not last long; on Palm Monday arrived a barbarian, sent expressly to call us back to the Iroquois country. This was under pretext of fear of the enemies but, in truth, to sacrifice me for the son of my first host—a man of influence, who was accounted dead—and for nine others who, in the summer preceding, had gone away to war without ever sending news of themselves. On the arrival of a certain man, the death of these men being announced, there was forthwith sacrificed a poor captive, who was in the house, of small renown. More than one such was therefore wanted, and I was to be the second. We arrived at the village on Holy Thursday, toward evening, I thinking to die there, like my Lord, on Friday; but He who had died on that day in order to give us the life of the soul, chose to give me also that of the body. The report that the warriors are not dead suddenly begins to be current—and, shortly after, that they are not only not dead, but that they are returning victorious, with twenty-two prisoners—and they, changing their minds, leave me in life; but I might every day expect the same fate. Oh, what a life, amid a thousand deaths!

My inclination was to withdraw as far as I could from the settlement, and seclude myself in the most secret part of the woods, in order to soothe and console myself with my God in the solitude; but — remembering that Lea, though tearful, was more fruitful than Rachel, and that it is the part of the Society to subordinate even spiritual consolations to the service of God, for the help of souls — I kept myself in the villages, and among the people, in order better to learn the language, and to be able more easily to baptize the dying children, and to instruct the adults; and I would have accounted myself guilty if, because of my absence, any one had not received the necessary aids at that time, at least for justifying the cause of God.

The 22 prisoners whom we have mentioned were finally led up by our warriors; they were of a nation that had never waged war with these, and nevertheless they were treated as is usual in the case of the fiercest enemies, — with beatings, mutilation of the fingers, fires, and most cruel outrages, etc. Five, who alone were adult men, were appointed to be burned alive; they retained the rest as slaves; of these some were women, but most were boys and girls. They spoke a language of which I had scarcely any knowledge; but, with the aid of a barbarian who knew both languages, I baptized them before they died, which was on Easter day. But what they did at Pentecost is horrible. They brought three women from the same nation, with their little children, and received them naked, with heavy blows of sticks; they cut off their fingers, and, after having roasted one of them over her entire body, they threw her, still alive, into a great fire, to make her die therein — an act uncommon, even there. And as often as they applied the fire to that unhappy one with torches and burning brands, an old man cried in a loud voice: "Aireskoi, we sacrifice to thee this victim, that thou mayst satisfy thyself with her flesh, and give us victory over our enemies." The pieces of this corpse were sent to the other villages, there to be eaten.

During the winter, at a solemn feast which they had made of

two bears, which they had offered to their demon, they had used this form of words: "Aireskoi, thou dost right to punish us, and to give us no more captives" (they were speaking of the Algonquins, of whom that year they had not taken one; these are, moreover, their chief enemies), "because we have sinned by not eating the bodies of those whom thou last gavest us; but we promise thee to eat the first ones whom thou shalt give us, as we now do with these two bears"—and so they did.

This woman died a Christian; and I, not having been able before, baptized her in the flames, on occasion of giving her to drink. The eve of Saint John the Baptist, a day of so much rejoicing, was for me most bitter by reason of seeing eleven Hurons and one Frenchman, lately taken prisoners, together with three others, killed—whose scalps they bore in triumph, with those of ten other Hurons, who had been treacherously deceived and slain under pretext of a friendly treaty of peace. My sins were changing, as for the Hebrew people, the new moons and feasts into days of mourning. I received at the same time the news of the captivity of a hundred others, taken, ill-used, and killed by others, their enemies.

I have often enough the opportunity to escape, but I will not do so while I can help, console, and confess the French or barbarian captives, assist the dying, baptize the children, etc. I have already baptized more than 70 among the children and adults of five different nations. Be it done for their good, for which perchance God has sent me hither and, as it were, wonderfully preserved me alive, nor permitted them to conduct me back to Kebek, or the Dutch to ransom me, although they have repeatedly tried to. I have twice visited them, and they have received me courteously; nor do they cease to attempt my ransom, and they make various little gifts to the barbarians who have charge of me, so that they may treat me well. I myself begin to grow weary of so long a letter, which I end by praying Your Reverence to recognize me as yours, although among the barbarians in the matter of living and clothing, and in almost everything similar to them.

I live in a continual tumult, as it were, far from my God;

but as a son of the Holy Roman Church and of the Society—in which I hope, although unworthy, always to live, and to die. Obtain for me from the Lord, not to abuse, more than I have done, so many occasions for sanctifying myself. Regard me as a needy man, whose faith is amid the obscure shadows of infidelity; his hope, amid frequent and protracted trials; his charity, amid a thousand carnalities, without help from the sacraments; his chastity, not indeed in the midst of delights, but amid a thousand liberties, nakedness, and indecencies, unavoidable by any one who is not altogether blind. These things make me complain to my God, to the end that He may not forsake me, so that, when He shall come He may unite us all, drawing us from various nations. I salute all our Fathers and brethren, and commend myself to their most holy Sacrifices and prayers. From the Colony of Ronselar (Rensselaer), in New Holland, August 5, 1643.

THE SWEET SONGS

The gentle tide of your melodies, beloved,
Floods my heart and pauses there.

I hear the sweet songs, beloved,
Standing by the door from morning
Till the sun sets, and dusk deepens.
I hear them late, until I sleep.

The gentle tide of your melodies, beloved,
Rocks me till I sleep in peace.
I sleep, content and warm,
Though my bed is hard.

But—when I wake,
I forget your songs.
Forgotten are all your songs
No sooner than heard.

—SO WOL KIM

ROMANCE

Written in the face of every child is a quest for love—to love and to be loved. Look into a child's eyes. Wrought by the hand of God, those eyes reach back into eternity. Love fashioned them and the desire in them.

Love permeates each tiny, living cell in a child's body. It is the sum total of a young soul's longing. It is the reason for a child's life. Without love, that life would be a chaos of frustration.

One day, perhaps, a child will find the object of its love in a human way. Let this love be denied and men deem it a tragedy. And so it is—deep tragedy.

Human love, however, is but a steppingstone to the search for the ultimate, the love of God. If this is missing, a child's life is the most tragic of all tragedies. For a child is then bereft of that for which it was made, that which is its completion, its perfection.

Need you wonder, then, why a missioner leaves father, mother, brother, sister, to bring God's love to the hearts of little children? A missioner's job is the most romantic adventure in the whole world.

—CYRIL V. HIRST, M.M.

LONG BOW

by Edward A. McGurkin

> Telling true lion stories can get a fellow into a lot of trouble.

In one of my diaries, I recorded a story told me by Father Bunders. It was about the time the White Fathers in Northern Rhodesia were awakened in the middle of the night by the ringing of the church bell and discovered that a lion was tugging at the rope. Meat juice on the rope had attracted the lion. The juice had been left there by the houseboy, who earlier that day was cutting up an animal when it suddenly came time to ring the Angelus. So far, so true.

When newspapers began to arrive from the States, we learned that the lion had moved to Shinyanga and was waking Maryknollers. U.S. papers filled in all the details. Their artists portrayed a Maryknoll Padre investigating the lion. He was dressed in a long nightshirt—the Padre, that is, not the lion—and was leaning against a tree, with long yawns and droopy eyes, waiting for the lion to finish his midnight lunch and quit ringing the bell.

London papers copied the story, which by this time was pretty good. These papers soon arrived in Tanganyika and were shortly in the hands of the White Fathers. Such embarrassing moments!

More excitement ensued when one of the Canadian Fathers received his *Messager du Sacré Coeur,* a rather serious monthly edited by the Canadian Jesuits and respected for its strict adherence to the truth and nothing but the truth. Here is their version translated from the French: "In the middle of the night, the Maryknoll missioners of Shinyanga, in what was formerly known as German East Africa, were awakened by the ringing of the church bell. Père Edward climbed into the bell tower — imagine his astonishment when he found a lion there, pulling away at the bell rope. The houseboy, it was learned later, had been dressing a gazelle, when remembering all of a sudden that he had forgotten the Angelus, he rushed to the church without washing his blood-dripping hands. That night, the lion scented the fresh blood and climbed into the belfry and quite innocently caused all the commotion that followed, which was unusual, to say the least."

Before the story stops rolling, we will perhaps read that the lion was discovered in the choir loft of the Shinyanga Cathedral, seated at the console of the tower chimes, playing "Oft in the Stilly Night," with tears bubbling out of his big dreamy blue eyes. It's our own fault, no doubt. As the school teacher used to say: "That will larn ya!"

But will it? Anyway Father John Martin is sending us a bell. All we need now is a greasy rope and a hungry lion, and maybe the story will come true.

Speaking of lions, we picked up another story when the Catholics of Mwanza had a party to welcome Bishop Blomjous on his return. Justice Harbord, who presided, said that he was not in favor of speeches on such occasions. He immediately gave a rather lengthy speech to explain why.

During the early persecutions it once happened that the fun of the mob was spoiled. The hungriest and fiercest lions were unleashed to satisfy the bloodthirsty mob in Rome's Madison Square Garden. On this day, Christians were huddled in the arena when a big hungry lion came bouncing into the amphitheater. A Christian man stood up, took the lion aside and whispered something in his ear. The lion gave a snort of disgust and walked away, leaving the Christians untouched.

This happened several times. After a whispered word in the ear, each lion stalked out of the place in a huff. The Emperor was enraged. He called up the Christian and demanded an explanation. The man explained: "I told each lion that if he ate us, you would call upon him to give an after-dinner speech."

African wit sparkled in a verbal tilt with colonial administrators, according to a story that came our way recently. It threw barrels of light into the obscure corners of impressive diplomatic verbiage. It seems that a certain commissioner of the regime was having his difficulties in convincing the people of the wonderful advantages of income tax.

"Income tax," he told them, "is a sound investment, paying off with an interest in benefits that no one could rightly estimate, so vast they might be. It is a tried means of security, to be inaugurated while the populace is riding comfortably on the ground swell of abundant years; a buoyant support to tide them over the lean years of want and depression; a guarantee of safe coasting through hard times and a protective insulation against the heart-trying preoccupations inevitably attendant on, and aggravating, the inner crisis that accompanies the ebbing tide of economical good times. It is your money that you pay out, to be sure; but it comes back to you in a new and fantastic, utterly amazing and incredible manner."

An old native listened attentively. Then, addressing the commissioner, but turning his head and speaking loud enough so that all might hear, he said: "Now I understand. It means, for example, that if I want to give my dog a nice piece of fresh meat, I just take a knife and chop off a part of his tail."

THE SOUND OF RAIN

The sound of falling rain
  is ceaseless on the eaves.
I want to catch the soothing sound
  in a brass bowl
And turn the sad tale of the day
  to foam and bubbles.

— "BLUEBIRD"

THE CHRIST CHILD

Little Babe in manger sleeping,
  Wake and see our tear-filled eyes.
Thou art author of our weeping,
  Thou, the God of Paradise!

For we weep that thou so holy,
  Creator Omnipotent,
Thus shouldst deign to be so lowly,
  Naked, cold, and impotent.

Yet we weep for pure rejoicing;
  Hast thou not Redemption's power?
Grateful adoration voicing,
  Angels join us in this hour.

Humble shepherds represent us
  Worshipping the Savior's birth;
Glorifying God who sent us
  Peace to right-willed men on earth.

—B. REILLY, O.P.

VISION OF A NEW WORLD

by Joseph A. Grassi

> St. Paul was confident that Jesus would act through
> him to change the world.

The life of Paul of Tarsus has always left the reader and student amazed. How account for the tremendous success of one man: the implanting of so many churches through Asia Minor and southern Europe? What was the source of his boundless energy in traveling hundreds of miles from city to city, always in danger from robbers, the most bitter persecutors, and even from former friends? In reading through his letters, and through the Acts of the Apostles, one searches in vain for a list of techniques or "gimmicks" that account for his achievements.

But Paul was a man convinced that God had established a certain goal in human history, that divine power was working in men to accomplish that goal, and that he himself had been chosen as a special instrument for God's work. To understand how Paul knew this, we must go back to the decisive turn in his life, on the road to Damascus.

Paul was only a young man when Jesus of Nazareth was crucified. The atmosphere of the Jewish world in which he lived was one of great hope and expectation, centering about the glorious future which Israel believed that God had destined for His own people and, through them, for the whole world. Many of the Prophets had foretold this triumphant age, and many people, including Paul, felt certain that it was just about to dawn.

Some thought of this new era in earthly and national terms, and looked to a restoration of the Davidic dynasty under a new leader, a Messiah. The anointed one would free Israel from foreign domination and win respect for her among the nations of the world. This group, however, although numbering many zealous adherents, was in the minority. Paul and most of his friends were more influenced by the abundant apocalyptic literature of the times which painted a brilliant picture of a super-earthly kingdom to come into existence through the powerful intervention of God. A mysterious "Son of Man" figured largely in these writings; he would be God's chosen instrument to inaugurate His kingdom on the day when the divine power would burst upon earth from heaven.

In these expectations, the Gentiles—the non-Jewish people of the world—played an important part. In God's plan out-lined by the Prophets the purified Gentiles would join Israel to worship side by side with her in God's world victory. Paul had read in the Scriptures the words of Sophonias:

"Then I will change and purify the lips of the peoples, that they all may call upon the name of the Lord to serve him with one accord; from beyond the rivers of Ethiopia and as far as the recesses of the North, they shall bring me offerings" (3:9–11).

He also knew the prophecy of Zacharias:

"All who are left of all nations that came against Jerusalem shall come up year after year to worship the King, the LORD of hosts, and to celebrate the feast of Tabernacles" (Zach. 14:16).

The young Paul was deeply moved by these intense mes-sianic hopes. He was keenly aware that only recently a young Prophet from Nazareth had been crucified by the Romans for proclaiming that he had initiated the long-awaited time of God's final intervention. The events that followed had deeply dis-turbed the young Pharisee. He was astonished to learn that there was a growing community in the holy city who believed that the crucified Jesus had risen again and was now present among them in His Spirit and power.

At first it is hard to understand why Paul took upon himself an almost one-man campaign against the new sect; after all, messianic groups were nothing new. Many of his compatriots were rather favorably inclined toward members of the sect, who had little externally to distinguish them from their fellow Jews. But Paul saw beneath the surface, for he had listened carefully to the young Stephen as he made his defense before his martyrdom.

Stephen was one of the "seven" whom the Twelve Apostles had chosen as their assistants. He was a Greek-speaking Jew and had quickly proved to be one of the most brilliant lights in the young community. Luke makes it a point to draw special attention to the power of the Spirit that moved him: he was a man "full of faith and the Holy Spirit" (Acts 6:5). His outspoken defense of the new faith soon brought about his arrest, the charges against him being that he had spoken "against the Holy Place and the Law"; "that he had claimed that Jesus had said that he would destroy this place [the temple] and change the traditions which Moses handed down to us" (6:13–14).

Although false witnesses had made these charges, there was a certain nucleus of truth behind them. Stephen was one of the first to see clearly that Jesus by His Resurrection and the sending of His Spirit into his people had become a new living temple that took the place of the old material temple of the Jews. He also saw that the new faith would eventually supersede the regulations of the old law. He was not the type of man to keep these insights to himself and had openly expressed his views.

After his arrest, when Stephen made his defense before the Sanhedrin, he forcibly pointed out that God's dwelling among his people was not limited or restricted by the temple: "not in houses made by hands does the Most High dwell . . . " (7:47). He accused them of restricting and opposing the Holy Spirit throughout the history of the people. At the end of his speech he looked up to heaven and saw Jesus standing at the right hand of God. The vision affirmed what he already knew, that the glory of God had entered into Jesus, who was now the Holy

Temple of God. He told the Sanhedrin, "I see the heavens opened, and the Son of Man standing at the right hand of God" (7:56). At this point they seized him, brought him outside the city and stoned him to death, for they saw that his claim that Jesus Himself was the Holy Temple of God would spell the end of worship in a material temple, and eventually nullify the cherished traditions of Moses.

Paul, however, understood the deeper meaning behind Stephen's words. If Stephen was right, then God had inaugurated the final age of the world through this man Jesus, and this went against everything that Paul held most dear and sacred. As a good Jew, he held that the Torah was the revelation of God and the source of Israel's hope. He believed along with his fellow Pharisees that only a strict and zealous adherence to the Law would hasten the messianic age. If God had now completely shown Himself in Jesus, independently of the Law, then the Law could only become secondary and eventually lose its meaning for those who believed in Jesus.

Since Paul saw the implicit conflict between Judaism and the new "Way" so clearly, there was nothing left for him to do but to devote all his energies to stamping out the believers in Jesus. Paul's whole life had been dedicated to bringing the blessings of the Law to as many men as possible in order to prepare the way for the final times. He had, in fact, probably been a Jewish missionary before he became a Christian missionary. He wrote, "I advanced in Judaism above many of my contemporaries in my nation, showing much more zeal for the traditions of my fathers" (Gal. 1:4). His belief that missionary work was one of the principal means for hastening the coming of the messianic age was based on the teachings of the Prophets, who had predicted that the dawn of the great age would coincide with the conversion of the nations. Paul saw clearly that this new sect was nullifying all his life's work by implicitly undermining the position of the Law.

It is understandable then that he literally "ravaged the Church of God" (Gal. 1:13). It was imperative that the new group be suppressed as soon as possible; it was not enough for him to seek out believers in Jerusalem; he even sought and obtained authority from the high priest to arrest members of the new sect in Damascus and bring them back in bonds to Jerusalem to face trial.

Little did Paul suspect that he would be the one to be brought back in bonds to Jerusalem. Jesus, the Son of God, captured him and Paul became His servant for life. Paul described this experience with the terse, indisputable statement, "Christ Jesus laid hold of me" (Phil. 3:12). We might well ask what it was that could have made such a startling and sudden change in a man who had been a violent persecutor of the Church. In the epistles, Paul sums it up briefly in Gal. 1:15–16; in the Acts of the Apostles, Luke gives us three parallel accounts of Paul's conversion (9:1–30; 22:3–21; 26:4–23).

In Acts, Luke has Paul tell the story of his conversion to King Agrippa in these words:

"I then thought it my duty to do many things contrary to the name of Jesus of Nazareth. And this I did in Jerusalem; and many of the saints I shut up in prison, having received authority from the chief priests to do so; and when they were put to death, I cast my vote against them; and oftentimes in all the synagogues I punished them and tried to force them to blaspheme; and in my extreme rage against them I even pursued them to foreign cities.

"But while I was journeying on this business to Damascus with authority and permission from the chief priests, at midday, O King, I saw on the way a light from heaven brighter than the sunshine round about me and my companions. We all fell to the ground, and I heard a voice saying to me in Hebrew, 'Saul, Saul, why dost thou persecute me? It is hard for thee to kick against the goad.' And I said, 'Who art thou, Lord?' And the Lord said, 'I am Jesus, whom thou art persecuting. But rise and stand upon thy feet; for I have appeared to thee for this purpose, to appoint thee to be a minister and a witness to what thou hast seen, and to the visions thou shalt have of men; delivering thee from the people and from the nations, to whom I am now sending thee, to open their eyes that they may turn from darkness to light and from the domination of Satan to God; that they may receive forgiveness of sins and an inheritance among those sanctified by faith in me" (Acts 26:9–18).

In Galatians, Paul describes this tremendous experience in words that are very simple yet pregnant with meaning: "it pleased him . . . to reveal his Son in me that I might preach him among the Gentiles" (1:15–16). Three great themes are compressed in this short statement: revelation, sonship, and preaching to the Gentile world.

The verb *reveal* itself points to the nature of his conversion. The Greek word for reveal or unfold is *apokalyptein,* which is very frequently linked with the final appearance or *Parousia* of the Messiah, the Son of Man. We see such a link in Luke 17:30, "In the same wise will it be on the day that the Son of Man is *revealed.*" Likewise Paul writes to the Thessalonians about "the *revelation* of the Lord Jesus" on the great day of His appearance (2 Thess. 1:7). The words, then, would lead us to understand that Paul had a vision of the Risen Son of Man coming in His great triumph in the midst of His people. Or we should say, "beginning to come in triumph," for this "revelation" was only beginning to take place, and would only come to pass completely at the last day, for as Paul writes in Romans, "The eager longing of creation awaits the *revelation* of the sons of God" (8:19).

The object of the revelation was the *Son* Himself. The vision unfolded to Paul in some way who the Son was: not by any external means or knowledge but by the presence of the Risen Son Himself through His Spirit. Joined to the Risen Christ, through sharing His Spirit, Paul could know what it meant to be a son of God. He describes this very simply later on in the same epistle: "God sent his Son, born of a woman . . . that we might receive the adoption of sons. And to prove that you are sons, God has sent the Spirit of his Son into our hearts crying, 'Abba, Father' " (Gal. 4:6).

Finally the words, "that I might *preach* him among the Gentiles," bring out some of the practical consequences of what had happened. If God had chosen Paul in such a striking man-

ner, it was that he could be a living witness of God's intervention—that others could have the same hope and confidence
of becoming true sons of God. Paul had received the Spirit that
was in Jesus precisely that he might share Him with others.
Previously Paul had *something* to give men in the Law; now he
had *someone* to share—Jesus Himself who in His Spirit wished
to enter into countless men in order to form a permanent community of true brothers.

From the brief description in Galatians we can surmise that
Paul's experience was essentially the same as that of Stephen as
he died in martyrdom, looking up to heaven: "He being full of
the Holy Spirit looked up to heaven and saw the glory of God,
and Jesus standing at the right hand of God" (Acts 7:55). It
was the light of the exalted Christ that blinded Paul on the road
to Damascus. He must have been reflecting on this experience
when he wrote in 2 Cor. 4:6, "God who commanded light to
shine out of darkness, has shone in our hearts, to give enlight-
enment concerning the knowledge of the glory of God shining
on the face of Christ Jesus."

Putting together the evidence from Acts and from Galatians
we can outline some of the far-reaching implications for Paul
in what happened to him in his encounter with Christ:

1) He suddenly realized that the Christian community, the
very group he had despised and so violently persecuted, was
the dwelling place of Jesus the Risen Messiah. When Paul had
asked, "Who are you, Lord?" (Acts 26:15), the answer came,
"I am Jesus whom you are persecuting." Paul immediately
understood the solidarity and identity of the Risen Jesus with
the new community: the Risen Messiah was now mightily at
work in His people.

2) From Galatians especially we learn that the Messiah was
at work in His people precisely in order to transform them into
His image—that they also might become sons of God. "To
reveal his Son in me" (Gal. 1:16) was God's design. God
wished to establish a community of true sons of God, brothers
of one another through the working of His Son. This was something that could have a beginning on earth but which must gradu-

ally unfold until the last day when there would be the final revelation of the sons of God and the perfect brotherhood of men at the Resurrection. "The eager longing of all creation awaits the *revelation* of the sons of God" (Rom. 8:19).

3) God's great plan for the universe now began to unfold itself to Paul: Jesus had become *kyrios* (Lord of all creation) by His resurrection and exaltation. His Spirit was now in those who believed in Him so they could have a hope of resurrection through joining themselves to Him. Jesus wished to be recognized as Lord by all men, to establish His rule of love over them and give them the same hope. Paul understood that Jesus was in the process of *becoming* Son of Man, insofar as it was His intention to live in power in countless human lives to bring about a community of men based on love and hope.

As the years went on, Paul developed his thought on this great plan. He wrote to the people of Colossae,

"I am to fulfill the word of God — the mystery which has been hidden for ages and generations, but now is clearly shown to his saints. To them God willed to make known how rich in glory is this mystery among the Gentiles — Christ in you, your hope of glory" (1:26).

In this way he made it plain that the very presence of the Risen Jesus in the community was the source of hope for future glory in the coming triumph of the Church.

4) Paul was surprised to find that the Messiah had come into the midst of *ordinary* people. He had bypassed his own colleagues, the fervent Pharisees who were convinced that they were best preparing the way for the Messiah. Jesus Himself had been one of the *'am ha'aretz* (Hebr.), "the people of the land," who were not able to observe the minutiae that were all-important to the Pharisees. The Master had mixed with sinners, tax collectors, the poor, and even women of doubtful reputation. Christianity was to be essentially a popular movement, not a monopoly of the elite.

All of this had far-reaching consequences for Paul. He understood that the impelling drive in the new movement was to be the pure initiative of the grace and mercy of God through Christ, not any well-ordered system of ethics or regulations. The urgent love of Christ would be the only force applied to men. It was likewise an indication that the poor would be best fitted to receive the good news; that is, the poor in spirit — those who realized their own insufficiency and would be open to a new force of love in their lives.

5) Paul quickly came to understand his own part in God's great plan, "that I might preach him among the Gentiles" (Gal. 1:16), or, in the words of the Risen Christ, "I have appeared to thee for this purpose, to appoint thee to be a minister and witness to what thou hast seen. . ." (Acts 26:16). His role was to be that of a Prophet in bearing witness to what he had seen. God had selected him and called him to be a witness of the Risen Jesus and to proclaim that He was now working in His people, preparing the way for a glorious return in the flesh at the end of the final age which was now dawning. Reflecting on the Scriptures, Paul recalled that those great men in the Old Testament who had witnessed the glory of God were selected for the same special purpose: to bear witness to others.

To help us understand Paul's prophetic mission, Luke describes Paul's conversion in Acts in terms that are used of the great Prophets, particularly Jeremias, Daniel, and Ezechiel. For example, like Paul, Daniel and Ezechiel fell to the ground when they beheld the vision of God's glory (Ez. 1:28; Dan. 8:17). Jeremias' call is similar to the words of the Lord to Ananias, who was ordered to go and receive Paul into the Damascus community. The Lord told him, "Go, for this man is a chosen vessel to me, to carry my name among nations and kings and the children of Israel" (Acts 9:15). Jeremias was also to be "a prophet to the nations" (Jer. 1:5), with "authority over the nations and kingdoms." So Paul was able to view his own vocation as that of a prophet: to bear witness in the world to God's glory now manifested in the Risen Jesus.

His witness became all the more urgent in view of the Jewish belief that the conversion of the nations must come about before the final stage of God's kingdom. The coming of the Messiah, in their belief, would usher in the final age of history. But before the final victory, the Gentiles must be received into the Kingdom. Paul then saw a special urgency in his message: since Jesus the Messiah had come to open up the final era of the world, the good news of His liberating death and Resurrection must be preached among all the nations of the earth so they could repent and prepare themselves for the return of Jesus. Paul felt that this had to be done before the Son of Man could come to achieve His complete victory. No doubt he was familiar with a logion of the Lord to this effect: "This gospel of the kingdom shall be preached in the whole world, for a witness to all nations; and then will come the end" (Matt. 24:14).

6) Paul's response to God's revelation to him in His Son was that of a supreme confidence in God's power. The vision of the Risen Son of Man could only mean that all the powers of God reserved for the final age had finally broken into the world. The divine plan for history had been revealed: to create in the Son of Man a glorious risen community of men. Henceforth all the divine power would be working to bring this great design to swift execution. Paul had been especially called and chosen in view of this new dispensation, hence he felt that he was to be a unique instrument of God in bringing all men to Christ. He knew that when God spoke and revealed Himself, His word was always effective; what God spoke, He did. If the Lord had revealed His plan, He would surely work in men to bring it about.

To sum up: Paul the Pharisee had set out for Damascus to capture the followers of Jesus. Instead, Jesus captured him and Paul became His follower. In his encounter with the Risen Jesus he learned that the Messiah had indeed come and was dwelling through His Spirit in the very community that Paul was ravaging. He understood that it was God's plan to reveal His Son to the world, to create a permanent community of sons of God united in brotherhood through fellowship with Christ. Paul's mission was to be a witness to the world of what God had done in him and in others who believed. Knowing that the Risen Jesus had become *Kyrios* of the universe, he was perfectly confident that Jesus would act in him and in others to accomplish His design in the world.

Applications for the Modern Apostle

After his conversion, Paul looked on the world with different eyes: it was a *world that could be won* for Christ. There are many today who would not look upon it in the same way, and in confirmation of their views they would point to the fact that after almost two thousand years, less than a quarter of the world's population can be called Christian in name. If we counted those who are truly committed Christians, they would constitute a small minority in the world today and, with the large population growth of the non-Christian world, a more and more diminishing minority. They also point with alarm to the renewed vigor of the great non-Christian religions of the world; e.g., Buddhism and Mohammedism, whose members have redoubled their missionary efforts.

Can we, then, have the same certainty that Paul had? If we have the same Christ that he had, then there is only one answer: we must have the same certainty that the world can be won. Once we say that it cannot, we lose that very faith which makes it possible to win the world. Paul did not look upon the encounter on the way to Damascus as an isolated event, now past, but as the beginning of a lifelong relationship. It is true that he came to know Christ through direct revelation, whereas we come to know Him through others. But it is the same Christ to whom we have been united. This Christ has not become weak or worn-out through the centuries; it is rather we who need to revive our faith that He can and will work through us.

However great our trust, we must be realistic in the face of how God is actually working in the world. We cannot conjure up our own image of what a victorious Church should be like. In view of the nature of the world, and the need to preach the Gospel anew to each generation, all victory must be progressive and can never be final at any one moment. This progression can never be measured in numbers; it must always be measured in regard to the way that Christ, the *Kyrios,* is actually extending His reign in the world. This will manifest itself in many ways; prominent in these will be an increasingly effective preaching of the Word in each generation and a correspondingly deeper penetration of Christian witness into every sphere of human influence.

We can answer, then, that we must have faith, as Paul had, that the *world can be won*. The slow progress is due first of all to our lack of confident trust that it can be done. Second, it is due to our making a human image of how this winning must be done, instead of leaving the mode of victory to Christ Himself.

PRAYER FOR A MISSIONER

Take my weariness that he may be energetic,
  depression that he may be inspired,
  inadequacy that he may be efficient,
  frustrations that he may find fulfillment,
  discomfort that he may have ease,
  aridity that he may have consolation,
  darkness that he may be enlightened,
  humiliations that he may have humility,
  patience that he may be meek,
  silence that he may be strong,
  failures that he may have success,
  disappointment that he may be gratified,
  loneliness that he may find you.
You who give joy, give him peace;
You who give peace, give him happiness;
You who are happiness, give him yourself.

— MOTHER M. ALICE, I.B.V.M.

COMMUNION FROM HEAVEN

by Patrick J. Byrne

> Old Father Nagata refused to leave his post until his
> task was done.

If an angel were to tell us of divinely given option on the time
and manner of our dying, what would we choose? As many
answers as men. Whether such an angel came to Father Aloysius
Nagata, of Kyoto, we know not, but from the exquisite beauty
of his last moments we might easily suppose 'twas so. The good
Padre had prepared for them by a long seventy-five years, consecrated unreservedly to the will and the work of his Divine
Master, with no minutest reserve held out for self. Through
the forty-three busy years of priesthood his humble, helpful
presence was a constant benediction to his beloved parishioners, who held joint ownership of his heart, his time, his
powers.

Came a recent Sunday Mass—like any other Sunday's, preceded by Saturday's confessions and the weekend demands
of a flourishing parish. Yet not like any other Sunday's, for
today's Mass will be ended in heaven. At Communion time
many of the congregation went to the railing. After communi-
cating a few, Father Nagata was seen to stagger as if dizzy,
then pause. Evidently fearing to drop a host, he had the altar
boy bring a chair, whereon he rested for a few moments. All

---

*From *Ambassador in Chains, the Life of Bishop Patrick James Byrne*, by
Raymond A. Lane. Copyright P. J. Kenedy & Sons, used by permission.

were watching him in anxious concern. None knew quite what to do, but the Padre knew, and well he knew, indeed.

Anon he rose; again he commenced the Communion. But again he faltered; again he was forced to rest, the while holding tightly to the ciborium. Now this time his children found voice — imploring voice — imperative that he remain resting. Some had rushed for a doctor; others would carry him away for proper care.

What! Leave before Communion was finished? Indeed, he would continue; no gainsaying that. He raised a host, and silence fell upon them. But himself he could no longer raise. And so, at his wish, they opened the gates of the Communion rail, and one by one they came to him, tears streaming down their cheeks, and reverently knelt before the stricken priest to receive a Holy Communion that not to their dying day will they cease to remember. It was a Communion reached down to them from heaven itself.

One more would have been too many. The dying Father finished his sacred task; then came weariness unutterable. His hand dropped. The altar boy, a seminarian, caught the ciborium from reluctant fingers and bore it safely to the tabernacle. All had communicated; the work was done.

Yet not entirely. Something still remained to be done! No one noticed that, although by now seemingly unconscious, the good Padre kept his thumb and forefinger closely pressed together, as must be done when one has touched the Sacred Host, until they are purified by the ablution.

The doctor arrived. He gave a hypodermic stimulant; consciousness flickered back to the eyes. The priest called for water. Someone held it to his lips.

"No, no," he said, "my fingers!" Feebly he moved them. The water was poured. His head fell back in death. The *Ite missa est* was said in heaven.

A NATIVE CHILD

by Isak Dinesen

The transformation of an African boy was completed
when the Prince of Wales gave compliment to his sauce.

Kamante was a small Kikuyu boy, the son of one of my squat-
ters. I used to know my squatter children well, for they both
worked for me on the farm, and used to be up round my house
herding their goats on the lawns, in the faith that here something of interest might always occur. But Kamante must have
lived on the farm for some years before I ever met him; I suppose that he had been leading a seclusive existence, like a sick
animal.

I came upon him for the first time one day when I was riding
across the plain of the farm, and he was herding his people's
goats there. He was the most pitiful object that you could set
eyes on. His head was big and his body terribly small and thin,
the elbows and knees stood out like knots on a stick and both
his legs were covered with deep running sores from the thigh to
the heel. Here on the plain he looked extraordinarily small, so
that it struck you as a strange thing that so much suffering could
be condensed into a single point. When I stopped and spoke to
him, he did not answer, and hardly appeared to see me. In his
flat, angular, harassed, and infinitely patient face, the eyes were
without glance, dim like the eyes of a dead person. He looked as

if he could not have more than a few weeks to live, and you expected to see the vultures, which are never far away from death on the plain, high up in the pale burning air over his head. I told him to come round to my house the next morning, so that I could try to cure him.

I was a doctor to the people on the farm most mornings from nine to ten, and like all great quacks I had a large circle of patients, and generally between two and a dozen sick people up by my house then.

The Kikuyu are adjusted for the unforeseen and accustomed to the unexpected. Here they differ from the white men, of whom the majority strive to insure themselves against the unknown and the assaults of fate. The Negro is on friendly terms with destiny, having been in her hands all his time; she is to him, in a way, his home, the familiar darkness of the hut, deep mould for his roots. He faces any change in life with great calm. Amongst the qualities that he will be looking for in a master or a doctor or in God, imagination, I believe, comes high up in the list. It may be on the strength of such a taste that the Caliph Haroun al Raschid maintains, to the hearts of Africa and Arabia, his position as an ideal ruler; with him nobody knew what to expect next, and you did not know where you had him. When the Africans speak of the personality of God they speak like the Arabian Nights or like the last chapters of the book of Job; it is the same quality, the infinite power of imagination, with which they are impressed.

To this characteristic in my people I myself owed my popularity, or my fame, as a doctor. When I first came out to Africa I travelled on the boat with a great German scientist, who was going out, for the twenty-third time, to experiment with cures for sleeping-sickness, and who had over a hundred rats and guinea-pigs on the boat with him. He told me that his difficulty with the native patients had never been any lack of courage in them—in the face of pain or of a great operation they generally showed little fear—but it was their deep dislike of regularity, of any repeated treatment or the systematization of the whole; and this the great German doctor could not understand. But when I myself got to know the natives, this quality in them was one of the things that I liked best. They had real courage: the unadulterated liking of danger—the true answer of creation to the announcement of their lot—the echo from the earth when heaven had spoken. I sometimes thought that what, at the bottom of their hearts, they feared from us was pedantry. In the hands of a pedant they die of grief.

My patients waited on a paved terrace outside my house. Here they squatted—the old skeletons of men with tearing coughs and running eyes, the young slim smooth brawlers with black eyes and bruised mouths, and the mothers with their feverish children, like little dry flowers, hanging upon their necks. I often had bad burns to treat, for the Kikuyu at night sleep round the fires in their huts, and the piles of burning wood or charcoal may collapse and slide down on them—when at times I had run out of my store of medicine, I found that honey was not a bad ointment for burns. The atmosphere of the terrace was animated, electric, like the atmosphere of the Casinos in Europe. The low lively flow of talk would stop when I came out, but the silence was pregnant with possibilities, now the moment had come when anything might happen. They did however always wait for me myself to choose my first patient.

I knew very little of doctoring, just what you learn at a first-aid course. But my renown as a doctor had been spread by a few chance lucky cures, and had not been decreased by the catastrophic mistakes that I had made.

If now I had been able to guarantee my patients a recovery in each single case, who knows but that their circle might have thinned out? I should then have attained a professional prestige—here evidently was a highly efficient doctor from *Volaia*—but would they still have been sure that the Lord was with me? For of the Lord they knew from the great years of drought, from the lions on the plains at night, and the leopards near the houses when the children were alone there, and from the swarms of grasshoppers that would come onto the land, nobody knew wherefrom, and leave not a leaf of grass where they had passed. They knew Him, too, from the unbelievable hours of happiness when the swarm passed over the maizefield and did not settle, or when in spring the rains would come early and plentiful, and make all the fields and plains flower and give rich crops. So that this highly capable doctor from Volaia might be after all a sort of outsider where the real great things in life were concerned.

Kamante to my surprise turned up at my house the morning after our first meeting. He stood there, a little away from the three or four other sick people present, erect, with his half-dead face, as if after all he had some feeling of attachment to life, and had now made up his mind to try this last chance of holding on to it.

He showed himself with time to be an excellent patient. He came when he was ordered to come, without fault, and he could keep account of time when he was told to come back every third or fourth day, which is an unusual thing with the natives. He bore the hard treatment of his sores with a stoicism that I have not known the like of. In all these respects I might have held him up as a model to the others, but I did not do so, for at the same time he caused me much uneasiness of mind.

Rarely, rarely, have I met such a wild creature, a human being who was so utterly isolated from the world, and, by a sort of firm deadly resignation, completely closed to all surrounding life. I could make him answer when I questioned him, but he never volunteered a word and never looked at me. He had no pity whatever in him, and kept a little scornful laughter of contempt, and of knowing better, for the tears of the other sick children, when they were washed and bandaged, but he never looked at them either. He had no wish for any sort of contact with the world round him, the contacts that he had known of had been too cruel for that. His fortitude of soul in the face of pain was the fortitude of an old warrior. A thing could never be so bad as to surprise him; he was, by his career and his philosophy, prepared for the worst.

All this was in the grand manner, and recalled the declaration of faith of Prometheus: "Pain is my element as hate is thine. Ye rend me now: I care not." And, "Ay, do thy worst. Thou art omnipotent." But in a person of his size it was uncomfortable, a thing to make you lose heart. And what will God think — I thought — confronted with this attitude in a small human being?

I remember well the first time that he ever looked at me and spoke to me of his own accord. This must have been some time along in our acquaintance, for I had given up my first mode of treatment, and was trying a new thing, a hot poultice that I had looked up in my books. In my eagerness to do the thing thoroughly, I made it too hot, and as I put it on his leg and clapped the dressing on the top of it Kamante spoke; "Msabu," he said, and gave me a great glance. The natives use this Indian word when they address white women, but they pronounce it a little differently, and change it into an African word, with a diverging ring to it. In Kamante's mouth now it was a cry for help, but also a word of warning, such as a loyal friend might give you, to stop you in a proceeding unworthy of you. I thought of it with hope afterwards. I had ambition as a doctor, and I was sorry to have put on the poultice too hot, but I was glad all the same, for this was the first glimpse of an understanding between the wild child and myself. The stark sufferer, who expected nothing but suffering, did not expect it from me.

As far as my doctoring of him went, things did not, however, look hopeful. For a long time I kept on washing and bandaging his leg, but the disease was beyond me. From time to time he would grow a little better, and then the sores would break out in new places. In the end I made up my mind to take him to the hospital of the Scotch Mission.

This decision of mine for once was sufficiently fatal, and had in it enough possibilities, to make an impression on Kamante — he did not want to go. He was prevented by his career and his philosophy from protesting much against anything, but when I drove him to the Mission, and delivered him there in the long hospital building, in surroundings entirely foreign and mysterious to him, he trembled.

I had the Church of Scotland Mission as a neighbor twelve miles to the North West, five hundred feet higher than the farm;

and the French Roman Catholic Mission ten miles to the East,
on the flatter land, and five hundred feet lower. I did not sympa-
thize with the Missions, but personally I was on friendly terms
with them both, and regretted that between themselves they
should live in a state of hostility.

The French Fathers were my best friends. I used to ride over
with Farah, to hear Mass with them on Sunday morning, partly
in order to speak French again, and partly because it was a
lovely ride to the Mission. For a long way the road ran through
the Forest Department's old wattle plantation, and the virile
fresh pinaceous scent of the wattle trees was sweet and cheering
in the mornings.

It was an extraordinary thing to see how the Church of Rome
was carrying her atmosphere with her wherever she went. The
Fathers had planned and built their Church themselves, with
the assistance of their native congregation, and they were with
reason very proud of it. There was here a fine big grey Church
with a bell-tower on it; it was laid out on a broad courtyard,
above terraces and stairs, in the midst of their coffee-plantation, which was the oldest in the Colony and very skillfully
run. On the two other sides of the court were the arcaded Refectory and the Convent buildings, with the school and the mill
down by the river, and to get into the drive up to the Church you
had to ride over an arched bridge. It was all built in grey stone,
and as you came riding down upon it, it looked neat and impressive in the landscape, and might have been lying in a Southern
canton of Switzerland, or in the North of Italy.

The friendly Fathers lay in wait for me at the Church door,
when Mass was over, to invite me to *un petit verre de vin*, across
the courtyard in the roomy and cool Refectory; there it was
wonderful to hear how they knew of everything that was going
on in the Colony, even to the remotest corners of it. They would
also, under the disguise of a sweet and benevolent conversation,
draw from you any sort of news that you might possibly have
in you, like a small lively group of brown, furry bees—for they
all grew long, thick beards—hanging on to a flower for its store
of honey. But while they were so interested in the life of the

Colony, they were all the time in their own French way exiles, patient and cheerful obeisants to some higher orders of a mysterious nature. If it had not been for the unknown authority that kept them in the place, you felt they would not be there, neither would the Church of grey stone with the tall bell-tower, nor the arcades, the school or any other part of their neat plantation and Mission station. For when the word of relief had been given, all of these would leave the affairs of the Colony to themselves and take a bee-line back to Paris.

Farah, who had been holding the two ponies while I had been to Church, and to the Refectory, on the way back to the farm would notice my cheerful spirits—he was himself a pious Mohammedan and did not touch alcohol, but he took the Mass and the wine as coordinate rites of my religion.

The French Fathers sometimes rode on their motor-bicycles to the farm and lunched there, they quoted the fables of Lafontaine to me, and gave me good advice on my coffee-plantation.

The Scotch Mission I did not know so well. There was a splendid view, from up there, over all the surrounding Kikuyu country, but all the same the Mission station gave me an impression of blindness, as if it could see nothing itself. The Church of Scotland was working hard to put the natives into European clothes, which, I thought, did them no good from any point of view. But they had a very good hospital at the Mission, and at the time when I was there, it was in charge of a philanthropic, clever head-doctor, Dr. Arthur. They saved the life of many of the people from the farm.

At the Scotch Mission they kept Kamante for three months. During that time I saw him once. I came riding past the Mission on my way to the Kikuyu railway station, and the road here for a while runs along the hospital grounds. I caught sight of Kamante in the grounds, he was standing by himself at a little distance from the groups of other convalescents. By this time he was already so much better that he could run. When he saw me he came up to the fence and ran with me as long as it was following the road. He trotted along, on his side of the fence,

like a foal in a paddock when you pass it on horseback, and kept
his eyes on my pony, but he did not say a word. At the corner
of the hospital grounds he had to stop, and when as I rode on,
I looked back, I saw him standing stock still, with his head up
in the air, and staring after me, in the exact manner of a foal
when you ride away from it. I waved my hand to him a couple
of times, the first time he did not react at all, then suddenly his
arm went straight up like a pump-spear, but he did not do it more
than once.

Kamante came back to my house on the morning of Easter
Sunday, and handed me a letter from the hospital people who
declared that he was much better and that they thought him
cured for good. He must have known something of its contents
for he watched my face attentively while I was reading it, but
he did not want to discuss it, he had greater things in his mind.
Kamante always carried himself with much collected or re-
strained dignity, but this time he shone with repressed triumph
as well.

All natives have a strong sense for dramatic effects. Kamante
had carefully tied old bandages round his legs all the way up
to the knee, to arrange a surprise for me. It was clear that he saw
the vital importance of the moment, not in his own good luck,
but, unselfishly, in the pleasure that he was to give me. He
probably remembered the times when he had seen me all upset
by the continual failures of my cures with him, and he knew
that the result of the hospital's treatment was an astounding
thing. As slowly, slowly, he unwound the bandages from his
knee to his heel there appeared, underneath them, a pair of
whole smooth legs, only slightly marked by grey scars.

When Kamante had thoroughly, and in his calm grand manner,
enjoyed my astonishment and pleasure, he again renewed the
impression by stating that he was now a Christian. "I am like
you," he said. He added that he thought that I might give him a
Rupee because Christ had risen on this same day.

He went away to call on his own people. His mother was a
widow, and lived a long way away on the farm. From what I

heard from her later I believe that he did upon this day make a digression from his habit and unloaded his heart to her of the impressions of strange people and ways that he had received at the hospital. But after his visit to his mother's hut, he came back to my house as if he took it for granted that now he belonged there. He was then in my service from this time till the time that I left the country—for about twelve years.

Kamante when I first met him looked as if he were six years old, but he had a brother who looked about eight, and both brothers agreed that Kamante was the elder of them, so I suppose he must have been set back in growth by his long illness; he was probably then nine years old. He grew up now, but he always made the impression of being a dwarf, or in some way deformed, although you could not put your finger on the precise spot that made him look so. His angular face was rounded with time, he walked and moved easily, and I myself did not think him bad-looking, but I may have looked upon him with something of a creator's eyes. His legs remained forever as thin as sticks. A fantastic figure he always was, half of fun and half of diabolism; with a very slight alteration, he might have sat and stared down, on the top of the Cathedral of Notre Dame in Paris. He had in him something bright and live; in a painting he would have made a spot of unusually intense coloring; with this he gave a stroke of picturesqueness to my household. He was never quite right in the head, or at least he was always what, in a white person, you would have called highly eccentric.

He was a thoughtful person. Perhaps the long years of suffering that he had lived through, had developed in him a tendency to reflect upon things, and to draw his own conclusions from everything he saw. He was all his life, in his own way, an isolated figure. Even when he did the same things as other people he would do them in a different way.

I had an Evening School for the people of the farm, with a native schoolmaster to teach them. I got my schoolmasters from one of the Missions, and in my time I have had all three—Roman Catholic, Church of England, and Church of Scotland schoolmasters. For the native education of the country is run rigorously on religious lines; so far as I know there are no other books translated into Swahili than the Bible and the hymn-books. I myself, during all my time in Africa, was planning to translate Aesop's fables, for the benefit of the natives, but I never found time to carry my plan through. Still, such as it was, my school was to me a favorite place on the farm, the centre of our spiritual life, and I spent many pleasant evening hours in the long old storehouse of corrugated iron in which it was kept.

Kamante would then come with me, but he would not join the children on the school-benches, he would stand a little away from them, as if consciously closing his ears to the learning, and exulting in the simplicity of those who consented to be taken in, and to listen. But in the privacy of my kitchen, I have seen him copying from memory, very slowly and preposterously, those same letters and figures that he had observed on the blackboard in the school. I do not think that he could have come in with other people if he had wanted to; early in his life something in him had been twisted or locked, and now it was, so to say, to him the normal thing to be out of the normal. He was aware of this separateness of his, himself, with the arrogant greatness of soul of the real dwarf, who, when he finds himself at a difference with the whole world, holds the world to be crooked.

Kamante was shrewd in money matters, he spent little, and did a number of wise deals with the other Kikuyu in goats, he married at an early age, and marriage in the Kikuyu world is an expensive undertaking. At the same time I have heard him philosophizing, soundly and originally, upon the worthlessness of money. He stood in a peculiar relation to existence on the whole; he mastered it, but he had no high opinion of it.

He had no gift whatever for admiration. He might acknowledge, and think well of the wisdom of animals, but there was, during all the time that I knew him, only one human being of whose good sense I heard him speak approvingly; it was a young Somali woman who some years later came to live on the farm. He had a little mocking laughter, of which he made use in all circumstances, but chiefly towards any self-confidence or grandiloquence in other people. All natives have in them a strong strain of malice, a shrill delight in things going wrong, which in itself is hurting and revolting to Europeans. Kamante brought this characteristic to a rare perfection, even to a special self-irony, that made him take pleasure in his own disappointments and disasters, nearly exactly as in those of other people.

I have met with the same kind of mentality in the old native women who have been roasted over many fires, who have mixed blood with Fate, and recognized her irony, wherever they meet it, with sympathy, as if it were that of a sister. On the farm I used to let my houseboys deal out snuff—*tombacco* the natives say—to the old women on Sunday mornings, while I myself was still in bed. On this account I had a queer lot of customers round my house on Sundays, like a very old, rumpled, bald and bony poultry yard; and their low cackling—for the natives will very rarely speak up loudly—made its way through the open windows of my bedroom. On one particular Sunday morning, the gentle lively flow of Kikuyu communications suddenly rose to ripples and cascades of mirth; some highly humorous incident was taking place out there, and I called in Farah to tell me about it. Farah did not like to tell me, for the matter was that he had forgotten to buy snuff, so that today the old women had come a long way, as they say themselves, *boori*—for nothing. This happening was later on a source of amusement to the old Kikuyu women. Sometimes, when I met one of them on a path in the maizefield, she would stand still in front of me, poke a crooked bony finger at me, and, with her old dark face dissolving into laughter, so that all the wrinkles of it were drawn and folded together as by one single secret string being pulled, she would remind me of the Sunday when she and her sisters in the snuff, had walked and walked up to my house, only to find that I had forgotten to get it, and that there was not a grain there—Ha ha Msabu!

The white people often say to the Kikuyu that they know nothing of gratitude. Kamante in any case was not ungrateful, he even gave words to his feeling of an obligation. A number of times, many years after our first meeting, he went out of his way to do me a service for which I had not asked him, and when I questioned him why he had done it, he said that if it had not been for me he should have been dead a long time ago. He showed his gratitude in another manner as well, in a particular kind of benevolent, helpful, or perhaps the right word is forbearing, attitude towards me. It may be that he kept in mind that he and I were of the same religion. In a world of fools, I was, I think, to him one of the greater fools. From the day when he came into my service and attached his fate to mine, I felt his watchful penetrating eyes on me, and my whole *modus vivendi* subject to clear unbiased criticism; I believe that from the beginning, he looked upon the trouble that I had taken to get him cured as upon a piece of hopeless eccentricity. But he showed me all the time great interest and sympathy, and he laid himself out to guide my great ignorance. On some occasions I found that he had given time and thought to the problem, and that he meant to prepare and illustrate his instructions, in order that they should be easier for me to understand.

Kamante began his life in my house as a dog-toto, later he became a medical assistant to me. There I found out what good hands he had, although you would not have thought so from the look of them, and I sent him into the kitchen to be a cook's boy, a marmiton, under my old cook Esa, who was murdered. After Esa's death he succeeded to him, and he was now my chef all the time that he was with me.

Natives have usually very little feeling for animals, but Kamante differed from type here, as in other things, he was an authoritative dog-boy, and he identified himself with the dogs, and would come and communicate to me what they wished, or missed, or generally thought of things. He kept the dogs free of fleas, which are a pest in Africa, and many times in the middle of the night, he and I, called by the howls of the dogs, have, by the light of a hurricane lamp, picked off them, one by one, the murderous big ants, the *Siafu*, which march along and eat up everything on their way.

He must also have used his eyes at the time when he had been in the Mission hospital—even if it had been as was ever the case with him, without the slightest reverence or prepossession—for he was a thoughtful, inventive doctor's assistant. After he had left this office, he would at times appear from the kitchen to interfere in a case of sickness, and give me very sound advice.

But as a chef he was a different thing, and precluded classification. Nature had here taken a leap and cut away from the order of precedence of faculties and talents, the thing now became mystic and inexplicable, as ever where you are dealing with genius. In the kitchen, in the culinary world, Kamante had all the attributes of genius, even to that doom of genius— the individual's powerlessness in the face of his own powers. If Kamante had been born in Europe, and had fallen into the hands of a clever teacher, he might have become famous, and would have cut a droll figure in history. And out here in Africa he made himself a name, his attitude to his art was that of a master.

I was much interested in cookery myself, and on my first visit back to Europe, I took lessons from a French chef at a celebrated restaurant, because I thought it would be an amusing thing to be able to make good food in Africa. The chef, Monsieur Perrochet, at that time made me an offer to come in with him in his business of the restaurant, for the sake of my devotion to the art. Now when I found Kamante at hand, as a familiar spirit to cook with, this devotion again took hold of me. There was to me a great perspective in our working together. Nothing, I thought, could be more mysterious than this natural instinct in a savage for our culinary art. It made me take another view of our civilization; after all it might be in some way divine and predestinated. I felt like the man who regained his faith in God because a phrenologist showed him the seat in the human brain of theological eloquence: if the existence of theological eloquence could be proved, the existence of theology itself was proved with it, and, in the end, God's existence.

Kamante, in all cooking matters, had a surprising manual adroitness. The great tricks and tours-de-force of the kitchen were child's play to his dark crooked hands; they knew on their own everything about omelettes, vol-au-vents, sauces, and mayonnaises. He had a special gift for making things light, as in the legend the infant Christ forms birds out of clay and tells them to fly. He scorned all complicated tools, as if impatient of too much independence in them, and when I gave him a machine for beating eggs he set it aside to rust and beat whites of egg with a weeding knife that I had had to weed the lawn with, and his whites of eggs towered up like light clouds. As a cook he had a penetrating, inspired eye, and would pick out the fattest chicken out of a whole poultry yard, and he gravely weighed an egg in his hand, and knew when it had been laid. He thought out schemes for improvement of my table, and by some means of communication, from a friend who was working for a doctor far away in the country, he got me seed of a really excellent sort of lettuce, such as I had myself for many years looked for in vain.

He had a great memory for recipes. He could not read, and he knew no English so that cookery-books were of no use to him, but he must have held all that he was ever taught stored up in his ungraceful head, according to some systematization of his own, which I should never know. He had named the dishes after some event which had taken place on the day they had been shown to him, and he spoke of the sauce of the lightning that struck the tree, and of the sauce of the grey horse that died. But he did not confound any two of these things. There was only one point that I tried to impress upon him without any success, that was the order of the courses within a meal. It became necessary to me, when I had guests for dinner, to draw up for my chef, as if it were a pictorial menu: first a soup-plate, then a fish, then a partridge, or an artichoke. I did not quite believe this shortcoming in him to be due to a faulty memory, but he did, I think, in his own heart, maintain that there is a limit to everything, and that upon anything so completely immaterial, he would not waste his time.

It is a moving thing to work together with a demon. Nominally the kitchen was mine, but in the course of our cooperations, I felt not only the kitchen, but the whole world in which we were cooperating, pass over into Kamante's hands. For here he understood to perfection what I wished of him, and sometimes he carried out my wishes even before I had told him of them; but as to me I could not make clear to myself how or indeed why he worked as he did. It seemed to me a strange thing that anyone could be so great in an art of which he did not understand the real meaning, and for which he felt nothing but contempt.

Kamante could have no idea as to how a dish of ours ought to taste, and he was, in spite of his conversion, and his connection with civilization, at heart an arrant Kikuyu, rooted in the traditions of his tribe and in his faith in them as in the only way of living worthy of a human being. He did at times taste the food that he cooked, but then with a distrustful face, like a witch who takes a sip out of her cauldron. He stuck to the maizecobs of his fathers. Here even his intelligence sometimes failed him, and he came and offered me a Kikuyu delicacy—a roasted sweet potato or a lump of sheep's fat—as even a civilized dog, that has lived for a long time with people, will place a bone on the floor before you, as a present. In his heart he did, I feel, all the time, look upon the trouble that we give ourselves about our food, as upon a lunacy. I sometimes tried to extract from him his views upon these things, but although he spoke with great frankness on many subjects, on others he was very close, so that we worked side by side in the kitchen, leaving one another's ideas on the importance of cooking, alone.

I sent Kamante in to the Muthaiga Club to learn, and to the cooks of my friends in Nairobi, when I had had a new good dish in their house, and by the time that he had served his apprenticeship, my own house became famous in the Colony for its table. This was a great pleasure to me. I longed to have an audience for my art, and I was glad when my friends came out to dine with me; but Kamante cared for the praise of no one. All the same he remembered the individual taste of those of my friends who came most often to the farm. "I shall cook the fish in white wine for Bwana Berkeley Cole," he said, gravely, as if he were speaking of a demented person. "He sends you out white wine himself to cook fish in." To get the opinion of an authority, I asked my old friend Mr. Charles Bulpett of Nairobi, out to dine with me. Mr. Bulpett was a great traveller of the former generation, themselves a generation away from Phineas Fogg; he had been all over the world and had tasted everywhere the best it had to offer, and he had not cared to secure his future so long as he could enjoy the present moment. The books about sport and mountaineering, of fifty years ago, tell of his exploits as an athlete, and of his mountain climbings in Switzerland and Mexico, and there is a book of famous bets called *Light Come Light Go,* in which you can read of how for a bet he swam the Thames in evening clothes and a high hat—but later on, and more romantically, he swam the Hellespont like Leander and Lord Byron. I was happy when he came out to the farm for a tête-à-tête dinner; there is a particular happiness in giving a man whom you like very much, good food that you have cooked yourself. In return he gave me his ideas on food, and on many other things in the world, and told me that he had nowhere dined better.

The Prince of Wales did me the great honor to come and dine at the farm, and to compliment me on a Cumberland Sauce. This is the only time that I have seen Kamante listening with deep interest when I repeated the praise of his cooking to him, for natives have very great ideas of kings and like to talk about them. Many months after, he felt a longing to hear it once more, and suddenly asked me, like a French reading-book, "Did the son of the Sultan like the sauce of the pig? Did he eat it all?"

Kamante showed his good will towards me, outside of the kitchen as well. He wanted to help me, in accordance with his own ideas of the advantages and dangers in life.

One night, after midnight, he suddenly walked into my bedroom with a hurricane-lamp in his hand, silent, as if on duty. It must have been only a short time after he first came into my house, for he was very small; he stood by my bedside like a dark bat that had strayed into the room, with very big spreading ears, or like a small African Will-o'-the-wisp, with his lamp in his hand. He spoke to me very solemnly, "Msabu," he said, "I think that you had better get up." I sat up in bed bewildered; I thought that if anything serious had happened, it would have been Farah who would have come to fetch me, but when I told Kamante to go away again, he did not move. "Msabu," he said again, "I think that you had better get up. I think that God is coming." When I heard this, I did get up, and asked him why he thought so. He gravely led me into the dining-room which looked West, towards the hills. From the door-windows I now saw a strange phenomenon. There was a big grass-fire going on, out in the hills, and the grass was burning all the way from the hill-top to the plain; when seen from the house it was a nearly vertical line. It did indeed look as if some gigantic figure was moving and coming towards us. I stood for some time and looked at it, with Kamante watching by my side, then I began to explain the thing to him. I meant to quiet him, for I thought that he had been terribly frightened. But the explanation did not seem to make much impression on him one way or the other; he clearly took his mission to have been fulfilled when he had called me. "Well yes," he said, "it may be so. But I thought that you had better get up in case it was God coming."

UNTIL I SHARE...

Listen to the agony of mankind.
  I who am fed, who never yet went hungry for a day,
  I see the dead, the children starved for lack of bread.
    I see and try to pray.

Listen to the agony of mankind.
  I who am warm, who never yet have lacked a sheltering home,
  In dull alarm, the dispossessed of hut and farm
    Aimless and transient roam.

Listen to the agony of mankind.
  I who am strong, with health and love, and laughter in my soul
  I see a throng of stunted children reared in wrong
    And wish to make them whole.

Listen to the agony of mankind.
  And know full well . . . that not until I share their bitter cry
  Their pain and hell, can God within my spirit dwell
    And bring America's blessing nigh.

— DR. TOM DOOLEY

A BELL FOR CAPODANNO

by Joseph F. Cloonan

Lieutenant Vincent R. Capodanno, a 38-year-old Navy Catholic Chaplain, was killed on September 4, 1967, by Viet Cong gun fire while ministering to wounded, combat Marines of the 1st Marine Division in Vietnam. Chaplain Capodanno had served with Marines in Vietnam since April 1966. Father Cloonan is a Navy Chaplain.

"Ask not for whom the bell tolls. It tolls for thee."

The mystical poet, Donne, wrote those words in a symbolic sense. No man, he said, was an island; each is part of the main. When any man dies, his death means some dying for everyone else.

In a graphic sense, he was showing how we are all tied up with one another, by bonds of love and even at times by other less worthy bonds, such as hate, etc.

Last night—which will be three weeks from last night as you read this—I got word of the death of a priest whom I have heard of but never met.

But I have a deep feeling of personal loss.

For what I have heard of this dedicated priest sums up this way: He was a man who tried as hard as he could to share in the struggles and sufferings of the men to whom he ministered.

* A guest editorial in *The Register*, Sept. 24, 1967. Reprinted by permission.

He worked among men who were in the constant threat of death and among them, he died.

He died in the act of assisting the wounded, Marines wounded in one of the fiercest actions of the Vietnam conflict.

Did he die willingly? Who knows what is in another man's mind at the moment of death. Was he there willingly? Yes.

He had already served his stint there and had been granted permission to extend it for another six months. He had also asked for a second extension, but death denied that request.

Last week I talked with another priest who had been in Vietnam for a year. He talked of suffering and death and of how fear can sneak up on you and take you by surprise just when you think you have yourself well in hand.

He also talked about how tough it was just being there . . . in a hot, heavy, humid climate that you wore like an envelope of penance . . . with prickly heat, skin rash, irritating itches, and the constant clamoring of the body for the feel of cool, clean water.

A wise man once said that poverty was bearable but that the things that accompany poverty are not. For the poor man is often despised, ignored, abused, ridiculed. These are harder to take than the poverty. War is hell, but the accompaniments of war are more hellish.

If he knew that the result of his sufferings would be quick success, and — more importantly — lasting success, it would be more bearable.

If he knew that the innocent and the helpless would be guaranteed protection after his help was withdrawn, his dying and, more costly, his living, might not seem to be in vain.

If he could, like the Man from La Mancha, dream the impossible dream . . . beat the unbeatable foe, his heart might lie peaceful and calm when he's laid to his rest.

But the Man from La Mancha was a tilter at windmills who left situations worse than he found them, who rode into a situation and out of it without lasting good.

But men like Father Capodanno, who knew the people and

the whole area from his work as a missioner, know that there is no magic formula for success, no quick recipe for victory.

They don't dream impossible dreams, they don't fight unbeatable foes. But they do reach out sweaty hands for reachable stars. Reachable and expensive. Bought only with blood, sweat, and tears.

Their goal is not the humiliation of the enemy but the exaltation of an enslaved people to the heady level of freedom.

I think that's why Father Capodanno stayed in Vietnam long after he could have been rotated home.

While less dedicated men yawn through monotonous days and nights and call them comfortable, he was uncomfortable in the knowledge of the terrible need of others who couldn't help themselves. He who as a missioner had extended his hand and his heart to those who didn't know God now, as a chaplain, extended his life among those who were fighting the cause of the helpless.

Most of us are the comfortable who are content with our lot. We are afraid of the elevators that can take us into outer space and up to the stars. We want to stay where the inaction is. We have compromised with the world, with our ideals; we have toned down the heartrending cries for help to muted sounds that are bearable, bearable enough that we don't have to commit ourselves to them.

But every once in a while, like a flash of heat lightning, the self-giving of someone like Father Capodanno illuminates the mystery of nobility in an ignoble world.

A PRAYER FOR MISSIONERS

O Divine Wayfarer,
Whose first shelter was a stable,
Whose first journey was a flight
*   for life,*
And who traveling oft had not
*   where to lay your head;*
Be to those who carry your message
*   a sure Guide and unfailing rest.*
Clothe them in the garment of charity
*   which is strange to no man,*
And teach them the language of sympathy
*   which is understood by all,*
That, while strangers in every land,
They may yet be welcomed
*   as citizens of the soul of man*
*   and as brothers of the human heart,*
*   for your Kingdom's sake. Amen.*

THE FATHER PRESIDENT: 1635

by Paul Horgan

A portrait of a Franciscan missioner and his approach to
his Indian people in seventeenth-century New Mexico.

Whenever the old father president of all the Franciscans and
their missions in New Mexico thought of the idea of "spring,"
he did not think of a time of year, but of a time in his life — his
youth. Newly ordained as a friar in Spain, he had come to the
City of Mexico, and then to Santa Fe in 1635 as a missioner. If
he then saw the country as dry, stony, and vacant, he bore
within him all the green and flowering certainties of growth,
the seeds of a new life that he would plant in the desert wastes
of the Indian soul, to the honor and glory of the two majesties
that governed him. These were his Divine Lord in Heaven and
his royal lord King Philip IV of Spain. In his enthusiasm and
inexperience the young friar believed that these two majesties
were by nature indivisible. He set out to serve them with his
whole being, adoring the One and revering the other.

If his convictions which he held so strongly gave him great
firmness of character, he was saved from hardness of mind by
a vein of comic irony that ran through his temperament and
made him a good companion, whether to Spaniard or Indian.
He was one of those whose views were often quoted by others
to win arguments, and whose drolleries were repeated by ,less

original men who did not always mention their source. Any reminder of him brought up his image.

He was of medium height, stockily built, quick and darting in movement, and, when still, quivering in fixed alertness like a jack rabbit. His hair was prematurely iron gray. Wiry black eyebrows curved upward above his brilliant gray eyes. Through his stubby pepper and salt mustache and beard gleamed his prominent upper teeth. Always showing, they seemed to give extra wit or force to the notions he was never at a loss to make articulate. The voluminous blue-gray cloth of his Franciscan habit was always awry, twisted against itself by the energy of his limbs. When he walked his rapid steps caused a bobbing motion. He could always be picked out of a procession, for he moved like nobody else. He spoke, read, and wrote Spanish, Latin, and Italian, and he could read and write French and German, and it would not be long before he could talk to Indians in their own tongue. He seemed to know things without learning them, which made some of his religious brothers envy even as they admired him.

When he felt their envy he sobered his humor and displayed a begging interest in their concerns, that they might show their own best selves, which, he believed, all men deserved to do, under the dignity which God had put into human nature.

It was in such spirit that he approached his Indians, in the springtime of his faith and work.

His duty in 1635 took him first to the mission and pueblo of El Agua de Santo Domingo, on the Galisteo Creek a few leagues east of the Rio Grande del Norte, which was the ecclesiastical capital of the kingdom of New Mexico. There he saw a large terraced city of clay rooms, clustered rather like cells in a great hive, to which at one end was attached the recently built mission church with its convent, its holy burying ground, and its animal corrals.

When he asked why the headquarters of the religious province was not at Santa Fe, where the Crown's governor had his seat, he was told by the then father president that the more distance that separated the two authorities, the better.

No, how could this be? wondered the new missioner. All of life on earth was made in the image of Cross and Crown combined, the two majesties upon which mankind depended. They must not contend in strife.

Nevertheless, stated his superior, no priest could get along with any governor.

To the young man this sounded like simple bad temper based, probably, on too many years of troubled labor in a harsh land. His own experience would surely be different. He was aware that he had a gift for dealing with people. With a smile of affectionate respect he concealed his confidence from his embittered old superior, and listened with suppressed eagerness to his assignment. He was to go as pastor to an unconverted pueblo near the Rio Grande upriver. In a few days he left for Santa Fe in the company of a party of Christian Indians who took a cargo of corn and beans to be delivered as a portion of their annual tribute to the royal governor. There through the pastor of Santa Fe the missioner was to apply for an escort of soldiers to protect him against war parties of plains Indians on his march to his new parish.

If he expected a squad to be turned out for him offhand, he was mistaken. The pastor made application on his behalf at the palace for his soldiery, but nothing happened. When the young friar made inquiries, he was told to moderate his impatience until his request could be acted upon one way or another. Not quite concealing his surprise that there should be any question about his needs, and that the petition of a holy friar should be treated as a nuisance, he gave the interim to gathering an impression of the royal city.

Its recent history, he thought, was best reflected in its churches. In the first years of the colony, people had attended Mass either in Saint Michael's chapel across the creek, or in the old parish church which was like a granary of upright posts and brush covering. But as the population grew, so did the need

for a larger and more solidly built parish of adobes on the same
site as the old one on the plaza. Now in 1635 Santa Fe counted
250 heads of families, of whom 100 were soldiers. With their
kinfolk and servants they made a population of almost a
thousand.

"The most important Spanish women" devoted themselves
to the housekeeping of the parish church. They swept the clay
floor, washed and stretched the altar linens, and gave special
attention to the propriety of their greatest treasure. This was
a statue of our Lady of the Holy Rosary, clothed in silk and
rayed with a gilded glory about her head. She had come from
Spain, like any other colonist, and in the shelter of those clay
walls she spoke not only of heaven but of the home kingdom, for
her style was European. She was small, scarcely a yard tall,
but her little oval face gleamed with a perfect complexion in
polished bisque. Through her fixed dark eyes shone a message
of innocence and love that would never change. Her presence
seemed to uplift the world's life and make it visible for those
who came to find the answer to all things in her rude chapel of
dried mud. She had power. The resident pastor told the new-
comer how the principal captains of an Apache nation, having
heard of her from missionaries, came to Santa Fe to see her,
and were at once converted, kissing her feet and saying proper
words.

"Yes," remarked the new missioner, the establishment
seemed complete, and he praised the ingenuity with which out
of the humblest native materials all elements of the church
had been contrived. "I shall make drawings and measurements
here."

"Drawings?" asked the pastor.

"Yes, to guide me as I build my own church at my pueblo."

"Yes," said the pastor, "well, in any case, you will not have
the benefit of a bishop's approval of your constructions, as we
have no bishop nearer to us than five hundred leagues."

It was true, even though the Crown had been asked thirty
years ago by Governor Oñate of San Juan to appoint a bishop
for New Mexico. The petition had been renewed since, but

without avail. Heaven only knew when it might be approved, sighed the pastor. It was possible, in his view, that recent governors had secretly opposed the appointment of a bishop, who might exert his power against them.

Again the missioner was struck by the hint of strife between the two majesties of Cross and Crown, and in the following weeks he came to think of himself as a victim of such contention, as his request for an armed escort received no attention. At last, having exhausted the resources of Santa Fe and his own eager patience, he one day filled a haversack with food and set out alone on foot for his new parish.

He was equipped with a conjectural map of his way drawn by the pastor of Sante Fe, who, having spoken of real and well-known hazards, let him go with a spoken blessing and one even more fervently made in the silence of his envious heart. What he envied were the confidence, the morninglike vitality, and the plain acceptance of the possibility of martyrdom that animated the younger man.

After several days of walking alone the young missioner came to a side valley with a shallow creekbed. He followed it rising upstream amid flattened hills of now rosy, now white earth. Late one afternoon he saw a flat hilltop stained by an ink-dark cloud shadow; and then the shadow was drawn aside by wind aloft, and he saw the pueblo on the hill's rim, and he nodded as if in recognition and hurried forward, thinking what a pleasure it would be to find other beings to talk to.

But when he stood near enough to see his people, there was nobody to be seen. The pueblo was inscrutable, without human sign. Slowly he went toward it, searching the rooftops where the entrances were, watching for a quiver along any of the tall poled ladders that stood up out of the interiors. Nothing stirred. He sank slowly to his knees, and then sat on his heels, rubbing his hands on his thighs. He was hungrily disappointed.

And then, suddenly, from behind a corner of the hive came a naked child in a tumbling run. It was a small girl. After her raced a thin gray dog. On seeing him they both stopped dead and stared. He sat still. They came a few steps nearer, and the dog began to snarl. The missioner put out his arms toward the two young animals. He said nothing, but smiled with his eyes brilliantly open.

Against their will, it seemed, the girl and the dog came to him. He picked up the child in his arms and spoke to her gently, in her very ear. The dog earnestly sniffed all about him, and then set its paw on his arm, and he patted it on the head. When next he looked toward the pueblo he saw the roof lines edged with men and women and other children, regarding him in silence. Bearing their child forward in his arms, he rose and went to them, and, coming down from their lofts, they received him impassively.

That night when he was to be fed a certain family asked him to their roof. He watched them prepare a dish. The ingredients were sand, corn meal, and two small field mice which they minced, fur and all. They then moistened the whole for stewing with the unmistakable contents of a night pot. As it cooked he thought of what he must do, and when it was placed before him as an act of deliberate offense, he threw back his sleeves, took up his stew, and ate it, nodding pleasantly.

For he thought that he must either eat it now and have done with it for good, or eat the meaning of such challenging hostility every day in many other ways, for as long as he should remain — and he intended to remain.

The Indians asked him in gestures how he could eat such filth, and he replied that for "a good appetite there is no bad bread." They gazed at him. A child trusted him, and a dog, and he did not sicken at eating ordure. He had passed certain tests, then, and beyond these, he could smile into their eyes with a perfect humanity unafraid. He remembered, even then, how earlier Franciscans had been struck to death, and how "Indians crushed the heads of three of these and ate them as fricassee, as it was said."

He asked where he might sleep, and was taken to the deepest cell of the hive. They pulled away his ladder and left him alone. During the night drums rumbled softly, and discussions were held, but he heard only the first sounds of such fateful mutterings. If they came to look at him in the night, he did not know it. In the morning he called for his ladder, and they brought it, lowering it to him. He thanked them, and came up, and symbolically embraced them all in a gesture of wide-flung arms. He then asked them to do as he did, and knelt down on the roof.

"Kneel with me," he said several times, smiling and blinking both eyes, until one by one they did so. Something shone out of him, some trapped, yet freed, sunlight. "Now," he said, and made the sign of the cross upon himself, slowly showing them how, until their right hands moved from brow to heart, and from shoulder to shoulder. His delight at their agreement was so joyful that they felt like creators of a fine spirit. That was something to which they could give respect. None of this came to him as a surprise, for he knew that the grace of God must work; but he admitted that he was gratified. For his breakfast then he was given long strips of dried melon, and shreds of dried meat heated in smoke that gave savor, and scorching hot thin cakes of corn meal. Again they watched him eat, and when he sighed heavenwards at such good fare, they hung their heads to conceal their satisfaction.

The only essential thing left for him to do, then, was to convince them that he wanted nothing of them but their souls, and those not for himself, but for the one God from whom they came. Accordingly, his next acts were acts of work, in which he labored as hard as they.

After the first exasperating yet comic weeks of learning to communicate with each other, the missioner and his people found time flying. No day seemed long enough to enclose all the tasks they met.

The hardest of these was to teach, on the one hand, and on the other, to listen. How should he manage? Perhaps if he said that God was the whole sky and all the earth, then Jesus Christ His Son was like a star, the brightest of all, among the stars of heaven, and among men, like any man, but the best of them. And then it would be necessary to modify all that, and remove misunderstanding, for his pupils too easily decided that Jesus was not *like* a star, but *was* a star, at the same time that He was *like* a man, but *was not* a man. . . .

It was easier to work at making adobes, bricks out of earth, with which to make a church. For months the long piled rows of these grew till there seemed to be enough. Then with a party of men the missioner went to Santa Fe and Santo Domingo to bring back tools, and instruments of measurements, and sacred vessels, and a set of vestments, and holy oil and wine, and candles, and a missal, and a crucifix, and a bell for his bell tower. Next they went to the mountains thirty miles away for timber large enough to support a roof. He showed them with his drawings of the Santa Fe church how these would look when placed, and, after many more months, there they were, high overhead, and for the first time his drawings had meaning for the builders.

His daily lessons were many, and they understood how everything else they worked at was tied in meaning to the making and use of their church. He held up a piece of Indian pottery and then indicated the mission chapel, and said that together they were all shaping with clay a new vessel. The gesture delighted them, and gave him an idea for a happy detail. Choosing the best potters from among the women he asked them to go within the church and paint the walls with designs like those on their pots — corn leaves, birds, lightning, clouds, all touched alive with the repeated symbol of the cross, with which they were now familiar.

He thought the church looked like a coffin, narrow at the head, wider at the elbows, and slim again at the foot. But this was his private fancy, and when he was ready for his first Mass, and the fresh clay room was decked with boughs of pine and starred with the still flames of candles, he knew it was a true container of life, and he thought his people knew it too.

The jobs never seemed to end. He worked fields with the Indians, planting and irrigating. He procured a few sheep, a small herd of cattle, some horses, and taught their care and breeding. He trained a group of children to sing — in Latin — and presently had a choir for the responses in the sung Mass. When the children showed him how to imitate the songs of birds by blowing through hollow straws into little bowls of water, he let them make bird song as an act of worship during the Consecration at the Mass. He appointed a sacristan who learned to ring the tower bell for all occasions. Spain rang out over the valley, and New Spain came to pray, to study, to wonder. All was new, all was creative. It was a season of budding and promise. It was his springtime.

During his years of residence with the Indians, he often reviewed notions about them long debated by Spaniards. For more than a century the question had been asked, "What is an Indian?" Was he a man? An animal? An intermediate species? A natural slave, such as Aristotle described? Was he capable of the faculty of reason? Such questions were argued for generations in courts of law and before ecclesiastical tribunals.

There were two sets of answers, as the missioner knew. One set, believed by the colonial conquerors and landowners and soldiers and governors, concluded that the Indian was a miserable creature, inferior by nature and degenerate in his ignorance, who existed only to serve his Spanish superiors. He could not read or write, he possessed no sense of property and did not even mine for gold, and his idolatries were obscene. He was a beast of burden and a source of work, that was all. Let him be used, therefore, to the advantage of his masters.

But the Crown, the law courts, and the Church held an opposite view. The Indian, they said, could be lifted up. What had Pope Paul II stated in his bull *Sublimis Deus* in 1537? With grand compassion he enunciated the doctrine that "the sublime God so loved the human race that . . . all are capable of receiving the doctrines of the faith. . . ." The Indians were truly men, elaborated the pontiff; they were not only able to understand the Catholic faith, but even desired exceedingly to receive it. The Pope commanded that "the said Indians and all other people who may later be discovered by Christians are by no means to be deprived of their liberty or the possession of their property, even though they be outside the faith of Jesus Christ;

and that they may and should, freely and legitimately, enjoy their liberty and the possession of their property; nor should they be in any way enslaved; should the contrary happen it shall be null and void and of no effect. . . ." "The said Indians," concluded His Holiness, "and other peoples should be converted to the faith of Jesus Christ by preaching the word of God and by the example of good and holy living." It was under these terms that the missioner lived with his people.

Knowing them well, he became devoted to them. They were peaceable. They governed themselves under an order that seemed to be theirs by natural law. They cherished their children and respected their old people. He considered them "the best infidel people" he knew. Yet since to his satisfaction they were human beings, they were of course capable of great error, and to this he did not shut his eyes, but labored to bring them to goodness through penitence and hope of salvation. He learned much about their pagan practices, and saw that at the base of their worship lay not love but fear. All objects and acts in nature were propitiated out of fear by forms of worship that must be allied to despair, for how could a tree, a stone, a cloud, the sun, the moon, a clutch of turkey feathers, answer prayer? He caught his breath in shame at some of the acts he saw performed when the Indians danced in community to call forth the powers of generation, whether out of the sky and earth in costumed imitation of the acts of the weather, or out of human loins in public, naked repetitions of acts of lust.

It took him years to do so, but in the end he persuaded them to desist from their seasonal enactments of dance worship. Their fear was even greater, at first, for they feared that if they ceased dancing for rain and corn, no rain or corn would come. But when after some years they saw that corn and rain returned after all under the laws of Divine Providence, they abided under their new faith and lived with their pastor of peace. They saw that he asked no more of them than of himself. They marveled. Was he really a Spaniard? They touched him in the simplicity of their uses of Christianity. Sometimes when they came to confession he saw them carrying bits of string made from yucca fiber with knots tied every so often. When he asked what the knots were for, they told him that these represented sins which they had made note of. "Of such was the Kingdom of Heaven . . ."

EARLY SPRING

Already the pine looks greener.
  Is it only because I think so?
The snow still lying in the mountain valley
  looks warmer.
The sounds of repairing an earth-walled house
  resound in the sunbeams.

Cannot I hear the sounds that
  seem to rise, then fade away?
Everywhere I see the movement of
  budding and growth
The butterfly would already be known,
  but his wings are slow to come.

The beautiful signs of early Spring
  are found through the length of the land.
While my thoughts are forming,
  the drifting cloud stops still.
Why not divulge the secret of Spring
  before blaming the halting pen?

—CHUNG IN-BO

MOTHER OF REFUGEES

by Sister M. Marcelline

Lady on the road to Egypt
   you pave the way to the hearts
   of refugees.
   For your dark path of pain
   and tribulation
   is just like theirs,
   as they flee from friendly climes
   to strangers' shores.

They carry the barest essentials.
They tread wearily under burning skies.
They walk to uncertainty,
   feeling separation and desolation.

Lady on the road to Egypt,
   how great must be your compassion
   for refugees from China!
   Your motherly love for them
   is deep consolation.
   It gives the strength of resignation;
   the hope that God will bring
   a final restoration in Christ,
   who also walked the road to Calvary
   that He might rule upon a cross,
   and conquer hearts for all eternity.

Lady in exile,
   seeking a roof for habitation,
   dreaming of a temple for adoration,
   praying for Joseph in search of a market
   for his heavy labor;
   as we find you in Egypt,
   faithful wife and fairest mother,
   suffering calmly the pain of exile,
   how truly you are the mother of all hope,
   the courage of China's refugees!

As you find them, then,
   clustered on the hills
   of Junk Bay and Kowloon Tsai;
   in Central District, Diamond Hill,
   King's Park, Kennedy Town,
   Cheung Sha Wan, Hung Hom,
   and Shek Kep Mi. . .

Take them all to your immaculate heart.
Make them feel its beat for each and every one.
You are their Mother.

Mother of Refugees, we cry to you.
We trust in you.
Bring them all to Christ, your Son!

THE GREAT WALL

Night after night,
All through the night
I build and break down
The Great Wall.

LATE AT NIGHT

Late at night,
Barely visible, the gleaming light.
A soft footstep,
Hardly audible;
A footstep, fading away.
Tried hard to sleep again.
But sleep would not come.

—SO WOL KIM

MY SOUL TO GOD . . . MY BODY TO MY COUNTRY

by John Tung

In an auditorium in Chungking, China (1951), a courageous priest speaks up to his Red masters.

Authorities of the Government, Dignitaries of the Church,
Christians who are loyal to your faith, and Gentlemen. The
subject of this speech will be: the sacrifice that I make of myself to the two supreme powers (my religion and the State).

Persons who do not believe in the existence of God, nor in
the existence of the soul, who do not recognize the Pope as
being the representative of Christ, who do not recognize the
Catholic hierarchy, present the Three-Self Movement as a
purely patriotic movement. These same persons recognize the
liberty to adhere to the Catholic faith; they admit purely spiritual
relations may exist between the faithful and the Pope. But this
movement, which has evolved outside the hierarchy, today
invites us to attack the representative of the Pope, Archbishop
Riberi. Tomorrow we shall perhaps be asked to attack the Pope
himself, who is Christ's representative. And the day after
tomorrow, why should we not be asked to attack our Lord and
God Jesus Christ Himself?

We may always, in the course of an attack, make distinctions.
But in reality God is one; the Pope is one; and the Pope's
representative is one. No distinction or division is admissible.
Such a development, the triple independence, would take from

me all possibility of remaining Catholic. A patriotic movement of such a nature is in fact incompatible with the Catholic Church.

Gentlemen, I have only one soul and I cannot divide it; I have a body which can be divided. It is best, it seems, to offer my whole soul to God and to the Holy Church; and my body to my country. If she is pleased with it, I do not refuse it to her. Good materialists, who deny the existence of the soul, cannot but be satisfied with the offering of my body only. I believe that if the State and the Church could collaborate, the movement for a triple autonomy, conformable to Catholic principles, would be recognized as a patriotic movement. If it were so, how much good would result both for the State and for the Church!

But on the contrary, the more the movement progresses the farther one is from the other. We have reached a point where almost any backward step is impossible. Very soon, the last thread to which we can attach our hope will be broken. How miserable I feel, unable to do anything, but as I am unable to remedy this situation, I can do nothing better than to offer my soul to one party and my body to the other, in the hope of promoting their mutual understanding. There is nothing else I can do as long as that understanding is not realized. I have no regrets. I only beseech God to have pity on my natural weakness and give me supernatural courage, then I shall be unshakable till death.

I beseech the authorities to accept my sacrifice and not to show me any sort of indulgence. And above all, if it happens that I weaken, I beseech them not to tolerate this weakness. Are not the weak the scourge of society? Therefore, to guard against all weakness, and in the event that I should lose control of my actions and speak words of weakness, I take this opportunity, while I am perfectly lucid, to solemnly declare that I disavow them and declare them right now null and void.

I am aware that the [civil] authorities have many times clearly declared their intention not to use force, but only to stimulate us. It is therefore my duty to speak in complete frankness and never to say what I do not mean. [The authorities wish that] I sign a declaration only if I sincerely approve of it, and if I do not approve, not to sign it hypocritically. Have not the authorities manifestly given us freedom of speech as well as the freedom of being silent? Why shouldn't we believe their declarations?

Suppose that, under the effect of I know not what fear, I should go against my conscience, talk contrary to my own opinions, sign what I disapprove of. Then I am deliberately deceiving the authorities. And if I say in secret that I made a mistake because I was forced, then I am equally deceiving the hierarchy. Would not such conduct sow discord between the government and the Church? If I stifle the voice of my conscience, deny my God, leave the Church, and cheat the government, I am nothing more than an opportunist and a coward. I would then be only one of those persons in whom nobody can have confidence, whose life has no value for anyone. Who then would want to have me, who would want to help me? I would only be a miserable outcast deserving of all punishment from the authorities in this world and eternal punishment in the next from divine justice.

It is true that I am a Catholic. But this does not prevent me from having a very great admiration for the Communists. They believe neither in God nor in the soul, still less in heaven or hell. It is my conviction that they are mistaken. However, they have more than one quality which compels admiration, shakes my own indolence, and brings me to recall vividly the millions of martyrs of our Church during the course of two thousand years. These martyrs are the ones who urge me to beseech God, day and night, to forgive my numerous sins and grant me the unparalleled gift of martyrdom.

The first admirable quality of the Communists is that they are capable of facing death. They never betray their cause and deceive others by giving some excuse, as General Li Ling did to rationalize his capitulation: "If I did not fight to death, it is because I was preserving myself for future deeds." Should I a Catholic be cowardly, or attached to life, and use the pretext of preserving myself for future service to the Church? A Christian who betrays his God also betrays his Church and his country. The Communists are wont to say: "For one who falls, ten thousand will rise." How could a Catholic forget: "the blood of martyrs is the seed of Christians."

The second admirable quality of the Communists is that they show no fear when accused of crimes and condemned to death: "The people's eyes," they say, "see clearly and are not mistaken." This is the reason why they face death with such pride. Now, how could a Christian fear to be falsely accused and abused; how could he fear that this unjust death is without value or meaning? How could he forget that our "supreme judge is almighty God, full of wisdom and kindness, justice and equity"?

The Communists also possess a third quality. When they are right but fail to convince others, they maintain their own faith intact. If it happens that they are beaten in an argument or discussion, they do not abandon their belief, quit or doubt the Party. How could a Christian forget that his faith comes to him from God? How could he feel the entire Church is defeated because he himself has been defeated? If he did that, he would soon falsify the Church's teaching and weaken its discipline, betray God and his own soul.

If I betray my God and my soul, who could then guarantee that I would not betray my motherland and my people? This is why I refuse to be shaken in my faith and be an instrument by which other Christians' faith should be shaken. This is why I refuse to abase my priesthood by misleading the faithful.

The Communists, whom I admire, have a true consideration for the Catholic Church which I love, and endeavor to win the support of the Christians. I confess that I feel much honored by it. Why then should I not redouble my efforts to be an unshakable Christian in answer to the noble intention of the government? I will not "exhibit a sheep's head and sell dog meat."

I do not content myself with admiring the unshakable courage of the Communists and thanking them for their noble intention of trying to win the support of Christians. I still have a great desire. It is to offer them the Catholic Church which is so dear to me: to bring them to God and to make them our brothers in the faith. Do not say I am a fool who prattles crazy things, and do not think that I am insincere! I say that, when the day comes that Communists of such ideals truly know the Catholic Church, they will make good Catholics completely devoted to their faith and will surpass a thousand times a Catholic such as I am. I also pray God that in the Communist Party there may be found many Sauls to become Pauls, who will far surpass the poor priest that I am. It is my most fervent prayer. To this end, I will withhold no sacrifice, praying with hope that the earthly life I offer today may bring the conversion of future generations.

This is my way of seeing things. The composition of this speech is faulty; please excuse a man who could not put the required care into it. Moreover, because I did not obtain ecclesiastical approval, my speech evidently cannot represent the Church's opinion. The speech is also without the approbation of the civil authorities. It is only the expression of what seems to be an ideal, but it is perhaps nothing but a beautiful personal dream.

I am a Catholic Chinese. I love my country but I also love my Church. I categorically disapprove of anything that is in opposition to the laws of my country or to the laws of my Church, and before all I strongly refuse anything that could breed discord. But if the Church and the government cannot achieve an accord, all Chinese Catholics, sooner or later, will have only to die.

Why not, then, immediately offer my life to hasten the mutual understanding of the two parties? If my offering is accepted, the only reason is that understanding is not wanted, that peace is rejected. I hardly believe that the government will permit itself to be drawn irrevocably into demanding the death of the 3,700,000 Chinese Catholics.

If a member of the Catholic hierarchy does not accept my prayer, or considers me as one out of order who mixes in things not of his concern, this person may punish me with suspension, but no one can forbid me to have recourse to higher authority, to the Pope himself if need be. But if in this desperate situation we both still have the courage to look for a solution, reconciliation can be attained. May I be pardoned for all the shortcomings of this speech.

In the name of the Father, and of the Son, and of the Holy Spirit. Amen.

A   PROPHET

Thou gavest to every land,
To the poor Arabia, nurse of camels,
A prophet to show the way and a holy book,
But to us Turks this grace has not been given.
We have followed prophets from divers lands
And set our faith in holy words,
But the way has not been shown us.
Lord, send us a prophet to show us that way.

— MAGHJAN JUMBAY

*From the book *The Soviet Empire,* O. K. Carol. New York: St. Martin's Press, 1953, p. 228. Reprinted by permission.

NEVER LESS ALONE

by Bishop James E. Walsh

> In a tiny hut on a island off China, Francis Xavier lay
> dying, his mission unaccomplished.

He felt queer, lightheaded, a little unsteady on his feet, as he
began to say Mass. He thought it was because he had been cutting corners on sleep. Not that he was very busy, but he had been
giving lavish hours to long bursts of rapt prayer. A mild re-
solve to get more sleep flashed through his mind. He lurched on
his feet a little and grasped the edge of the rude altar to support
himself when Antonio presented the wine and water. He felt
dizzy. And what made it so hot all of a sudden? Had the weather
changed? The cool, fresh wind of South China's idyllic November stole through the gaping apertures of the ramshackle little
hut, even as he thought about it. The candles flickered. The
breeze was refreshing, but he was still parched and hot. Then
he completely forgot about it, as he extended his hands over the
chalice and the little bell tinkled.

"This is my Body." The white host gleamed aloft for an instant in his trembling hands. "This is the chalice of my blood
. . . which shall be shed for you and for many unto the remission
of sins." He braced himself as he raised and lowered the chalice
with infinite care. On the instant the whole universe changed.
He was no longer just a fever-wracked wanderer, stranded at
the end of the world with little hope of going on and still less of

return. "Why, You came with me. You are here—and I want nothing," was the instinctive thought that flashed across his mind. He was where he belonged—and the whole heavenly court was with him. It was not a new thought. It was one that had come to him countless times since that day many years ago when he first stood at the altar to welcome the Living Bread that came down from heaven. It had been more and more with him in the recent years of his long, lonely voyages. He dismissed it now with a conscious effort and went on slowly and painstakingly with the Mass. But his soul felt lifted as if on wings.

He was a little embarrassed to be caught huddled up on the floor when Antonio returned with three of the Portuguese sailors from the *Santa Croce*. But he really was feeling very ill. He had known the Chinese boy was up to something when he left the hut that afternoon. The missioner's refusal to eat all day had plainly worried his faithful young companion. He did not think he would feel any better on the ship, but it was kind of these good men to come for him. He knew that from the Captain down they already thought he was a little crazy to have remained on the island, and he did not wish to estrange them further. He decided to let them take him along.

The Captain met him. "I told you that Chinese boat would never come back for you, Father Francis," was his greeting. "Not a chance in my opinion. They have your bargain money, and that's all they wanted."

The sick man did not find this very consoling. But he was too sick to feel that it mattered much. He rallied his forces to return a kindly answer. "It is good of you to take me aboard, Captain," he replied. "I am not feeling very well. I should like to wait a little longer for the boat to China. It is only a few days overdue. Any little accident could have delayed it. It will be as God wills."

The sound of retching and stifled groans stopped a sailor leaving his watch the next morning and brought him into the missioner's tiny cabin. The wind had freshened during the night, and the ship was dancing and rolling. One glance showed that the prostrate sick man was finding it very trying. His labored breath, flushed face, and restless limbs made him a picture of misery.

Antonio was watching beside him, looking his own misery. The sailor went to call the medical officer and the Captain.

"We'll take the Father back," said the Captain, after he and the doctor had seen the sick priest and listened to Antonio. "The doctor will go with him and bleed him for the fever. The ship is rolling too much." He bent over the sick man. His look was kindly, as if he meant to comfort him. "I'll call a sampan and put you back on shore, Father Francis," he said. "Maybe the fresh air will help you. But I told you you should have gone back with our fleet when it started for Malacca day before yesterday. No use staying in this desolate place. But anyhow, we'll do what we can for you."

The priest thanked him. With the help of Antonio and one of the sailors he staggered out of the cabin. He almost fell into the water as they guided him into the little sampan. The Captain wrapped a coarse ship's blanket around his shoulders. The sailor reached in his pocket and gave Antonio a handful of almonds as the sampan was pushing off. The man burning with fever did not need either, but he looked his gratitude for the simple acts.

Antonio got more and more worried as the days passed. The bleeding had had no effect except to make the sick man weaker. Visitors to the little hut were few. Except for the simple fishermen of the island, Sancian was deserted. All the traders had left. The marketplace was dismantled. Christopher, the Tamil boy, looked in once, but Father Francis had not seemed pleased with him. He roused himself from his torpor to scold the boy about his bad conduct, but Christopher only looked sullen and hung his head and said nothing. The boy slunk away and did not come back again. After that nobody came and Antonio remained with the priest alone.

Mostly the sick man lay in a stupor but, at times when the fever was strong, he seemed to pass into a state of delirium. Then he spoke rapidly, sometimes raising his voice to a shout and again trailing off in a whisper. Antonio did not understand the languages he was speaking. Most of his talk sounded like Latin of the psalms he had heard in the churches at Goa and Malacca. There was another language that sounded very much like Portu-

guese and yet was not Portuguese, and there was another that
rang out more sonorous than either. There were snatches of the
catechism in Tamil and in Japanese. And there was one language
completely strange — and this he seemed to speak more flowingly
and meaningfully than any other, as if it might have been the
language of his inmost thoughts from his childhood. Antonio
could only sit and wonder. He could not get the missioner to
eat anything. He watched him growing weaker day by day.

Father Francis wanted the crucifix. It helped him to pray.
He took it from the boy, kissed it, and propped it on the blanket
where he could see it without turning his head. "Everything went
wrong," he whispered. "But if it is right with You, it is right with
me." The effort was difficult for him. He did not try to speak
again.

His mind was clear, and he let his thoughts wander. China just
across the bay. He would never reach it. That trouble with the
Commandant at Malacca was fatal. God forgive the poor man.
If only we could have gone with our own Ambassador! That was
the way to get to China. Might still go with the Ambassador of
Siam? But when is he going — and will he take me? Nobody
knows. Maybe I should have gone back with the ships to Malacca. Was I just foolish — and stubborn? This wasn't the best
way to get to China. Brother Alvaro deserted me. Christopher
is lost to me. Anthony has forgotten all his Chinese. The boat
hasn't come. And here I am. Everything went wrong from the
start. But I couldn't go back — I had to keep on. Ignatius will
understand. And so will You. He felt comforted. He smiled. He
had made his report. The crucifix slid off the blanket. His eyes
were closed and he did not notice it. He seemed asleep.

Antonio watched him closely. His head lay listless on the
sacking that took the place of a pillow. His breathing was faint.
Antonio thought it was time. He picked up the crucifix and
propped it up on the matting where the missioner could see it
when he opened his eyes. The boy saw his lips moving as if in
prayer, but no sound came forth. He arose and got the little stub
of Mass candle that was left. He lighted it and held it against the

missioner's nerveless hand, as he had seen the priests do in Malacca.

The lips were still moving. It must be a long prayer. There was the trace of a smile, as if the haggard face were lit up by some inner vision. Suddenly the eyes opened. They reached towards the crucifix. The sick man strained forward. He had come to the end of his prayer. "In Te, Domine, speravi: non confundar in aeternum," came the Latin words haltingly but in a clear, strong voice. The missioner sank back on the tumbled matting. Antonio heard a little sigh, almost as if a breath of wind had stirred through the hut. There was the slightest of tremors and the gaunt form lay inert. Antonio leaned over. There was no breathing. Father Francis was still.

The candle still flickered where Antonio had set it down in the drafty hut. It was a symbol. The greatest mission undertaking in history was over. The great soul of Xavier had flown to God. But a flame had been lighted in the East that would never die.

"I AM THE WAY"

Thou art the Way.
Hadst Thou been nothing but the goal,
* I cannot say*
If Thou hadst ever met my soul.

* I cannot see—*
I, child of process—if there lies
* An end for me,*
Full of repose, full of replies.

* I'll not reproach*
The road that winds, my feet that err.
* Access, approach*
Art Thou, Time, Way, and Wayfarer.

—ALICE MEYNELL

THE WHEAT

I rode up to the highest hill
To watch the pastures green and still;
And I saw the ripe and blowing wheat,
Golden in the summer heat.
It stood beneath a vaulting sky,
And rippled in the breeze's sigh!
I saw the wheat—a golden sea
Spread out for miles in majesty.
The wheat! The wheat! The golden wheat!
A field of grandeur at my feet!
The wheat that soon would make the bread,
By which a hungry child is fed.
While my faithful gelding grazed,
Long at this sun-lit field I gazed—
And as I watched I thought the wheat
Resembled Christ—Our Savior sweet!
Let the snow fall, freezing cold—
The wheat will come up—green and bold!
Let the sun burn and madly beat
Upon the earth with cruel heat;
Bravely the sprout will break the clod
And raise its grass-like blade to God!
Let the floods come and tempests blow,
Somehow the wheat will try to grow!
So is Christ like a field of grain,
For His Word lives on in joy and pain.
If persecution reaps the field—
A slender stem will bravely yield
New grains of faith to sow
The love of God where it will grow—
Just as the blowing, golden grain
That grows in splendor upon the plain.

—CASSIE EUGENIA DIXSON

WE ARE THE HARVEST

by Joseph Michenfelder and Albert J. Nevins

Our roots are buried in the mainlands of five continents; from the arid, thirsty soil of many nations, we have burst forth two billion times. Our fruit ripens at the mouths of uncharted rivers, in hidden windswept valleys, and upon wastelands of forgotten ice. You will find us clustered in the heart of steaming jungles and on deserts of sand that lead to the sun.

We are the harvest.

We are countless centuries old, but in our life this is youth. And there is something within us like the wind, telling us that we shall continue to live and bear fruit as long as there is any life at all.

The skin that covers us is in shades of red, black, yellow, white, and brown. We speak as many languages and dialects and tongues as there are stars in the night. We work, sing, laugh, cry, beget children, and die. And so let it never be said that we are merely numbers — or categories or statistics, or lines on a chart. We are real, living, breathing persons, who desire to love and be loved as persons.

We are the harvest.

Our homes are made from the things at hand — mud, grass, ice, adobe, wood, cardboard, sheet metal, shingle. We eat what we are able to grow—corn, wheat, rice, beans, peanuts, chili, co-coconut. Sometimes we kill the beasts that fly, swim, or crawl.

We cover our bodies with cotton, wool, silk, hemp, grass, skins, fur, and sometimes with nothing at all. Our limbs are decorated with paint, ivory, flowers, metals, pearls from under the sea, gems from within the earth.

But mostly we are poor. Every night many of us go to bed hungry, even though we have labored from the very rising of the sun. If there is famine or flood, we starve. When the snows come, we freeze.

And always there is sickness. Many of our children die even while at the breast; and of those who grow into manhood or womanhood, few will walk thirty-six years of this life. For there are terrible things that afflict us—dysentery, malaria, leprosy, beriberi, goiter, sleeping sickness, typhoid, rickets, typhus, blindness, paralysis.

We are the harvest.

Our gods are legion, and most of them we fear. We believe in predestination, ancestor worship, reincarnation. We consult witch doctors, and we practice voodoo, black magic, devil worship.

And yet, we suspect that behind this life there is something mysterious, something beautiful.

We have heard it said that there is a God who loves us, a God who made us to live as long as He lives. We have even heard it said that color and race and language fall away before the majesty of His Fatherhood. If this is true, then we are all God's children, members of one family and brothers beyond blood.

But this is hard to believe. If someone would come to teach us, perhaps we could understand it. Perhaps we could learn the reasons for the suffering that surrounds us. Perhaps our wounds would then be bathed, our children nourished, our stomachs fed, our prayers answered, our sins forgiven. No longer should we spend our lives regretting the fact of our birth.

Come to us! We do want to be children of this God who made us, and loves us, and (we have heard it) died for us.

Like sheaves of grain that wave full golden heads, we are ready as we have never been ready before. Come to us! Come wherever we are — at the mouths of uncharted rivers, in hidden windswept valleys, upon wastelands of forgotten ice, in the heart of steaming jungles, on deserts of sand that lead to the sun.

We are the harvest.

I WAS TOO NAÏVE

"Once parted, never will meet again."
I was too naïve to understand the words.
If only I could meet her again,
Whom I bade farewell long ago
On the crest of Mansoo mountain.

I was too naïve, then.
Now, the pains and pleasures of life
  being understood,
A gentler tone could come into
My talk with her . . .
And yet, would that I could
  live naïvely, even now!

—SO WOL KIM

FROM THE ENCYCLICAL ON
THE DEVELOPMENT OF PEOPLES

We want to be clearly understood: the present situation must be faced with courage and the injustices linked with it must be fought against and overcome. Development demands bold transformations, innovations that go deep. Urgent reforms should be undertaken without delay. It is for each one to take his share in them with generosity, particularly those whose education, position, and opportunities afford them wide scope for action. May they show an example and give of their own possessions as several of our brothers in the episcopacy have done. In so doing they will live up to men's expectations and be faithful to the Spirit of God, since it is "the ferment of the gospel which has aroused and continues to arouse in man's heart the irresistible requirements of his dignity" (Constitution on the Church in the Modern World, #26).

— POPE PAUL VI

NEWNESS

When Paul preached the Good News, it was the "newness" of the Christian faith that won such fervent adherents; everyone felt that they could break from the past and make a new start by an immediate response to a "young" Risen Christ who was not bound by the past, nor by any age. The apostle of today must give modern man the same opportunity that Paul gave his hearers.

—JOSEPH A. GRASSI, M.M.

LONG TRAIL HOME

by Sister Maria del Rey

To this day no one knows what happened to gentle Sister Hyacinth on the lonely mountain in Igorot-land.

Sister Hyacinth pulled her feet up under her and tried to stretch her cramped body without putting them out into the rain. She could hear the steady splash and gurgle outside the cave as big drops hit the leafy forest, the sodden ground, the once-tiny mountain stream now dangerously high. She heard it running down the canvas tacked at the cave's mouth and dripping off the bottom, some four inches from the ground.

Plainly it had no intention of stopping. Could go like this for days and probably would. Sixteen years in the mountains of northern Luzon told her that much about the Philippines' rainy season.

"Dear God," she thought, just stating the case for His consideration, "this won't be so good for the laundry tomorrow. Living like this we need a bit of sun to dry things in."

She was painfully thin—TB did that to one. The wad of rice straw, intended to soften the bare ground, felt like nothing at all. The dampness of the earth seemed to seep through the straw and the blanket wrapped around her. A thin blanket, yet she knew it was the best one they had. Sister Una and Sister Carmencita on either side of her had far thinner ones.

For a second or two she played with the idea of what would

*From *Dust on My Toes,* by Sister Maria del Rey; Scribner's. Copyright Maryknoll Sisters.

happen if she did luxuriate in stretching out to her full 5' 7". Her head would touch the rocky cave-wall as it did now; her feet and ankles would be out in that rain. She might catch pneumonia. In her condition it could mean death. Well, that wouldn't be so terrible. She would be at rest like those seven Adoration Sisters buried in the bomb crater up in Tuba clearing. The bomb that killed them *en masse* had conveniently dug a common grave for them.

"Stick my feet out and die of pneumonia," she said almost aloud. "But it wouldn't be that simple. I'd linger for weeks; the Sisters would stay to take care of me; they'd miss their chance to get through to the American lines. For sure, we can't stay here much longer."

Gingerly she shifted so as to lie on the other side, careful not to wake the other two. It eased her cramped body a bit. Her eyes closed. She slept.

It was Good Friday night, 1945.

*   *   *   *   *

It *was* strange! How did Antoinette Kunkel, once one of those trim New York business girls, find herself spending the night in a mountain cave in the northern part of Luzon? Well, it's a complicated story.

New York in the '20's! The Postwar Generation was running wild and grannies clucked in dismay. But Nettie Kunkel and the Ostermann girls and the Kelly boys and Ed Tobin and Mary McKeon and Frank Kleindeinst gathered round the Ostermann piano on West 50th Street. "Old McDonald's Farm," "Donderbeck's Machine," were done to a turn; "Sing Me to Sleep" or something like it trembled forth as Nettie Kunkel sang soprano and Bertie Ostermann manned the alto.

Hilarity swung round the piano with Celia Ostermann playing. Ernest Baedeker clowned all evening. Gene Kelly and his brother Bill would head out to the kitchen for *heimgemacht* pies and strudel, and everyone would dash after them.

Nettie, Bertie, and Mary McKeon were "The Trinity," inseparable friends. With the boys, they played tennis and skated and had many snowball fights in Central Park. They danced and saw movies and went to the beach. They sat at concerts — not in the boxes, nor yet in Peanut Heaven. And Nettie's eyes glowed as the glorious music poured through her whole person. How she loved music!

She got a good salary as secretary at the Rolls Royce Company. She took up French at night school, bowled one night a week at the Pastime Bowling Club, attended Sodality meetings regularly. She was twenty-three years old.

"Nettie?" everyone said. "Quiet, pleasant, and friendly. Never shows any temper. A good strong will though. She'll never set the world on fire but she's so easy to live with! A really nice girl."

The crowd began to break up. Bertha Ostermann married Gene Kelly. Several of the boys went to the seminary; eventually they were Father Frank and Father Joe; even Msgr. Will and Msgr. Frank. Mary married Harry Ostermann.

It was almost at the beginning of this break-up that Nettie went off to Maryknoll. That she entered the convent was no surprise, but going in for foreign missions was something a bit different. Maryknoll itself, only thirty miles away, was rather a mystery, too. A colony of priests, Brothers and Sisters, working in real poverty, with the odd objective of training young Americans for the Catholic foreign missions. It was an idea that was gaining a foothold in the American Catholic's consciousness. But it was definitely strange. Some said peculiar.

But Nettie went to Maryknoll. She slept on top of the carriage shed, sharing the loft with several other giggling postulants. She ate in St. Joseph's, the former barn; worked with Sister Genevieve and Sister Corde setting up, taking down, and cleaning type; she cleaned vegetables and washed endless dishes in the kitchens; she prayed at St. Martha's, the little stone chapel in the middle of the compound, stamping the snow off her feet in winter, shaking her umbrella in spring as she entered the little vestibule.

At entertainments she found herself much in demand. Nettie

could mimic anybody in the most precise and yet the kindest way. Often Mother Mary Joseph declared a "Simplicity Night." They were all buoyant young women, Mother included, and there was nothing they liked better than to put on an act. Nettie would come on to the makeshift stage and, with a flip of the wrist, a turn of the head, she brought to life somebody they all knew. It might be a farmer down the road, a boyish seminarian, a Very Important Person who had come to look them over, or one of the Sisters who took it in good part.

One evening, with a girl from Lonsdale, Rhode Island, Monica Coupe by name, Nettie sang "Whispering Hope." It was an instant success. Nettie's voice, like herself, was not strong but sweet and true. They sang it twice and yet again. It became a staple for any Simplicity Night. Even after the girls became Sister Eucharista and Sister Hyacinth, even after they were professed Sisters and even in their estimation, Ancients in the Ranks, still "Whispering Hope" was demanded by their all-too-friendly audience.

"We could feel it coming," Sister Eucharista later confessed. "Mother would say, 'All the acts were very fine indeed. And now, before we part, I am going to ask. . . .!' Yes, Sister Hyacinth and I were to do 'Whispering Hope' again!

"Sister was assigned to the Philippines in 1927. We sang it just before she left. After that Sister said to me, 'Let's bury 'Whispering Hope.' Thank goodness, I'll never sing it again!' "

But when the Sisters got together in the Philippines after the hot day's work, often they would ask Sister Hyacinth to sing that song. She always was very nice about it; few suspected that the small triumph had become in fact a real cross. She hated the song.

Just a year or so in Manila's crowded, dusty, broiling slum section emphasized her chest weakness. Doctors ordered Sister Hyacinth up to the mountains where the Maryknoll Sisters had recently opened a house. She stayed there sixteen years.

It was a new house. Money was scarce and sometimes vanished entirely. The Sisters opened a small school. It had its up and downs, but gradually it took root and flourished.

Then there was the mission work among the Igorot tribes people. Maryknoll was out on the fringes of town. Igorot women often took a short cut through the property as they toted baskets of sweet potatoes, bananas, rice, and babies to the Baguio market. Often they stopped at the back door, hoping to sell some of the burden en route.

Before long, the process was reversed. The Sisters went out to the Igorot homes walking the mountain trails, or riding the squat Philippine ponies. Catholic Igorots then numbered less than a dozen. Soon children came to the convent for catechism; then parents listened in on Sister Hyacinth's classes. In ten years' time, the chapel was full on Sunday mornings. Dark, stringy-haired youngsters sat on burlap mats all over the middle aisle; the benches in back groaned under the weight of women and men in their tribal dress and undress.

The Filipinos, lowlanders by birth, who had migrated to Baguio for work, came in increasing numbers, too. On Sunday mornings, the house swarmed with doctrine classes for big children and little ones, grown-ups and First Communicants.

In all this mission work Sister Hyacinth did what she could. She took over several of the classes, but pony trips and long walks were ruled out. To release someone stronger, she offered to take over odd jobs in the house. When the Sisters returned in the evening with tales of new classes started in far-off clearings, her eyes would glow as she bent them over her less thrilling work. She was like an elder daughter in the house, never pushing forward, always on hand to help the younger members. Like Sister Constance, the Superior, she aided and abetted all the work, but claimed no personal part in the satisfaction attached to it.

Then came war.

She was fairly well in December 1941; the old TB suspicion had been pretty well laid to rest. But rushing out of the house to lie on the hillside for several hours at night, while Japanese planes bombed and strafed the city and roadsides, was not exactly doctor's orders. Tension and anxiety ate into her, too. So many of the refugees streaming out of the city stopped at their door. "Hide, madres! Hide! Come with us to the hills." But they stayed. They were as safe at home as anywhere, even though it was on the edge of town where anything might happen.

Three years of Japanese occupation followed, when there were only rumors to live on. Rumors lived and died, kept the spirits high and let them down. This was the dream world, the phantasms. Reality brought scares, midnight searches, inspections and lastly, the long gruelling of Sister Constance concerning a simple note she had written. The Sisters were taken off to internment camp and carted home again. Some of them were shipped down to Manila; some returned to Baguio. In July '44 they were all taken except Sister Carmencita, a Filipino; Sister Una, who in spite of her long years in the States was an Irish national; and Sister Hyacinth, by then too sick to be moved. She was in bed most of the time. Once a week, a Filipino woman doctor used to slip in quietly to give her a calcium shot.

So the three had stayed in the big convent on the hill until Christmas Day '44. From the front windows they saw far, far away and 5,000 feet down, Lingayen Gulf where the Americans would probably land just as the Japanese forces had landed in 1941. How that shining scrap of sea used to glint up at them in three years!

Sister Una was a tower of strength those days; Sister Carmencita a constant joy. Between them, with their neutral nationalities, they wove a curtain for Sister Hyacinth's Americanism. Gregorio, faithful Gregorio, once the gardener who made the grounds of Maryknoll School something to stop the passersby, now produced sweet potatoes, squash, onions, and carrots.

On Christmas Day, the Japanese commandeered the house. They, too, would like to keep an eye on Lingayen Gulf. The three Sisters hauled everything they could to the chapel. They piled it in, closed and locked the door, and turned the house keys over to the commandant. Then they went to Adoration

Convent to live with "The Pink Sisters" who opened wide their hospitable arms. They were cloistered Sisters, but their convent was open to all comers those days.

A Japanese radio transmitter and a military prison had been set up in the house across the road from Adoration Convent. Bombings from American planes were endless. All too often the place was machinegunned and bullets spattered on the convent's tin roof. Bombings shook the ground; the flimsy building shuddered; the steep mountainside began to slough away until the very foundations were imperilled.

They stood it for a month or more. Then, on February first Bessie Akop with deep satisfaction led them on a two-hour hike over the pine-covered trails to her family's clearing, Tuba.

Most of the huts had been burned just a few months before. Four remained in fairly good condition. They stood on stilts six feet or so from the ground. Bessie and her old father owned them in a haphazard, nonlegal way.

It was a strange caravan she led to this haven. Some dozen Adoration Sisters, German and Filipino, had come along. The three Maryknoll Sisters and the ever-faithful Gregorio who would not leave them. A Spanish Dominican priest took a cave nearby.

"You should have come here to begin with!" Bessie grumped as she wrestled with the canvas folding chair Gregorio had carried for Sister Hyacinth. She had stood the hike well but she was, oh, so grateful just to lie still and to know that Tuba was too insignificant a clearing to attract notice from the skies.

So it was for five weeks.

Of course, planes flew overhead often in the five weeks. Sometimes the thunder of bombing penetrated softly to little Tuba. But morning succeeded morning and night succeeded night peacefully enough. It was heaven! They had only to stay in Tuba and await the liberation of the whole Baguio area.

They were a compact little community. As Superior, Sister Una kept the Maryknoll Sisters' hut in good order. Bessie Akop lived nearby. Mass saw them all kneeling in the Maryknoll hut.

Then they scattered to the various tasks of the day. Now and then Bessie had some choice morsel of news from a guerilla runner. Americans had landed at Lingayen; they had a foothold at La Union. They all swallowed it eagerly and said with one accord, "It won't be long now!"

Came March seventh. It was after Mass. Sister Una and good Bessie were inspecting a vegetable bin cut out of the hillside. It was perhaps three feet high and not more than that deep and wide. A piece of corrugated tin was to be the door; it wasn't quite ready yet.

"It ought to do nicely for storing sweet potatoes and things," Sister Una had just said. "If you have anything you want to keep in it, Bessie . . . ."

"Quick! Quick!" and Bessie was shoving her into the vegetable bin. "Get the others! Sisters, come!" She called to Sister Carmencita fixing breakfast in the hut and to Sister Hyacinth reading her office outside. Not knowing just why, they too ran.

"Run! Hide!" called Bessie to the Adoration Sisters some little distance away. Most of them were outside their hut praying or reading; one was inside preparing breakfast.

But the roar of motors drowned out the warning.

Bessie and the Maryknoll three squeezed into the vegetable bin. Bessie and Sister Carmencita pulled the corrugated iron over the opening and held it tight from the inside.

Then hell broke loose! Whining, diving, zooming, the planes swirled like a tornado. Bullets sprayed mud and stones against the sheet of iron. Then came a thunderous boom! Inside, there was no room even to tremble. Calm Sister Una prayed steadily. Sister Carmencita answered quietly. That saved the day for them all.

The motors began to fade. One after another the planes zipped past and went off. Then they recognized that part of the thunder against the corrugated iron came from someone screaming and pounding on it from the outside.

They opened immediately. A woman flung herself in on them. It was Sister Remedios, a Filipino Adoration Sister. Her veil was torn off. Her clothes hung in rags upon her. Blood spattered her face and arms. She sobbed in hysteria. "They're dead! They're all dead!"

A bomb crater twenty feet wide spread itself in the center of the clearing. In grotesque poses, six Adoration Sisters lay on the edge, half in and half out. Two stirred a little and were still. A seventh, in a daze, was dragging her useless legs along the ground. A piece of shrapnel had lodged in her spine. She died, blessedly for her and conveniently for the other refugees, in time to be buried with her Sisters in the bomb crater a few hours later.

The Dominican Padre, the Divine Word Father, the La Salle Brothers who were hiding out in the woods, came to pray beside the seven, and remained to bury them. It was an easy burial. The soft soil in the bomb crater received them gently. It rolled back softly over the black habits, the hands folded in prayer, the mangled faces covered with their own veils.

That afternoon it was decided. Even a clearing, if visible from the air, was not safe. Sister Una consulted with her army of two and they moved down the stream bed to the cave. Trees arched over the stream. There was no path. More than once they sat on one rock and slid down to the next. Just at the cave the stream took a bend before plunging down another gorge. Here a small sandy bank had formed. They called it "the Beach." Sister Hyacinth's chair was set up here. When three women have had no new clothes for more than three years, sewing and repairing are quite an item on the agenda. Sister Hyacinth did this for all of them. She helped wash the dishes; she set up the makeshift altar for Mass; she even knit socks out of cotton twine. But most of the time she rested.

There is a battle of soul in resting. It is not easy to lie still and watch others work hard. Self-respect, if nothing else, keeps nagging. One who would cheerfully work her fingers to the bone crumples before the command to rest. There's no glamor in resting; there isn't even hard work—least of all, any sense of accomplishment.

But so it was. That battle had been won. Sister Hyacinth had learned obedience even in difficult things.

She slept in her cave with an easy conscience.

*   *   *   *   *

An hour or so later the rain stopped as totally as it had poured all the day before.

As the last raindrops pattered off over the mountain ridge, Sister Hyacinth uncoiled herself and put her feet out straight. She breathed gratefully and dropped off into deep slumber.

A quarter-mile upstream, Father Gutierrez peered out of his much smaller cave, looked gladly at the Paschal moon emerging from clouds and retired again to rest.

In her hut on the Tuba clearing, Bessie Akop lay still and listened to a muffled knock on the floor boards of her hut. A messenger had slipped under the house from the pine forest. He tapped on the boards above his head — one, two, one-two. Again, one, two, one-two.

Quickly her tough brown hands pulled up two short boards. Joseph Kitma swung himself up through the hole and stood before her.

Bessie's glad cry was quickly suppressed. She leaped to get food for him. Joseph had been closest to her husband in those long months the guerillas lay hidden in caves. Tomas Akop had always sent Joseph to get the medicine for his men. Bessie got it from the Sisters; the Sisters got it from the nurses in the hospital. Joseph got it from Bessie and took it to the hide-outs where Akop's men tossed in alternate fever and chills.

But that was before the hide-outs were discovered and Akop's company was taken to Manila for execution. "Poor fellows," Bessie often said, "it would have been easier to let them die of malaria."

Joseph went to her side and covered the work-worn hands with his own. "No, Bessie, no food for me. I'm not hungry."

"Not hungry! Everybody's hungry these days."

"No, no, Bessie. Really! You forget that the American Army isn't far away. I'm with them. We get plenty to eat. Look, I can give you some." He pulled out of his pockets several cans of K rations.

"But listen," he went on. "I'm here on business. The Army is asking several of us Igorots who know the district well to lead out the civilians. We're getting caravans of about five hundred together and taking them out of Baguio. I tell you, Bessie, you and the Sisters must go. Especially them. For when the retreating army has to leave, they'll take it out on any whites around. They won't be thinking clearly then. No defeated army is reasonable."

"But Sister Hyacinth — she is sick. Sister Carmencita has never been strong. Sister Una is worn to a thread, she works so hard. Aren't they safe down in that cave?"

"No, no! The Japanese will take to the caves, just as we did three years ago when we were defeated. They won't argue as to who got the cave first. Take the Sisters out, Bessie. We're forming a caravan now to start 2 A.M. Monday morning. Down at Kilometro 4. I'll stop by at Gregorio's house and tell him. He can help carry their things."

Bessie looked up at him and made a simple statement. "Joseph, you're a good man."

"Don't talk that way. Who taught me about God? Sister Hyacinth. Who made me a real soldier? Your Tomas. Just be there, that's all. Kilometro 4, 2 A.M. Monday. Easter Monday!"

He was gone. He slid into the wet pine forest without a rustle.

*　　*　　*　　*　　*

By four o'clock Easter Sunday afternoon they were ready. They single-filed along the forest paths, Igorot fashion. Gregorio went first, carrying their rice supply and a clay cooking stove. Sister Una came next with her own bed roll, her own clothes, and one of Sister Hyacinth's blankets tied to her back.

Sister Carmencita's bundle had the sacred vessels for Mass, her own blankets, and the second for Sister Hyacinth.

Sister Hyacinth had resigned herself to carrying only her own extra clothing such as it was, a small bundle fitted to her shoulders. She looked with envy at Bessie behind her. Bessie's heavy basket lay on her broad, short back, suspended from a leather band around her forehead. She thrust her powerful neck forward; at each step her brown toes clung to the grass and pebbles, her calves bulged and pushed her ahead another foot or so.

They climbed the creek bed to Tuba clearing. Gregorio headed for the woods. He could have made better time and had easier walking on the wide dirt road which went part of the way to Kilometro 4, but Gregorio took no chance of encountering Japanese road patrols. He headed for the woods and his little troop followed. Just as she stepped from clearing to pine-shadow, Sister Hyacinth stopped and looked back at the four huts, and the circle of loose earth in the center.

"All right, dear God," she said. "I'll not die here. Just as You wish. I'll go on to safety; I'll go back to the States; I'll die anywhere You want me to. I want what You want."

With a smile she turned to Bessie. "You should learn the 'Star Spangled Banner' before you get to the American Army camp," she said. "I'll teach it to you along the way." And she set off singing.

When they reached the assembly point at seven that evening, some five hundred people were milling around the few huts at Kilometro 4. They were polyglot as only a crowd in the Orient can be: Spaniards, Swedes, Chinese, Belgians, Germans, Irish, Filipinos from the lowland provinces and the mountain Igorots. Sister Hyacinth was probably the only American in this caravan now girding itself for a five-day hike to La Union in the lowlands.

Clustered in family groups around small cooking fires, many waved and called greetings to the Sisters. Old friends from school, the market, the hospital in Baguio. Some had known Sister Una at St. Paul's Hospital in Manila. Some were Sister Carmencita's old kindergarten children. Sister Hyacinth waved to her catechism pupils. Others brightened at the sight of the Maryknoll habit although they did not know these particular Sisters.

The Yeuns were there—wealthy Chinese with an old father, very sick. They had him on a litter by their fire and, standing by, two Igorots who were to be paid $1,000 each to carry him.

Arsenio and his family from near the Maryknoll Convent were there. The old woman, his mother, was curled up under a bush, a moaning heap. He had carried her on his shoulders to Kilometro 4.

"What shall I do?" he asked Sister Una. "I can't carry her for five days over the mountains. I must leave her here."

"Oh, no!" Sister said, shocked.

"Does it not say in the Bible," he argued, "that a man must leave his mother and father and cleave to his wife? What I must do, I must do."

Around another camp-fire were the Pasquales. Manuela, the mother, lay prone on the ground. "She gave birth this afternoon," said her husband. "Tonight we must go on with the new baby. She must rest as much as possible this evening." There were four other children, none of them over five.

"I don't know how we will get along," he said simply.

"I don't know either," Sister Una replied. She gave him a can of milk. "But this might help. You need it more than we do."

Four Adoration Sisters had been among the early birds. They had a hut for the night and gladly moved over to accommodate Bessie and the Sisters on their floor for a few hours' rest. There were many religious—Belgian Sisters, Filipino Jesuits, Spanish Dominicans. There was a good deal of joking, old friends seeing each other, three years of hardship nearing the end. It all summed up to a joyous, "It won't be long now!"

All fires were doused.

Two A.M. The caravan formed. Igorot runners scouted ahead. Orders passed down the line. "No smoking." "No lights." "Keep sight of the person ahead." "All right? Let's go!"

Arsenio carried his mother into the hut evacuated by the

Adoration Sisters. "I know, son, I know," he heard her say softly. "God keep you safe." He turned his face resolutely and left.

Sister Una slipped in as she heard his heavy footsteps clump down the three wooden stairs from the house. She put a coconut shell full of cooked rice beside the old woman. "Here's a bottle of drinking water, too," she said, her heart full of pity. "Is there anything at all we can do? Don't worry. Someone will be coming through this clearing soon. They'll not forget you."

"Yes, yes," said the weak voice. "Death will be coming soon." It was a sigh of expectation.

The Pasquale family rose to go. Manuela took her newborn and put him in a pouch-like affair on her back. Her husband carried the one-year-old. They tied a rope around the other three children and, like a pack of mountain climbers, took their place in the line-up.

Sister Hyacinth shouldered her pack. She resolutely took the climbing stick Gregorio had whittled for her. It was a friendly stick; her hand fitted nicely around it. She took her place behind Sister Carmencita and noted the small Filipino hand clasping also a burly stick. Once again she thought as she always did when she saw Sister Carmencita's hands, "Just like a kitten's paws, so soft, so seemingly ineffective. But believe me, there's spiritual strength in that constant little smile, that soft voice, those hands. Lord, give me that kind of strength right now. I'll need it."

They had hardly started when it rained. Rain was steady throughout the days of hiking. The Sisters' skirts were tucked up; their veils reduced to a minimum. They were soaked through and soon thought nothing of it. They slept in wet clothes anywhere the caravan stopped for the night.

As the crow flies, La Union was only fifteen miles away. But crows were taking no passengers on their flight those days; if they did, they would probably have charged black-market prices. The walking distance has been estimated anywhere from fifty to seventy miles. The guides took a circuitous route to avoid Japanese encampments. It was, moreover, a matter of climbing mountainsides and slithering down valleys, of wading through mountain streams, clambering over rocks, stumbling over pebbly paths. Several months later, Sister Constance passed over this same ground. She was so exhausted she lay flat on the ground several times.

Going over part of this trail later, American soldiers found five bodies in the space of two kilometers (about a mile and a quarter) people who had tried the trip and failed. "I marvel that any women were able to complete it," testified an Army chaplain.

But Sister Hyacinth seemed fairly well. "She must have been tired," Sister Carmencita says, "but whether it was sheer will power or not, her apparent strength those days amazed us. She had never walked any great distance before that and all of a sudden she was crossing mountains for one, two, three, and four days. Still, she didn't seem to have any ill effects."

As the hours passed, the caravan strung out loosely. The road was less than three feet wide. Some people, impatient of slower ones, pushed ahead; some lagged behind and even dropped out. Others joined the caravan from their forest huts. The wealthy Chinese on his litter made a bottleneck of every stream fording. Sometimes the guides stood waist-deep in the water and passed the children from hand to hand. It was all a slow tortuous passage.

Many times Sister Una, looking behind her, found that others had wedged themselves between herself and Sister Carmencita. Sometimes she saw Sister Hyacinth's tall head far behind. There were friends all along the route; she did not worry. Usually, she dropped out of line herself and waited for them to catch up.

Every few hours, when passing a clearing, the leaders called a halt for rest and water. The caravan swarmed into the huts, deserted now, and made themselves at home lying flat on the dusty floor boards, panting for water.

At these times Gregorio and the other Igorot men went scouting for water. He seemed indefatigable. His strong brown toes gripped the rain-soaked earth as he helped each of them to climb the hills. His back carried their dwindling rice sack. All his life he had been loping along paths like these. His bolo swung from his belt, ready to lop off branches which might smack back into their faces. His beady eyes glinted over the high cheekbones, ever watchful, ever cautious. He rarely talked; even the Igorots called him "the Silent One." Many a time the Sisters and Bessie took the tin cup of water he offered with a heartfelt, "God bless you, Gregorio!"

Thus it was at Ambusi on Wednesday noon. They were halfway there, the guides said, and the rest of the way would be easier going. The mountains were nearly passed; the lowlands were near. Indeed, fresh guides came from the American camp at La Union to lead them the day and a half left of the journey. A great shout went up from the huts of Ambusi when these runners came into the clearing. A day and a half! La Union by Friday morning! And this was Wednesday noon!

"All right? Ready? Let's go! "

Five hundred pairs of arms reached for their packs and buckled them on. Five hundred pairs of legs, weary no longer, stood up. Smiles broke out; snatches of songs were begun. It won't be long now!

"Oh dear! " said Sister Carmencita. "This pack is wearing a hole through the corner. If Gregorio would put the straps this way . . . Don't wait for me, Sister Una. I'll catch up."

Bessie and Sister Una set out. They could get things ready at the next stop. Sister Hyacinth reached for her pack. "That's a good idea," she said to Sister Carmencita. "The pack will be easier to carry that way. Maybe Gregorio will fix mine, too."

She had been talking to two Adoration Sisters. They were sick and exhausted. Of all the caravan, they alone seemed too far gone to have picked up any strength during the Ambusi stop. Plainly, they were glad of a chance to delay their departure.

"We'll wait and go with you," they said to Sister Hyacinth.

Sister Carmencita's bag was soon fixed. "You go on ahead,"

said Sister Hyacinth. "I'll come with the Adoration Sisters."
Sister Carmencita moved on with the caravan.

And there, properly speaking, the story of Sister Hyacinth
ends.

*   *   *   *   *

Half an hour later Sister Carmencita found Sister Una standing under a banana tree. It was raining as usual, and the leaves
gave some protection. The spurt of vigor at Ambusi had quickly
worn off; the guides had called another halt for water and rest.
There was only one hut in this clearing. In it water was being
handed out to the stream of bedraggled people who filed through
to get it. They sat in groups under the house or out among the
trees, their conversation as sodden as their clothes.

"Do you want a drink, Sister?" Sister Una asked. "Let's
wait for Sister Hyacinth and we'll get it together."

"She'll be coming along any moment," said Sister Carmencita.
"Gregorio was fixing her pack for her when I left Ambusi. She
is coming with the Adoration Sisters."

"Bessie has gone ahead to the night-stop," said Sister Una.
"She will have the rice cooked when we get there."

They sat down on a log under the banana tree. The stream
of now familiar faces passed on to the hut — Mrs. Yeun and her
daughter beside the litter-borne old man who, like King Midas,
was so grateful for a simple cup of water; Arsenio and his family,
Manuela and her three-day-old son; the Filipino Jesuits, the
German Benedictines, the Belgian Sisters.

Then came the two Adoration Sisters walking very slowly.
They were barefoot, bruised and muddy.

"Where is Sister Hyacinth?"

"Isn't she with you?" they asked. "She went ahead of us to
catch up with you."

Gregorio came. He put down his heavy load.

"I fixed her pack," he said, "and she started off with these

Sisters. I stayed behind to fix my basket. The bottom was falling out. She has not come?"

They searched among the sodden groups. She was not there.

"I go back. I go back." Gregorio left his pack with the Sisters and started over the trail to Ambusi.

They waited under the tree. The caravan got itself together and pushed on. People trudged past the two bedraggled figures in streaming wet clothes. The few who knew their plight were encouraging. "Don't worry; she'll be along. Probably stopped to rest someplace."

The last of them went by. The hours passed. No Sister Hyacinth; no Gregorio! The other two did not talk any more. Three o'clock, five o'clock, seven o'clock. The sudden night of the tropics was almost upon them. Then the ashy grey face of Gregorio loomed out of the twilight. They did not have to ask. Not in the Ambusi hut. Not on the roadside. Not behind the bushes near the road. He had looked everywhere.

He picked up his pack; they shouldered theirs. "We must go on," he said. And they agreed.

They found the caravan stopped for the night on the rocky banks of a river. The guides, in spite of the grumbling of many, had decided to wait for the Sisters. Joseph Kitma was among them. "Any news?" he said.

"None."

"Don't worry, Sisters," he reassured them. "There is a short cut to Pitugan, our next overnight stop. Steeper, but shorter. We will find Sister there. Perhaps a group of people went that way and took her."

Nevertheless, he and a friend went back over the trail that night.

Sister Carmencita tried to settle herself for the night among the hard rocks. It was past nine o'clock. She was exhausted; every muscle and bone cried out for sleep. Still her small fingers kept the rosary going and her eyes searched into the darkness. Where could Sister be? If she took the short-cut, why didn't somebody see her? Why didn't she tell somebody to inform Sister Una that she was going by another way? She knew they would worry to death; Sister Hyacinth was always thinking of others. If she dropped by the way, why didn't Gregorio find her body? Surely, somebody would have seen her drop. How could she wander down a side road leading to the Japanese garrison they had been warned against, when five hundred others were taking the right road?

Over and over again. Back to the beginning and through it again. Why, how, where? There were no answers. Sister Una stirred on the rock beside her. The two minds had but one thought. The same thought over and over again.

Sister Hyacinth was not at Pitugan when they reached there Thursday night. She was not at La Union Friday morning when the bedraggled crowd limped into the American camp. She was not found by searching parties sent out immediately. The Igorots, who know every cave and crevice in the mountains, did not find her. She has never been seen or heard from since.

GETHSEMANE

Breathes there a man who claimeth not
One lonely spot,
His own Gethsemane,
Whither with his inmost pain
He fain
Would weary plod,
Find the surcease that is known
In wind a-moan
And sobbing sea,
Cry his sorrow hid of men,
And then—
Touch hands with God.

—EDMUND LEAMY

BEATITUDES FOR FRIENDS OF THE AGED

BLESSED are they who understand
my faltering steps and shaking hand.
BLESSED are they who know that my ears today
must strain to catch the words they say.
BLESSED are they who seem to know
that my eyes are dim and my wits are slow.
BLESSED are they who looked away
when coffee spilled today.
BLESSED are they with a cheery smile
who stop to chat for a while.
BLESSED are they who never say,
"You've told that story twice today."
BLESSED are they who know the ways
to bring back lovely yesterdays.
BLESSED are they who make it known
that I am loved, not left alone.
BLESSED are they who know the loss
of strength I need to bear the cross.
BLESSED are they who ease the days
on my journey home in so many loving ways.

ANOTHER MEXICO

by Graham Greene

Observations on the preservation of the Faith in Mexico
by a noted English author.

In July 1926, Father Miguel Pro landed at Veracruz. He was
twenty-five years old and a Jesuit. He came back to his own
country from a foreign seminary much as Campion returned
to England from Douai. We know how he was dressed when a
year and a half later he came out into the prison yard to be shot,
and he may well have worn the same disguise when he landed
(the equivalent of Campion's doublet and hose): a dark lounge
suit, soft collar and tie, a bright cardigan. Most priests wear
their mufti with a kind of uneasiness, but Pro was a good actor.

He needed to be. Within two months of Pro's landing, President Calles had begun the fiercest persecution of religion anywhere since the reign of Elizabeth. The churches were closed,
Mass had to be said secretly in private houses, to administer
the Sacraments was a serious offence. Nevertheless, Pro gave
Communion daily to some three hundred people, confessions
were heard in half-built houses in darkness, retreats were held
in garages. Pro escaped the plain-clothes police again and again.
Once he found them at the entrance to a house where he was
supposed to say Mass; he posed as a police officer, showing
an imaginary badge and remarking: "There's a cat bagged in
here," and passed into the house and out again with his cassock

under his arm. Followed by detectives when he left a Catholic house and with only fifty yards' start, he disappeared altogether from their sight round a corner—the only man they overtook was a lover out with his girl. The prisons were filling up, priests were being shot, yet on three successive first Fridays Pro gave the Sacrament to nine hundred, thirteen hundred, and fifteen hundred people.

They got him, of course, at last (they had got him earlier if only they had known it, but they let him go). This time they made no mistake, or else the biggest mistake of all. Somebody had thrown a bomb at Obregón's car in Chapultepec Park— from another car. The evidence since then points to Government complicity. All the assailants escaped but the driver, who was shot dead. A young Indian called Tirado was passing by, fled at the explosion, and was arrested. He was tortured without effect: he persisted in declaring himself innocent. The police pounced on those they feared most—Pro and his two brothers, Humberto and Roberto, and Luis Segovia Vilchis, a young engineer and Catholic leader. No evidence was brought against them; they were not tried by the courts. The American ambassador thought he could do more good by not intervening and left next day with the President and Will Rogers, the humorist, on a Pullman tour; one South American ambassador intervened and got a reprieve—timed too late to save any but Roberto. Pro was photographed by the official photographer, praying for his enemies by the pitted wall, receiving the *coup de grâce;* the photographs were sent to the press—to show the firmness of the Government—but within a few weeks it became a penal offence to possess them, for they had had an effect which Calles had not foreseen.

For Mexico remained Catholic; it was only the governing class—politicians and pistoleros—which was anti-Catholic. It was a war—they admitted it—for the soul of the Indian, a war in which they could use the army consisting mainly of Indians attracted by a dollar a day pay. (The individuals who composed the army too were Catholic, but it is quite easy to keep an uneducated soldier in ignorance of what he is doing.) By the time

I left for Mexico, Calles had been gone some years—flown over into exile by his rival, Cárdenas. The antireligious laws were still enforced except in one state, San Luis Potosí, but the pressure from the Catholic population was beginning to make itself felt. Churches—now Government property—were allowed to open in most of the states, except for the hundreds that had been turned into cinemas, newspaper offices, garages. A proportion of priests calculated according to the size of the population was allowed to serve by the state governments. The ratio was seldom more favourable than one priest to ten thousand people, but the law, particularly in the Federal District of Mexico City, was slackly enforced. But in some other states the persecution was maintained. In Veracruz the churches remained closed until the peasants rose when a child was shot, early in 1937, in Orizaba; in Tabasco, the tropical state of river and swamp and banana grove, every church was believed to have been destroyed by the local dictator, Garrido Canabal, before he fled to Costa Rica—there wasn't a priest in the state; in Chiapas no church was open for Mass, the bishop was in exile, and little news came out of that mountainous untravelled region where the only railway-line runs along the coast to Guatemala. Nowhere were priests allowed to open schools. Educational programmes everywhere were laid down by the Government on dusty rationalist lines—nineteenth-century materialism reminiscent of Herbert Spencer and the Thinkers' Library, alpaca jackets and bookshops on Ludgate Hill. . . .

I went with Dr. C. to call on the Bishop of Chiapas. People had told me he was regarded by the Government as one of the most dangerous and astute of the Mexican bishops. A month or two before, he had tried to return to his diocese, but he was put into a motor-car and driven back across the state border. I don't quite know what I had expected to see—some plump blue-chinned ecclesiastic with a quick eye and a cautious mouth, certainly not this unsophisticated good old man living with the utmost simplicity in surroundings of pious ugliness. He looked like a village priest and showed a kind of humble confused embarrassment at the genuflexion. The little dark curtained room was stuffy with images and big obscure brown paintings of the love of God. No priests, he said, were officially allowed in Chiapas, although some of the churches were open now for the people to use. It was hard travelling there except in the south near the Pacific where there was the railway to Guatemala and a few roads. But in the north it was all mountain and forest and Indians who could speak no Spanish and could not even understand the language of the next village. He doubted very much whether it was possible to find a guide from Palenque to Las Casas.

San Cristóbal de Las Casas—he spoke of it with gentle regret, the old capital before the Government removed to Tuxtla and the plain, lying eight thousand feet and more up in the mountains. It was, he said, "a very Catholic town"; there were many churches, and one in particular, Santo Domingo, was among the most beautiful in Mexico. But most of the churches of Chiapas were not like those one saw in other parts of Mexico. Chiapas had always been a poor wild state, and the churches were very simple. . . . He spoke of it gently as a foreign land to which he would never now be able to return. It touched my imagination so that I began to regard the city of Las Casas hidden there in the mountains at the end of a mule track, with only one rough road running south, as the real object of my journey—and the beginning of going home.

The anonymity of Sunday seems peculiarly unnatural in Mexico; a man going hunting in the marshes with his dog and his gun, a young people's fiesta, shops closing after noon— nothing else to divide this day from all the other days, no bell to ring. I sat at the head of the stairs and had my shoes cleaned by a little blond bootblack—a thin tired child in tattered trousers like someone out of Dickens. Only his brown eyes were Mexican—not his transparent skin and his fine gold hair. I was afraid to ask his name, for it might have been Greene. I gave him twice what I usually gave (twenty centavos—say, five cents) and he returned me ten centavos' change, going wearily down the stairs with his heavy box into the great heat of Sunday.

Garrido has fled to Costa Rica and yet nothing is done. "We die like dogs." There were no secret Masses in private houses such as are found in the neighboring state, only a dreadful lethargy as the Catholics died slowly out—without Confession, without the Sacraments, the child unbaptized, and the dying man unshriven. I thought of Rilke's phrase: "An empty, horrible alley, an alley in a foreign town, in a town where nothing is forgiven."

There are, I suppose, geographical and racial excuses for the lethargy. Tabasco is a state of river and swamp and extreme heat; in northern Chiapas there is no choice between a mule and the rare plane for a traveller, and in Tabasco no choice between plane and boat. But a mule is a sociable form of transport—nights spent with strangers huddling together in the cold mountain air, talk over the beans and the embers; while in a boat you are isolated with the mosquitoes between the banana plantations.

And then there are no Indians in Tabasco, with their wild beliefs and their enormous if perverted veneration, to shame the Catholic into *some* action. Too much foreign blood came into Tabasco when it was a prosperous country; the faith with the Grahams and Greenes goes back only a few generations. They haven't the stability of the old Spanish families in Chiapas.

Nothing in a tropical town can fill the place of a church for the most mundane use; a church is the one spot of coolness out of the vertical sun, a place to sit, a place where the senses can rest a little while from ugliness; it offers to the poor man what a rich man may get in a theatre—though not in Tabasco. Now in Villahermosa, in the blinding heat and the mosquito-noisy air, there is no escape at all for anyone. Garrido did his job well: he knew that the stones cry out, and he didn't leave any stones. There is a kind of cattle-tick you catch in Chiapas, which fastens its head in the flesh; you have to burn it out, otherwise the head remains embedded and festers. It is an ugly metaphor to use, but an exact one: in northern Chiapas the churches still stand, shuttered and ruined and empty, but they fester—the whole village festers away from the door; the plaza is the first to go.

So in Villahermosa there is nothing to do all the long Sundays that go on and on but sit in Victorian rocking-chairs, swinging back and forth waiting for the sunset and the mosquitoes. The hideous buzzards group themselves on the roofs like pigeons: the tiny moron head, long neck, masked face, and dusty plumage peering this way and that attentively for a death. I counted twenty on one roof. They looked domesticated, as if they were going to lay an egg. And I suppose even a bird of prey does sometimes lay an egg.

Nothing to do but drink gassy fruit drinks (no miracle in the Godless state will turn this aerated water into wine) and watch the horrifying abundance of just life. You can't open a book without some tiny scrap of life scuttling across the page; the stalls are laden with great pulpy tasteless fruits, and when the lights come out, so do the beetles: the pavement by the green sour riverside is black with them. You kill them on your bed-room floor, and by morning, as I have said, they have been drained away by more life—the hordes of ants which come up between the tiles at the scent of death or sweetness. I bought some sugar one morning to take with me to Chiapas, and when I lay down in the afternoon an army of ants was trooping along three sides of my room.

The only place where you can find some symbol of your faith is in the cemetery up on a hill above the town—a great white classical portico and the legend "SILENCIO" in big black letters, the blind wall round the corner where Garrido shot his prisoners, and inside the enormous tombs of above-ground burial, glass-houses for flowers and portraits and images, crosses and weeping angels, the sense of a far better and cleaner city than that of the living at the bottom of the hill.

Herr R. had left Germany as a boy. His father wanted to send him to a military college, and he had told his father: "If you do, I will run away." He had run away and with the help of a friendly burgomaster had got papers and reached America. After that he'd never gone back. He had come down to Mexico as agent for various firms, and now he was settled on his own *finca*. There had been revolutions of course — he had lost crops and cattle to the soldiers and he had been fired on as he stood on his porch. But he took things with a dry cynical Lutheran humour; he had a standard of morality which nobody here paid even lip service to, and he fought them with their own weapons. When the *agraristos* demanded land he gave them it — a barren fifty acres he had not had the means to develop — and saved himself taxes. There had been, I suppose, that beautiful daughter (his wife was dead) and there were two sons at school now in Las Casas. He said of Las Casas: "It's a very moral town." I promised to take them out when I arrived: I should be in time for the great spring fair.

Walking in to the village to send his mail, we talked of the Church and Garrido. Though R. was a Lutheran, he had no ill to say of any priest he had known here in the old days. Palenque had not been able to support a permanent priest, and the priests who came to serve Mass on feast days stayed usually with R. at the *finca*. He had an honest Lutheran distaste for their dogmas which took him to queer lengths. There was one priest who was so sick and underfed that R. insisted he should not go to Mass before he had breakfasted. To ensure this, when his guest was asleep, he locked him in, but when he went to call him he found the priest had escaped to church through the window. One felt that the Mexican priesthood in that politely unobtrusive act had shown up rather well. Another priest, one who sometimes came to Palenque, was an old friend of Garrido. He had great skill in brickwork, and Garrido invited him under safe conduct to come into Tabasco and undertake a building job. But friendship and safe conduct didn't save him — when the work was finished he was murdered, though possibly Garrido's followers had gone too far and the dictator may have had no hand in his friend's death.

Garrido's activities did not stop at the border. He sent his men over into Chiapas, and though in this state the churches still stand, great white shells like the skulls you find bleached beside the forest paths, he has left his mark in sacked interiors and ruined roofs. He organized an *auto da-fé* in Palenque village, and R. was there to see. The evil work was not done by the villagers themselves. Garrido ordered every man with a horse in Tabascan Montecristo to ride over the fifty-six kilometres and superintend — on pain of a fine of twenty-five pesos. And a relative of Garrido came with his wife by private plane to see that people were doing as they were told. The statues were carried out of the church while the inhabitants watched, sheepishly, and saw their own children encouraged to chop up the images in return for little presents of candy.

TWO GRAVES

(The resting place of our Founders in the Maryknoll God's Acre prompts some verse from a seminarian.)

Like burnished silver, even's starlight falls
Upon the ebbing river's dancing waves,
While falling night through waning twilight calls
The children to their Fathers' hallowed graves.
Here sleep the forms that sounded forth the plea,
Which roused a mighty nation's youthful soul,
To send her sons across the farthest sea,
For Christ, and for the Queen of Maryknoll.
O Fathers, rest; your wondrous work is done,
And in your places many sons arise.
Their hands will bring the blest Eternal Sun
To pierce the darksome clouds of pagan skies;
For in their hearts they hold that living flame,
Which found its source in Mary's loving name.

—J. N. W.

THE PARABLE OF THE EAGLE

by James Aggrey

You are what you think.

A certain man went through a forest seeking any bird of interest he might find. He caught a young eagle, brought it home and put it among his fowls and ducks and turkeys, and gave it chickens' food to eat even though it was an eagle, the king of birds.

Five years later a naturalist came to see him and, after passing through his garden, said: "That bird is an eagle, not a chicken."

"Yes," said its owner, "but I have trained it to be a chicken. It is no longer an eagle, it is a chicken, even though it measures fifteen feet from tip to tip of its wings."

"No," said the naturalist, "it is an eagle still: it has the heart of an eagle, and I will make it soar high up to the heavens."

"No," said the owner, "it is a chicken, and it will never fly."

They agreed to test it. The naturalist picked up the eagle, held it up, and said with great intensity: "Eagle, thou art an eagle; thou dost belong to the sky and not to this earth; stretch forth thy wings and fly."

The eagle turned this way and that, and then, looking down, saw the chickens eating their food, and down he jumped.

The owner said: "I told you it was a chicken."

"No," said the naturalist, "it is an eagle. Give it another chance tomorrow."

*From *African Voices*, edited by Peggy Rutherford. New York: Vanguard Press, Inc., 1960.

So the next day he took it to the top of the house and said: "Eagle, thou art an eagle; stretch forth thy wings and fly." But again the eagle, seeing the chickens feeding, jumped down and fed with them.

Then the owner said: "I told you it was a chicken."

"No," asserted the naturalist, "it is an eagle, and it still has the heart of an eagle; only give it one more chance, and I will make it fly tomorrow."

The next morning he rose early and took the eagle outside the city, away from the houses, to the foot of a high mountain. The sun was just rising, gilding the top of the mountain with gold, and every crag was glistening in the joy of that beautiful morning.

He picked up the eagle and said to it: "Eagle, thou art an eagle; thou dost belong to the sky and not to this earth; stretch forth thy wings and fly!"

The eagle looked around and trembled as if new life were coming to it; but it did not fly. The naturalist then made it look straight at the sun. Suddenly it stretched out its wings and, with the screech of an eagle, it mounted higher and higher and never returned. It was an eagle, though it had been kept and tamed as a chicken!

My people of Africa, we were created in the image of God, but men have made us think that we are chickens, and we still think we are; but we are eagles. Stretch forth your wings and fly! Don't be content with the food of chickens!

CHINATOWN U.S.A.

by Edward Fox

In this legendary community, old ways rule unchallenged.

In New York's Chinatown they used to say if Bacigalupo didn't bury, you wouldn't see heaven.

And Bacigalupo's, the staid and solemn old Italian undertaking parlor on Mulberry Street, said goodby to many an Oriental man.

Such was, and is, the spirit and heart of the Chinatown man: even in the noon of life he ponders the night of death. He lives in legend, moves in peace, and seeks his celestial home.

He is born of a civilization ancient beyond reach of our New World. While Egypt built her pyramids, his people were already turning the Yellow River plains into a garden; when the Crusaders marched against the Holy Land, his land flourished with art, philosophy, music, astronomy, and architecture.

His civilization, a timeless strength, endures.

Flanked by the Bowery and Little Italy, Chinatown extends ten blocks along Manhattan's lower East Side, has a population of some 10,000 — mostly Cantonese. Wander the length of Mott Street, the Broadway of Chinatown, and you are enveloped in an old peaceful and dreaming world.

Here is the Temple House, incensed and many-splendored, its altar Buddha-banked in etchings, embroideries, tapestries; its happy Buddha full-stomached and laughing (9 million tourists have rubbed it for good luck) . . . the upper-floor family and

*From *Telephone Review*.

229

civic associations, meeting places for social and community groups (families with the same last names form their own associations for mutual help—Lees, Wongs, Ngs, Leongs, Hongs, Quons, Changs, Moys, Chins, Chus, etc.) . . . outdoors Chinese newspapers pasted to the walls of buildings . . . restaurants crowding in on one another—the Port Arthur, Tingyatsak, Lichee Wan, The Golden Dragon, Shavey Lee, Pacific, Joy Garden—their quiet rooms pungent with the steam and savor of wonton, egg roll, terrapin, bean curd, shark fin, bamboo shoots, the rich and full-heaped dishes of Moo Goo Guy Pan (chicken with mushrooms), Dow Jay Yok Soong (pork, string beans, bamboo shoots, water chestnuts), Jow Haw Kow (breaded shrimps) . . . curio shops, filled to tourist-brimming with back-scratchers, abacuses, fans, lampshades, mandarin jackets, sandals, ivory pagodas, crystal glass, jade, and the inevitable wood-piece puzzles . . . the plain-floored groceries and herb shops, lighted by bare electric bulbs, with all their strange provender of spearmint, moonflowers, sea horses, clear Szechwan fungus, refined tiger balm, sticky rice flour, sea urchins, dried squid and octopus, lichee nuts, rhinoceros horn, sliced deer horn, and gall of boa constrictor . . . over all flying from apartments the flags of America and Nationalist China.

Three generations may live under one roof. The wife takes care of the house, the husband takes care of business. Some families don't cook in their apartments and live on the prepared meals sent in from groceries and restaurants. Chinese women rarely go out and find their greatest social prestige when they give birth to a son. Children tell their troubles to their mother, who in turn discusses them with father.

Young Chinese women, declares the gentle tradition, walk erect and paint not their faces. Young men must walk near the curb to let the women see the shops, obey their family's wishes, and always use both hands when pouring tea.

At the heart of Chinatown life are the principles of Benevolence, Righteousness, Politeness, Wisdom, and Truth, so lucidly espoused by Confucius (Christianity, Taoism, Confucianism, and Buddhism are the major religions of Chinatown).

This gentle, tranquil disposition shines through social amenities and everyday business conduct alike.

Such gentleness of spirit marks the actions of young as well as old. And Chinatown's great hope is her youth. Filial piety, for example, is so respectfully practiced that juvenile delinquency (as well as crime in general) is unknown in Chinatown. A lad who transgresses incurs loss of face not only for himself but for all his friends and all his family.

Besides, the younger generation has little time for mischief. Consider Joyce Wong.

To Joyce, fair flower of Chinese gentility and for the past five years a telephone supplies auditing clerk, Chinatown is home. She was born there, and after spending twelve years in China returned for once and all to her New York home.

Sunday afternoons, year in, year out, when all Chinatown is crowded with Chinese visiting from their scattered colonies in Upstate, New Jersey, and Connecticut, she makes her way through the thronging streets, walks quickly to a quiet, flower-bordered classroom in the Transfiguration Church School on Mott Street. Here, working with Maryknoll priests and Sisters, she teaches Chinese and catechism to forty or fifty little Chinatown folk. For their tender years, these grammar-school tots carry a sizable burden:

"Chinatown's children must go to school twice. After their American school, at 4 P.M. they go to Chinese language school."

This burden Joyce shares each Sunday: whereas English has but 26 letters, Chinese has something like 28,000 picture symbols, each made with distinctive, intricate fine strokes. As a spoken language it has four main tongues, as well as over two hundred separate dialects.

"But I say to the children: 'Do not despair. Listen to Father Moore.' Father is a young priest and speaks Chinese well. I encourage boys and girls to be like him in study and sometimes one says, 'Boy, Father, you speak better Chinese than my pop, and you're an Irishman!' "

Chinatown's children watch television, read American newspapers, and applaud Elvis Presley, but their deeper sentiments are steeped in all the lore of the ancients. They read of the dim past of their ancestors on the plains of China . . . the temples and tearooms and moon gardens . . . the faceless millions ranging from mountain to sea . . .

The past is theirs.

They meet their Western destiny with Eastern heart and heritage.

So Chinatown, like its motherland, endures.

CHILD OF THE WORLD

I am the child by the Yangtze running
In the wind and the cold
To find a crack in the rocky shelter;
For my few years I am old.

I have no bench, no quilt, no pillow
On which my head is laid.
I am the child of the earth, hungry,
The one afraid.

You heard me cry in the dark,
You knew me and tossed in your sleep,
But the night is huge, and the river
Is wide and deep.

You knew of the waves, the wind rising,
Snow on the rocks —
I have a coat like paper, my feet
Have mud for socks.

I am the child of the world, hungry,
Savage and wild,
Inarticulate, forgotten.
I am your child.

— EDNA L.S. BARKER

REMARKABLE EFFECTS OF A MIRROR

by E. D. Edwards

The product of civilization almost wrecks the basis of it.

A young Korean was going on a journey to Seoul. As he was leaving home his wife called him back.

"Hé," she said. "Listen a moment. I have heard Mr. Kim's mother speak of a very lovely thing made of glass and metal. She says that when you look into it you see very curious things. I want you to buy one for me in the city."

"Is it expensive?" asked the husband.

"No," replied his wife. "You will have to pay something for it, but not really very much."

When he had finished his own business in Seoul the husband set out to fulfil his wife's commission. He made enquiries among his acquaintances in the city, discovered that the object in question was called a mirror, and bought one without any difficulty. In his eagerness to get home he put it into his wallet without even looking at it properly.

When he reached home his wife almost snatched the mirror from him in her impatience. But when she looked into it and saw the face of a woman in it, she burst into tears and began to scold:

"Oh, the villain! Not content with disporting himself in the

*From *Bamboo, Lotus and Palm,* by E. D. Edwards. London: William Hodge and Co., Ltd. Reprinted by permission.

city, he brings home a concubine! Who is this woman you have brought to insult me?"

The husband, taken aback by this unwarranted attack, looked into the mirror over his wife's shoulder, and seeing a man's face there, became violently angry.

"What sort of conduct is this for the wife of a respectable man?" he cried, almost black in the face with anger. "How dare you bring a libertine like that into the house?"

So incensed was he that he would probably have murdered his wife had not his old mother hurried in to find out why they were fighting. Each began to accuse the other. The weeping daughter-in-law raved about a concubine; the angry son, of a paramour, and both pointed to the mirror.

The old woman tried to pacify them. "Don't be vexed," she began quietly. Then, looking into the mirror she saw the face of an old woman looking at her and broke into a laugh.

"Is it this old woman the argument is all about?" she asked. "It is only the widow Pak from next door come to borrow some fire." So saying she went out to speak to her.

But not finding anyone, she went in again to her husband, and said in puzzled tones, "There is something very odd in the children's room. You can see all kinds of queer things in it and they are quarrelling over it. You had better come and see what it is."

The old man rose and went into the room where his son and daughter-in-law were still abusing each other. His wife handed him the mirror, and in it he saw the face of an old man.

"Ai-ya!" he exclaimed, "here's that old dog of a teacher come to collect his fees and I haven't a penny for him. This is not too good!"

One by one and two by two, the villagers looked into the mirror, and with every new arrival the uproar grew. At last they decided to take it to the magistrate, who might know more about such things than country-folk like themselves. So the village repaired as one man to the *yamen*.

But the magistrate was more astonished than anyone by what he saw in the mirror. Hastily summoning his officers, he bade them prepare horses and pack his baggage at once. "For," said he, "a new magistrate has come to take over my office, though I have no idea what I have done to lose my place."

Really believing that he had been cashiered, he was so busy making preparations for a hurried departure that it was some time before he could be dissuaded by a junior officer who, after a careful examination, pointed out how the mirror reflected the face of each individual in turn.

SAMPANS

Sampans, sampans,
  Out on the bay,
Sailing forever,
  Forever away;

Stop for a while
  On Malayan sands,
Then take me with you
  To far-away lands;

Sampans, sampans,
  With great black wings,
Take me to where
  The flower-pecker sings;

Take me across
  Your blue-white seas
To magic islands
  Of gold rain-trees;

Sampans, sampans,
  Out on the bay,
Sailing forever,
  Forever away.

—MARGARET LEONG

FROM THE ENCYCLICAL ON THE DEVELOPMENT OF PEOPLES

May individuals, social groups, and nations join hands in brotherly fashion, the strong aiding the weak to grow, exerting all their competence, enthusiasm, and disinterested love. More than any other, the individual who is animated by true charity labors skillfully to discover the causes of misery, to find the means to combat it and to overcome it resolutely. A creator of peace, he "will follow his path, lighting the lamps of joy and playing their brilliance and loveliness on the hearts of men across the surface of the globe, leading them to recognize, across all frontiers, the faces of their brothers, the faces of their friends (Pope John XXIII upon reception of the zalzan prize for peace).

EPIPHANY, 1968

The Epiphany presents two great topics: The first, how God manifested Himself in Christ; the second, how men can find Christ and in Christ can find God.

This second topic concerns all of us intimately. In other words, it envelops the lived experience of each of us with a fundamental word: Are we seekers of God? God, in order to reveal Himself in the light which must guide our life and bring us to salvation, must be sought. . . . Beloved children, searching for God in Christ represents the compass of life; it is a search which can be unfolded on every path of human experience—that of conscience, that of thought, that of action, that of history, that of politics, that of work, that of sorrow, that of love, that of progress.

Christ stands at the intersection of all human paths, for those who know how to search for Him and to find Him. And in Him God is reached and true life is achieved.

—Pope Paul VI

TEX

by Francis X. Lyons

The river that claimed Tex was shortly to take Brother's own life.

Brother had thought earlier that a nice long siesta this quiet Sunday would be just what the doctor ordered. But when he saw Jaimé Ruiz, Alberto Ferrufino, and little Tex join Armando in the doorway, he decided that he might as well go along.

Outside the sacristy the heat was even more intense as they walked down to the riverbank. The boys had wet their bathing suits and placed them on their heads, but by the time they came to the river the suits were almost dry again. They found eight more of the boys waiting for them near the canoes and suddenly it occurred to Brother Gonzaga that he was going to have a job on his hands to watch over so many of them. He knew that a couple of them, including Tex and Jaimé Ruiz, couldn't swim very well and the current in the center of the river was quite strong. On the mission side the river had dropped so far that they had to walk some distance over the dried cracked river bed to the water. On the other side, shining in the sun, was a long stretch of sandy beach. In the middle the river flowed swiftly.

He decided to check the boys out. He asked each one of them separately if he had permission to go swimming. When he came

* From *Something for God*, by Francis X. Lyons. Copyright Catholic Foreign Mission Society of America, Inc. Reprinted by permission of P. J. Kenedy & Sons.

to Tex, he saw the boy hesitate, then shake his head in the nega-
tive. Brother knew that the boy's parents kept a pretty close
watch over him, "Tex, I'm sorry but you can't come along without permission."

"But, *Hermano,*" Tex pleaded, "if I go back for permission
you will go off without me."

Brother looked at the eager brown face, contorted now with
anxiety, and thought how much he liked this little Japanese kid
who had become almost his shadow, helping around the workshop, running errands, and in the jungle pointing out the best
spots to hunt. *"Corre! corre!* run," he said, "and we will wait."
He watched the tiny figure scamper up the steep embankment
and turned back to the other boys.

"Armando, you take charge of the second canoe and take the
best swimmers with you. I'll take the other canoe with the
smaller lads."

They had hardly gotten settled in the canoes when Tex came
running back. Out of breath he jumped into the canoe with
Brother Gonzaga. They paddled slowly across the river, drifting
downstream a bit, and then when close to the other shore where
the current was negligible, worked their way back up to the
beach. They stuck the paddles in the wet sand and tied the
canoes with a vine.

They shouted and yelled as their bare feet hit the hot sand.
They were out of the jungle seconds later, changing their trunks
before Brother had finished checking the canoes. Gonzaga
donned his bathing suit slowly in the dense foliage as he watched
them frolic in the water. He never really enjoyed these trips.
It was good to watch the boys enjoying themselves and he
enjoyed their affection and confidence in him, but he always
felt the weight of responsibility. He was constantly worried that
something might happen to them. They were so used to their
environment that they were inclined to underestimate the
dangers that lurked on all sides.

"Hermano," one of them shouted, "hurry up, we're going to
play *piti.*" They had played it before and Brother dashed into
the water scattering them on all sides. In this game he acted

out the part of the *caiman,* the alligator, diving under water and grabbing them by the legs, careful not to hurt them, but giving them a good ducking just the same. They shouted and squealed and did their best to avoid him.

They were exhausted after an hour or so and dropped on the beach on large leaves they had brought out of the jungle. Brother was always amused at the simplicity of the arrangements. Back in the States people went to the beach with blankets, sun lotion, thermos bottles, beach umbrellas, portable radios, picnic lunches, and folding chairs. Here the boys changed in the jungle in a matter of seconds, drank the river water, stretched out on leaves that were cooler than blankets, and found fresh fruits and berries among the trees when they were hungry. It was all so simple and so uncomplicated. He stretched out with them, relaxing now that his charges were out of the water.

They dozed for a while, then someone started a mock fight with the wet sand, flinging it with abandon. In a few minutes they were all involved and Brother himself was plastered with sand. Jaimé, one of the smaller lads, got the sand in his eyes and began to cry. Brother cleaned him up while the rest went back into the river to wash off.

Gonzaga was enjoying a last dip. He was on the verge of calling everyone in to get dressed when there was a frantic shout, *"Hermano, Hermano, ayuda, ayuda!"*

He turned to see three of the younger boys struggling in deep water. Alberto Ferrufino was the closest and Gonzaga started for him at top speed. Just then Alberto got his footing and breathless, struggled to shore. Brother went on and grabbed Jaimé Ruiz whose pale, scared face was only a few yards away. He dumped him unceremoniously on the sand and turned to see Tex being dragged along in the current. At that moment Armando, a strong swimmer who had raced down the beach, dove in for Tex. Brother scampered up the beach and ran downstream, the wet sand clinging to his feet and holding him back. He could see Armando grab Tex by the hair and heard Tex screaming and struggling. Then Tex disappeared and Armando was alone in the water, fighting his way in against the current. Brother dove in near the spot where Tex had gone down, groping desperately in the murky, muddy water, praying and probing, but his outstretched hands encountered only emptiness. He surfaced, then he dove again. Then again and again, till exhausted and half mad, he made it back to the shore assisted by Armando.

Brother Gonzaga had no hope now of finding Tex alive, but after sending Armando back to town for help he continued to dive in the spot where Tex had gone down. Presently all the young men of the town, including the Japanese, who were excellent swimmers, joined him. They continued to search until nightfall, then built fires on the beach keeping vigil till the dawn. Brother went back to town and spent the night in chapel on his knees. He wept uncontrollably when he thought of little Tex, how he had first come into the workshop that day with the slingshot in his shy attempt to make friends.

After Mass and Communion Brother went back and resumed diving with the others. Twenty-four hours after the drowning, at three o'clock in the afternoon someone on the bank shouted, "There he is!" A canoe with three men in it brought the tiny body to shore. Brother helped them lift Tex out of the water, wrap him in a sheet, and take him back to town.

Tex's father, a pagan, collapsed when they brought the body into the house. His mother was hysterical.

Brother stayed with them as long as he could bear the sight of their agony and then he went back to the chapel and spent the next several hours on his knees in prayer. He told himself that it was God's divine will; he remembered that Tex had been to Communion that morning and that perhaps if he had lived he would have lost his innocence over the years and quite possibly his soul. He tried to tell himself that he had not been responsible, that it was an accident that could have happened to anyone. And yet he would not be consoled. "I shouldn't have let him come along," he told himself, "I knew he couldn't swim well. I should have checked again when he came back to the canoe, whether or not he had permission." For Tex's mother had been shouting that the boy had never been given permission to go swimming.

They don't keep bodies long in the tropics. There are no facilities for embalming and the law says that the body must be buried before sundown to prevent the possible spread of disease. Mass is said in the church after the burial with a catafalque in lieu of the dead person. Brother Gonzaga, exhausted by his self-recriminations, washed and changed, stopped by his work-table a moment to pick up an object there, and went out to the interment. The whole town was present, and as Brother pushed his way through the group, many murmured little consolatory words to him.

"No te preoccupes," they said to him, *"era su destino.* Do not fret, it was his destiny." And so they summed up their philosophy of life in an attempt to lessen his sorrows. They lived a hard life, beset with sickness and accidents, poverty and revolutions, and they had come to accept everything with a fateful shrug of the shoulders. If a man drowned in the river, it was his destiny; if a woman died in childbirth, it was her destiny too. It was their favorite phrase in their songs and in their conversation.

Brother numbly nodded his thanks to them and finally stood at the grave beside the mother and father of little Tex, watching Father Gallagher, the pastor of Riberalta, give the last blessing. The immediate relatives of the boy were sobbing uncontrollably as was the custom among these people, and the words of the service could hardly be heard above the weeping. At last, when Gonzaga thought he could bear it no longer, they lowered the rough-hewn casket into the grave. Father Gallagher shoveled in the symbolic first bit of dirt and the relatives dropped the sweet-smelling jungle flowers on top. There was a silence then, and Brother felt that all eyes were on him. He looked around slowly at the tearful faces. Stepping forward he reached into his cassock pocket. He took out the slingshot that Tex had given him, held it momentarily in the hot sunlight and then

dropped it into the grave. He didn't wait for the rest of the ceremony. He hurried back to his room and flung himself on his
cot, cassock and all, the hot tears welling up.

When Father Gallagher came back from the cemetery he
looked into Brother's room. Gonzaga was still stretched out on
the bed, murmuring one phrase over and over again. Father
Gallagher came up closer to hear what he was saying. "Never
again, never again," he kept repeating.

Father Gallagher, who himself had been so moved by the
tragedy that he could not bring himself earlier to visit the house
of Tex, thought that he knew what Brother was going through.
He sat down on the bed and began to massage Brother's neck
with his long fingers.

After a few minutes Gonzaga rolled over, blew his nose, and
said vehemently, "Never again will I let one of these people
get inside me, It hurts too much. That kid was like a little brother
to me."

"I guess we've all said that at one time or another, Brother,"
the priest said. "We've all made the same promise. You come
down here fresh and eager and zealous, wanting to love these
people and to devote your life to them. You go into a little town,
and you're lonely at first and then someone comes around shyly
with a grapefruit or a chicken; and then another one comes,
trying to show you how much they appreciate your being there;
and then all at once you know everyone in town is your friend,
and in many ways they have taken the place of the family and
friends you have left behind. Then you are changed to another
town. They come out on the riverbank and watch you leave and
the kids look at you kind of funny as though you were deserting
them and some of the women begin to cry softly. The men try
to make jokes about it, but you know that they feel it just the
same. You try to keep up a bold front as the launch pulls away,
but all the way down the river you keep telling yourself it's
the last time you'll leave a hunk of your heart behind.

"But there never is a last time, thank God. You go on to the
next town and the next, and after a while you realize that God

has given a missioner a special kind of heart. You grow a new piece for all the pieces you leave behind."

Brother, dry eyed, was watching him now, and Father Gallagher thought he had understood enough for the time being. He slapped him roughly on the shoulder and got up to leave. "Get some sleep now, Bro," he said not unkindly, "and don't let me see your face before ten o'clock in the morning. That's an order. I'll say Mass late and you can serve me."

When he had gone, Gonzaga, too exhausted to think about what the priest had said, his emotions spent for the moment, rolled over and fell asleep.

Two weeks after Tex's drowning, Brother Gonzaga went up to the Center House in Cochabamba for his annual vacation. It was a pleasure to be in the mountains after the jungle heat, and to forget about the motors for awhile. Not that he could completely forget them, for he spent a great deal of his time running from store to store buying the spare parts that could not be bought in Riberalta. Gradually, as the days wore on, the hurt grew less, till finally he was able to see that the accident had not been his fault. The sorrow found a hidden spot down deep in his being, coming to the surface only once in a while now, when he saw a lad like Tex playing in the street, or when he saw the same expression mirrored in the face of a boy who stopped him in the street and asked him for a holy card.

Coming back to town after his vacation Father Thomas Collins nudged Father Gallagher. "Do you see what I see?" he asked. Up ahead of them Brother was walking around surrounded by a bunch of small fry. They were laughing and shouting and trying to trip each other up.

"I sure do," Father Gallagher said, "and he's the one that said, 'Never again will I let them get close to me.'"

They had come up behind Brother by this time and he turned around grinning. "Okay," he said, "I heard you. Go on, rub it in."

I AM A CHRISTIAN

by Reina Maria Gutierrez

I am a Christian.
That's the way we put it,
simply but with pride,
in four plain words.
I am a Christian.

They are more than mere words. They are the sum of the lives
of a vast multitude of men, women and children.

They are a manifesto to mankind.

Speak those four words anywhere in the world—yes, anywhere—and people who hear them will recognize their
meaning.

They are a pledge—a pledge that stems from an ancient slab
which says: "I am the Lord your God. You shall not have
strange gods before me."

A pledge to those who dreamed that dream before divinity
came down two steps and became a Babe in a manger.

They are a covenant with a great host of martyrs and saints,
selfless souls who put their share of meaning into them.

Listen . . . and you can hear them echoing through the ages—
words that sprang alive from grateful lips, prayerful lips,
lips a-tremble with love for mankind.

You can hear them spoken before Nero in the arena, hear the
prayers as our brothers and sisters waited for their hour and
produced a testimony for the ages of man.

You can hear them in Moscow, Hungary, Korea, China.

You can hear them in the tinkling of coins handed to a beggar,
in the lullaby of a mother,
in the advice of a friend,
in the admonishing of a sinner,
in the stillness of a Sunday dawn,
in the laughter of an innocent child,
in the hammering in a laborer's workshop.
You can hear them in the farthest shack,
in the sun-baked desert,
in the endless sea,
in the byways,
in the closeness of a home,
in human wreckage,
in the densest jungle.
They are a pattern of life as lived by redeemed people . . . redemption that has its rights and obligations.
The right to heaven—the obligation to obey the Commandments.
The right to be sons of God—the obligation to do the Father's will.
The right to be priests—the obligation to sacrifice.
The right to hope, to dream, to live—the obligation to serve.
These are some of the meanings of those four words—meanings we don't often stop to realize or think about.
They are plain words, those four simple words.
You can shout them to anyone.
You can sweep them across the sky,
horizon to horizon.
You can carve them on the highest peak or grave them on your tombstone.
You can sing them to the tune of Ave Maria,
But you need not.
You need not do any of those things,
For those words are engraved in the hearts of 400 million people on the face of the earth.
They are known to 400 million people, every word and every syllable.

They are familiar to the brown, black, and yellow . . . to every-
one, including you and me.
That is why you need not shout them.
We can just speak those words. . . .
    but when we do, we speak them humbly, thankfully, reverently:
I am a Christian.

AN AFRICAN CANTICLE

by girls at Maryknoll's Marian College

in Tanzania

TANZANIA, bless the Lord,
And all your tribes and districts, bless the Lord.
From Tanga to Mbeya, all bless ye the Lord,
From Lindi to Bukoba, all bless ye the Lord.
Here let all the works of the Lord bless the Lord,
Praise and extol Him forever and ever.

ALL you BIG things, bless the Lord.
    Mount Kilimanjaro and Lake Victoria,
    The Rift Valley and the Serengeti Plain,
    Fat baobabs and shady mango trees,
    All eucalyptus and tamarind trees, bless the Lord.
    Ye hippos and rhinos and elephants, bless the Lord.
Praise and extol Him forever and ever.

ALL you TINY things, bless the Lord.
    Busy black ants and hopping fleas,
    Wriggling tadpoles and mosquito larvae,
    Flying locusts and water drops,
    Pollen dust and tsetse flies,
    Millet seeds and dried *dagaa*, bless ye the Lord.
Praise and extol Him forever and ever.

All you SHARP things, bless the Lord.
  Sisal plant tips and tall lake reeds,
  Masai spears and hunting arrows,
  A rhino's horn and crocodiles' teeth, bless the Lord.
Praise and extol Him forever and ever.

All you SOFT things, bless the Lord.
  Sawdust and ashes and kapok wool,
  Sponges and porridge and golden-ripe mangoes,
Praise and extol Him forever and ever.

All you SWEET things, bless the Lord.
  Wild honey and pawpaws and coconut milk,
  Pineapples and sugar cane and sun-dried dates,
  Slow-roasted yams and banana juice, bless the Lord.
Praise and extol Him forever and ever.

All you BITTER things, bless the Lord.
  Quinine and blue soap,
  Sour milk and maize beer, bless ye the Lord.
Praise and extol Him forever and ever.

All you SWIFT things, bless the Lord.
  Wild goats and honking lorries,
  Frightened centipedes and lightning flashes,
    bless ye the Lord.
Praise and extol Him forever and ever.

All you SLOW things, bless the Lord.
  Curious giraffes and old bony cows,
  Long-tailed chameleons, grass-munching sheep,
    bless ye the Lord.
Praise and extol Him forever and ever.

All you LOUD things, bless the Lord.
  Monsoon rains on aluminum roofs,
  Midnight hyenas and feast-day drums,

Train stations and carpenter shops, bless ye the Lord.
Praise and extol Him forever and ever.

All you QUIET things, bless the Lord.
   Candle flames and just-sown furrows,
   Heaps of clouds and sunny libraries,
   Our Uluguru Mountains and sleeping *pupas,*
   Land snails and crawling turtles,
   Grazing zebras and stalking lions, bless the Lord.
Praise and extol Him forever and ever.

All you creatures that never talk, still bless ye the Lord.
Praise and extol Him forever and ever.

THE SWING

Seen from a distance,
   the fluttering figure
Looks like a butterfly
   that soars up high and plunges down.
The song of a nightingale echoes
   in the green willows around.
Stepping lightly down from the swing
   as if awaiting her lover,
Holding her blue hair pin between her teeth
   and tidying her hairdo,
She adjusts her jacket
   breathing a little sigh.

—CHUNG IN-BO

SECOND NOVITIATE

by Robert W. Greene

> Thoughts came fast and harsh in the solitude of his
> Chinese prison.

Now I was alone. In my solitude, my great consolation was that
I was still able to offer the Holy Sacrifice of the Mass. I can
never explain why my Mass equipment was not confiscated. I
was certain the officers had seen the vestments in the attic when
I was offering Mass there. Later, when it became too cold in
the attic and I brought the vestments downstairs, they saw the
articles in my dresser drawer. A few days after I transferred
the vestments, the attic door was sealed with strips of paper,
and I thanked God that I had rescued the equipment for Mass
from that room.

Long before the Reds came into our area, anticipating possible trouble, I had bought a bushel of wheat, a grain we did
not grow in our section of China. I had hidden the wheat in
small boxes under the rice bin. But after the Sisters were sent
away, my greatest difficulty was in connection with making the
altar breads for the Sacrifice of the Mass. I used two stones to
grind a bit of the wheat by hand, and sift out a little flour every
two or three weeks. Then I would make the hosts on an iron.

Like so many other things I had taken for granted, I presumed
that always there would be others — the Sisters or the catechist —
to take care of making hosts for me. All I would have to do would

be to offer the Mass. Others would prepare the necessary articles for the ceremony. I had never learned to make hosts myself.

At first, I made a terrible mess of them, and I was very discouraged. It seemed such a simple thing when I watched the Sisters turn them out so beautifully. As I squatted there dejectedly in the smoke of the twig fire, I knew I needed help desperately, and instinctively my thoughts went to St. Martha, whom I always regarded as an expert in matters of cookery. So I begged St. Martha to help me, and she generously came to my assistance, although it was, I believe, the first time I had ever seriously sought her intercession.

After a bit, the wafers began to come off the iron in one piece and I had a sense of proud achievement as I held them in my hands, round and smooth. Then I would slip them between the pages of my bible and press them flat and crisp.

My baking efforts were a great mystery to the soldiers who came upon me as I was making the hosts. It had evidently been rumored about that I was getting a bit queer anyhow, and when they would ask me what I was making, I'd say, "Baking cookies for a festive day." They would ask me to let them try one of the "cookies," but immediately they would spit out the tasteless unseasoned, unleavened bread, shake their heads in a pitying gesture and wonder how I could enjoy eating them on a "fiesta." I simply told them, "That's the way I like them," and they would leave the rest of them alone.

By some patient maneuvering I was able to remove the locks from the storeroom door and get out a bottle of Mass wine. It took me three days to perform the trick, using a small piece of iron at rare moments when I was left alone. I saw soldiers look at the small bottle later in the day, but they shied clear of it — no doubt feeling that it might be poison. They were searching for guns and radios and other spy weapons. The Mass wine and vestments were of no importance to them, although in other areas I learned that the Youth Corps desecrated the vestments by parading through the streets with them on.

While the Mastermind was living in the room with me, I

would rise long before dawn and go to the attic to offer my Mass. There was hardly room to stand erect, but it seemed the safest spot for the Holy Sacrifice. During those days of watching the executions on market days, and feeling the pressure of mounting tension due to the continual questionings and threats, it was a great consolation thus to prepare myself spiritually for whatever the day might bring. Needless to say, my Mass each morning was unhurried and devout, for it required no stretch of the imagination to remind myself that each Mass I offered might very well be my last.

Then again I was happy in the thought that even though all the other priests had been forced to leave this area of China the Sacrifice of the Mass was to be celebrated each morning here in this spiritual wilderness. I begged courage for all who had been led astray by this new evil.

Now my whole day became a preparation for the next morning's Mass. I would pray that I might not be detected in my pre-dawn hideout in the attic. I wondered about the Mastermind during the four months he was with me. It seemed almost certain that he had heard me rise and ascend to the attic—yet he never mentioned it, nor did I. Even the flea-ridden police dog made no stir. One morning, as I had daily feared it might, the inspection of our quarters took place before dawn: I was but halfway through the Holy Sacrifice.

The soldiers downstairs banged on the door with their rifles. I heard them yell, "Open up!" I felt panicky and my heart sank. It seemed an eternity before the Mastermind yelled back, "What do you want so early?" They answered, "We've come for inspection, open up." Then my sleepy, dull-witted personal guard cursed them and said: "Everything is all right, we are still in bed. Come back later and I'll open the door." For these words, despite the curse and the lie, I shall always be grateful to the Mastermind, and as I finished my Mass I asked God to be kind to this Communist. When I came down from the attic, he made no reference to the pre-dawn visit of the soldiers—nor did I. But I saw something decent in this rough young Red soldier that I had never noticed before. On this one point, at least, we understood each other. He would not oppose my worship. After he departed, morning Mass became less of a problem in many ways, and I began to entertain the idea of reserving the Blessed Sacrament. Back a year ago, when Fathers Gilmartin and Nugent were still with me, we did have the Blessed Sacrament hidden and sometimes we would take it to the Sisters in the storeroom, so that they would be able to adore the Eucharistic Presence. With the guard in the rectory, I did not dare take a chance. However, now that I was alone, perhaps I should.

Then came the doubts — what if the soldiers should discover it in their search? Suppose I was taken away suddenly and did not have time to consume it? Would it be fitting to hide the Blessed Sacrament in miserable surroundings such as these? When I thought of all these difficulties, I would decide that it might be better not to reserve the Blessed Sacrament.

Then the next day I would tell myself that the Blessed Sacrament would be a great consolation to me and I would get strength from the prayers said in its presence. I could make up now for the hours in the past which I might have spent before the tabernacle, but did not. I told myself, "Here in Tung-an, you are alone in all this vast area of Southwest China; there are no other priests, there are no other places where our Eucharistic Lord is being adored. Maybe it is for this reason that you are here in Tung-an, that you may adore our Blessed Lord in the Eucharist."

Thus, for many days I weighed each side of the argument: The good reasons for it and the possible danger of desecration in reserving it.

I decided to reserve it. And as I look back now, it is clear to me that if I had not had the Blessed Sacrament, the constant questionings, the torture of those visits to the marketplace, the ridicule of the youngsters, the poor diet, the recurring physical ailments would have driven me beyond the point of endurance.

Now, in my aloneness, there were hours in the darkness of evening when I would enter the small room adjoining my quarters and kneel down before the Blessed Sacrament, which was reserved and hidden there in a small caskbox, to pray for China and for my people for whom I could now do nothing else.

I had one of the four volumes of my breviary and my Bible and it was a comfort to return to them throughout the day. I must confess that for the first time, I recited the words of the breviary with deliberate leisureliness. I relished the Divine Office more than ever before, I made my special prayers the Psalms of David: "I cried to the Lord, when I was in distress and he heard me . . . O Lord, deliver me from the unjust lip, and from the deceitful tongue . . . too long has my soul dwelt with those who hate peace . . . I lift up my eyes to the mountains: whence shall help come to me? My help is from the Lord, who made heaven and earth . . ." These words of David had new meaning for me here imprisoned in my rectory room. I wondered if there were Reds in David's day when I read: "They have opened a wicked and deceitful tongue against me . . . they have surrounded me with words of hatred and have attacked me without cause . . . in return for my love, they accuse me . . . they repay me evil for good and hatred for love." But David's consolations and his courage and hope became my own: "The Lord watches over thee, the Lord is thy protection at thy right hand . . . the Lord shall keep thee from all evil: he shall keep thy soul."

The months became a sort of tertianship, as practiced in the Society of Jesus, the "Solitude" of the Sulpician Fathers. This was my opportunity to reflect and appraise things in their proper prospective. Fundamentals became clearer, my own strength was seen as the weakness it really is. I formerly foolishly thought I was too busy for hours of prayer. I now had it forced upon me. In the past, sheer activity often created the illusion of accomplishment; now I was completely inactive. This life of an anchorite wasn't easy for me. My mission life had been a very active one, with much work for refugees, the sick, and the dying. Always there were many mission stations, miles away, to be visited, catechumens to be instructed and baptized. Now I was restless in my enforced idleness. I would tell myself: you are a missioner, ordained to preach Christ in foreign lands. Look at you now, you are wasting your time: no baptisms, no anointings, no preaching.

I would beg the officials again and again to permit me to do some work for the people, to let me reopen my dispensary, take care of the sick, go elsewhere in China to work if they did not wish to let me work here. All of which was greeted as usual with a sneering, "You're to stay here and not do anything for anyone."

I would try to tell myself that it was God's will that I should remain physically inactive, that I might grow spiritually. And I would pace my room again and say my beads. I would make novena after novena, especially those preceding the feasts of Our Lady. But often it seemed impossible to pray. The loneliness was oppressive, even at those times when I knelt in the blackness before the Blessed Sacrament. No consolation came from my prayers. Often the prayers and the psalms of the breviary I would have to read and reread many times to know what I was reading. Things didn't register so well any more.

For my solitude I made a daily schedule, and tried sedulously to follow it. I would rise before dawn and prepare for my Mass — the only Mass, I would remind myself, to be offered in this whole vast area of Southwest China. Though there was no one privileged to follow the august ceremony, I found myself watching the rubrics of the Mass more closely than ever. How deliberately I pronounced the words! How reverently I touched the Sacred Host! And my thanksgiving — why hadn't I realized before the value of that time when Christ is literally within me? I thanked God that it was still possible for me to offer Mass — to offer myself to God in union with Christ. Nothing else could have pacified my life and raised it above the degradation and sordidness which surrounded me.

Then after my Mass, if there was no inspection or visitors, I would prepare a little rice for my late breakfast, after which I would straighten up my room, wash some clothes (if I could get the water from the well), and then I would walk back and forth and say my rosary, or read a bit of the Bible or my breviary. Then I would make a visit to the Blessed Sacrament.

When I found it impossible to concentrate, I would pace the floor or gaze out the west window overlooking the mission court- yard. I could see the Youth Corps there at their meetings or stare at the soldiers coming and going through the mission gate—acting as though it was their very own military property. Or I would look out the east window at the people slowly going to or coming from the market, or listen to one of the now less frequent accusation meetings on the platform in the field. I felt that I was getting jumpy and nervous and I wondered what was to become of me. What plans did these men have in store for me? Why didn't they come to visit me any more? I'd try to tell myself not to be concerned about my future. I told myself, as I had admonished my Christians so often, I am in the hands of God, He knows I am here. He will strengthen me and watch over me. "Brace yourself," I'd say, "surrender your own will; present your body as a sacrifice living, holy, and pleasing to God."

In the afternoon, about three o'clock, I would start my little twig fire and prepare my evening meal—more rice and vege- tables, and an egg if I had been fortunate enough to have one sold to me in the market. From four o'clock until I retired seemed a long stretch then. I would say fifteen decades of the rosary, walking back and forth; and then as it grew dark, I would again go to the little room where I reserved the Blessed Sacrament. I had no oil or lamp now of any kind so my evening intruders were few and far between. I would spend an hour and a half or two hours before the Blessed Sacrament and this seemed not only to console me but to put my mind at rest. A calmness settled upon my whole being: "Come to me, all you who are weary and I will refresh you." In the quiet darkness there, I would remind myself that my troubles were small compared to those of others. They were as nothing compared to His. I was better able to sleep after my evening period of adoration. Each day I was getting more and more tired as I paced the floor, each night I would drop exhausted on my bed.

Sometimes as I lay on my hard board bed, I would picture myself on the morrow, dying a martyr's death. I would see myself holding aloft my mission cross, giving absolution to my weeping Christians as so many martyrs had done throughout the long glorious history of the Church. It was wishful thinking, full of pride. I would remind myself that my tormentors had not demanded that I deny my faith, or that I step on the crucifix, or sin against any of the virtues. I was convinced that to suffer in such a fashion would be a joy in comparison. I reminded myself of the priests and nuns martyred in North China. That privilege would not be given me; that honor was denied me. No doubt the principal reason was that I was not worthy—these priests and nuns, like the thousands who had won the crown before them, deserved the reward of martyrdom by their holy lives. What had I done to merit such a prize? I would fall asleep telling myself that such a consolation was not for me.

Then the next day it would start all over again, and I would begin another page in the story of utter failure in Tung-an. But my Mass would save me. In those moments I would remind myself that Christ foresaw and foretold and forelived just such a failure as mine years ago. He explained how the grain of wheat must go underground and rot in order to live again and bear fruit. It was the failure of Good Friday, the failure of the Mass. It could be man's greatest hour.

So I would say to myself, "If you can endure this inactivity now, you are a successful missioner. St. Paul's most difficult days were those he spent inactive in chains—not his travels nor his shipwrecks nor his labors for his people."

Still, I was tempted again and again to think of the priestly work I might have been doing had I never left my diocese in Indiana, where I knew priests were needed so badly. Was it a mistake to have entered Maryknoll and waste my life here alone in the hills of Southwest China among a people who have repaid my efforts to help them with torture more trying than death? Maybe my years at Maryknoll and my fifteen years of labor in South China were all in vain.

Then the thought would come to me that to endure patiently here in my mission prison in Tung-an perhaps was the best possible job I could do for our Lord for souls. My prayers for my people were from my heart, and maybe our Blessed Lord would accept them as readily as He would my physical labors for my flock, were I free. I would think that throughout the world there were many others—hundreds of loyal priests and lay people—enduring, far more patiently, far more suffering than I. I know too, that my people were praying for me and my fellow Maryknollers were praying for me and my friends were praying for me at home, offering their sufferings for me, wanting me to endure and to be strong in enduring.

ON THE DAY OF PRAYER FOR VOCATIONS, 1968

. . . Nevertheless the Church, gripped, as we were saying, by its characteristic need, awaits, asks, calls. It calls particularly young men and women because it knows that youth still has a good ear to understand its voice. It is the voice which invites one to do difficult things, heroic things, true things. It is the voice which implores understanding and aid for the countless needs of the brethren deprived of those who would speak to them of Christ and of God; of the brethren who are little, suffering, and poor; of brethren who are launched in the great, though equivocal, scientific technical, economic, social, political conquest of the temporal world, who are likewise in need of comfort, of light, of ideal transfiguration. It is the humble and penetrating voice of Christ who, today as well as yesterday, and more so than yesterday, says: Come.

—POPE PAUL VI

FLORIDA, SIXTEENTH CENTURY

The missionaries had no other purpose than to elevate the mind and spirit of the Indians among whom they dwelled. They did not expropriate their lands or push them back along an ever-receding frontier, as happened later in the Indian lands of the Anglo-American country to the north. To the Indians the missionaries took not only the catechism of Christianity, but the rudiments of European arts and crafts. To nearly 30,000 aborigines the missionaries taught farming, cattle raising, carpentry, weaving, and in many instances reading and writing. It was the first Headstart Program in America.

And note that these were men who gave themselves in service not just for a couple of years, as in the Peace Corps or Vista, but for 20, 30, or 40 years, until the ultimate hardship of death set the final seal on their sacrifice. Theirs was one of the most heroic humanitarian efforts for the amelioration and spiritual development of backward peoples that the American nation has experienced, and the story the missionaries wrote here in Florida is one that we in our time might well ponder when we reflect on the selflessness of the service that we en-lightened moderns have exhibited toward the disadvantaged — in the ghettos, in the migrant farmer huts, in the pockets or rural poverty.

— FATHER MICHAEL V. GANNON

POPE GREGORY II ASSIGNS BONIFACE

A letter dated May 15, 719, charges St. Boniface with the conversion of Germany.

Gregory, the servant of the servants of God, to Boniface, a holy priest.

Your holy purpose, as it has been explained to us, and your well-tried faith lead us to make use of your services in spreading the gospel, which by the grace of God has been committed to our care. Knowing that from your childhood you have been a student of Sacred Scripture and that you now wish to use the talent entrusted to you by God in dedicating yourself to missionary work, we rejoice in your faith and desire to have you as our colleague in this enterprise. Wherefore, since you have humbly submitted to us your plans regarding this mission, like a member of the body deferring to the head, and have shown yourself to be a true member of the body by following the directions given by the head, therefore, in the name of the indivisible Trinity and by the authority of St. Peter, Prince of the Apostles, whose government we administer in this See by the dispensation of God, we now place your humble and devout work upon a secure basis and decree that you go forth to preach the Word of God to those people who are still bound by the shackles of paganism. You are to teach them the service of the kingdom of God by persuading them to accept the truth in the name of

*From *The Anglo-Saxon Missionaries in Germany,* translated and edited by C. H. Talbot. Copyright 1954 Sheed and Ward, Inc., New York.

Christ, the Lord our God. You will instil into their minds the teaching of the Old and New Testaments, doing this in a spirit of love and moderation, and with arguments suited to their understanding. Finally, we command you that in admitting within the Church those who have some kind of belief in God you will insist upon using the sacramental discipline prescribed in the official ritual formulary of the Holy Apostolic See. Whatever means you find lacking in the furtherance of your work, you are to report to us as opportunity occurs.

Fare you well.

Given on the Ides of May in the third year of our most august Lord, Leo, by God crowned emperor, in the third year of his consulship, in the second indiction.

AFTER THE RAINS

After the tides have risen
  After the heavy rains,
We like to sail our boats,
  In the giant monsoon drains;

O some boats overturn
  And some are cast ashore;
While others are carried out to sea
  And those are seen no more.

— MARGARET LEONG

THE SUPREME VICTORY

by James M. Darby

> One year after the martyrdom of Peter Chanel the en-
> tire island of Futuna was baptized and has remained
> entirely Catholic ever since.

On the morning of April 28, 1841, after celebrating Holy Mass
at daybreak, as was his custom, and making his meditation
followed by part of his breviary, Father Chanel, all alone in his
compound, was attending to the household chores.

Then it was that a certain Filitika, a daring young fellow in
the service of Musumusu, popped into the hut quite unan-
nounced, as was the custom on Futuna. Finding no one, he
headed for the garden and there he saw Father feeding the
chickens.

As soon as the missionary noticed the native, he walked
over to him. Father knew what they were plotting against him.
But, without the least hesitation, he asked in his usual pleasant
manner, "Can I help you?"

"I have come to get something for Musumusu's wound."

Filitika was very careful not to explain how a few hours before, in the village of Vele, Musumusu and his gang had hate-
fully mistreated Meitala and the catechumens and set their
homes on fire, and how in the scuffle their ringleader had a bad
cut. He simply said that he had come along with the wounded
Musumusu.

* From *In the Land of Taboos,* by James M. Darby, S. M. Copyright 1957 St.
Anthony's Guild Press. Reprinted by permission.

While Filitika was still speaking, another man came forward and, noticing that Father had a good-sized stick in his hand, asked him to lend it to him. Having no desire to defend himself, Father Chanel handed it over immediately. So, when Musumusu with his desperadoes entered the compound, they confronted a man who was not only devoid of any malice toward them but also completely unarmed.

"Where are you coming from?" calmly inquired the priest.

"From Assoa."

"Can I do anything for you?"

"I came to get something to put on a bruise."

"How did it happen?"

"While I was knocking down coconuts," replied the scheming Musumusu, without twitching a muscle.

"That's too bad. Wait here a minute and I'll find you something to put on it."

Father went inside. As he was coming out of his room laden with medical supplies, he saw that two natives had followed him into the hut. One was carrying off an armful of linen; so Father spoke up.

"Filitika! Why are you taking my things?"

Filitika made no answer, but without the least scruple he ran out to the fence and tossed his haul over the top. Following his example, the others worked havoc in the hut, and before Father's very eyes they ransacked the place from top to bottom.

Musumusu, however, had not come just to rob a hut. Enraged, he gave away his purpose by shouting loudly enough for Father to hear him, "Say, who's going to do the murdering?"

His angry words had their effect. Filitika rushed at the priest and, knocking him down, cried out, "Quick, smash him one, and let him die!"

Another native immediately brandished his club.

In a flash Father grasped their awful seriousness: these men whom he had hoped to convert were about to become his assassins.

"Don't! Don't do that!" he protested, raising his right arm to ward off the blow.

The massive weapon came crashing down on the arm and literally crushed it, and the wounded man reeled back several feet. But the executioner gave him no respite, and while a new attacker dealt him fresh blows—using the very club that Father had loaned him—the first man violently struck his left temple. Blood began to stream down over his face.

Then, as happens with the dying, the most precious memories of Father's life must have flashed through his mind. There was La Potière, the place of his birth. . . . He saw his mother finishing prayer with the exhortation: "Be strong, O my soul, time passes away, eternity will soon be here!" . . . There was Monsols, Cras, the rectory where he had read the Annals of the Foreign Missions and thrilled to the idea of giving his blood for Jesus Christ. . . . There was Crozet, his first assignment as pastor . . . Rome, the catacombs, the Colosseum, where he had breathed in the air "redolent," as it were, "with the blood of the martyrs." . . . There was Belley; the chapel where he pronounced his holy vows, the reception room of the Marists, his sister Mary Frances, and the Superioress who made the distinction for him between the rewards of daily religious life and the palm of martyrdom. . . . There was Fourvière; the tiny *ex voto* of the missionaries who were about to set sail, a heart-shaped silver locket containing their names and placed by him around the neck of the Child Jesus. . . . There was Paris; the seminary on the Rue du Bac where "so many holy priests were made ready for martyrdom"; the room enshrining their relics. . . . There was Havre; the singing of the *Ave, Maris Stella;* the gangplank hoisted on deck. . . . Finally, Futuna, "his poor little Futuna!" . . . And now his warm blood was flowing from a deadly wound. Thus all his most precious hopes were being realized. He, the humble shepherd of Bresse, had the honor of giving his life for his sheep! From the bottom of his heart he whispered, "*Malie fuai*—It's quite all right!"

These same words he had used in answer to their threats, and he now repeated them over and over as the threats gave way to blows: "*Malie fuai!*" And, because he firmly agreed that it was "quite all right," he did not allow himself to utter the least complaint or to shed a single bitter tear, as we were to be informed later on by eyewitnesses of the beating.

But the attack is not over. One native brandished his lance; its point was actually a bayonet. The wooden shaft struck Father on the chest; the iron blade slid in beneath his arm. He staggered under the thrust and sank to the ground. Once again the blows of the club hammered him. Slumped onto the gravel floor of the hut, his back pressed up against the bamboo siding, his head bowed in pain, the missionary wiped the flowing blood from his face.

Without bothering any more about him, the murderers finished ransacking the place and then went off with their ill-gotten loot. One took a cloak, another a small chest, and still others a hatchet, the priestly vestments, or some other religious articles, including the crucifix and the chalice; these were destined to be returned later on. Before long the hut was completely empty. To a couple of natives who were still rooting around, Musumusu kept whining, "Someone ought to kill him off!" Then, referring to the ones who had run away, he added, "Did they come here just to enrich themselves?"

At that moment two catechumens arrived. Seeing that the wounded priest was still alive, they called him by name:

"*Patele Petelo*—Father Peter!"

Father Chanel focused on them a kindly glance. "Where is Maligi?" he asked after a moment.

Chief of Poi, the head minister Maligi would have been strong enough to oppose Musumusu himself. Unfortunately he was on another island. When the catechumen answered, "He is on Alofi," Father understood that nothing then could save him from his persecutors. Once again he said, "*Malie fuai loku mate*—My death will be a blessing to me!"

But the catechumens intended to defend him.

"Why injure this poor priest so badly?" cried one of them to Musumusu in horror.

"Get this man out of here," snarled Musumusu. "He's one of the converts."

But despite this, the catechumen bent over Father, took him

by the arm, and tried to help him up so that he could lead him away.

"Leave me here; death will be a blessing," Father repeated.

Then, terror-stricken at the impending danger, the catechumen left without him.

Musumusu was furious that no one had stayed to finish the job. Climbing through a window which led to Brother Marie-Nizier's room, he seized a little hatchet with a curved cutting edge. With this he dealt the dying priest so savage a blow that the steel penetrated the skull. The apostle of Futuna gasped for his final breath.

A little while afterward, the mother of the catechumen who had tried to save him risked approaching the spot of the murder. With the help of two other women she washed the blood from the body and, in accordance with the native burial custom, anointed it with coconut oil before wrapping it carefully in papyrus matting.

"I ask for nothing for my body; it is too insignificant for me to bother about it after my death," Father had stated two years previously when he was drawing up his last will and testament. But Providence wished otherwise.

Near the compound, Niuliki and Musumusu dug a grave. Before noon the same day the king, quite convinced that by interring the missionary he also was interring the religion, presided over the burial of the priest whom four years earlier he had promised to protect.

At the very moment of the burial, though the heavens had been clear as on the finest of days, an unusual rumbling resounded overhead. The sky darkened suddenly and a frightening clap, like thunder, broke just above the hut. According to some of the natives, a bright cross appeared in the very center of the darkness. Be that as it may, the darkness disappeared right after the crack of thunder. Terrified by this mysterious phenomenon, the islanders looked at one another in consternation. Trembling with fright, the murderers and pillagers let drop their booty and cringed down close to the ground.

As he was making his way back home with a cassock he had

stripped from his victim, Musumusu met a stout-hearted warrior from Poi hurrying to the priest's help. The would-be rescuer could hardly contain himself.

"Don't get excited!" interposed Musumusu, and tossing him the blood-stained cassock, he added, "Here, take your treasure. . . . This is all your God is worth!" Then he fled.

In an effort to erase all memory of the priest and his religion, the king issued an immediate order to clear away the mission hut. He himself smashed to pieces the harmonium, whose sweet sounds had so recently fascinated him; and on the spot of the crime he gave a banquet featuring his best kava to commemorate the triumph. After all, he had announced the "fall of the sun"! And had not the "fall of the sun" occurred just exactly as he had predicted?

Arriving on the scene too late came the warrior Misa, who had rushed to the aid of his friend; also the son of Niuliki, Meitala, who willingly would have given his own life for the priest; and the chief minister Maligi, who wept openly at the grave and scraped his face and chest with shells, thus grieving as he would for a close relative.

Brother Marie-Nizier, meanwhile, was not yet to kneel at the grave of his confrere. As he made his way toward Poi knowing nothing at all about the terrible drama, Brother met a native who told him. This man had, like the others, plundered the hut of Father Chanel, but being deprived by the king of his part of the loot, he resolved to take revenge by saving Brother Marie-Nizier. So now he advised him to go back to the valley of the "conquered" tribe.

The next day Niuliki paid a visit to Sigave to encourage the Brother to return to Poi. He even shed tears as he told of the death of the priest, though he himself had had him murdered! But Brother Marie-Nizier saw through the trickery.

"You can have me killed right here, if you care to, but I'll not go back to Poi."

Two weeks later he was forced, in order to avoid the fury of the king, to request asylum on board a ship that stopped at

Sigave, and so, with three or four other white men on the island who were also in danger, he left Futuna.

"The priest is dead; the religion has perished with him!" insolently proclaimed the enemies of the true God.

But the catechumens, young and old alike, did not slacken in their faith.

"I too wish to die for God. I want to join the good Father!" exclaimed the youngster of ten years, while the grown-ups repeated over and over again the words of the priest: "Whether they kill me or not, the Catholic Faith, once it has taken root on the island, will never be destroyed!"

MAYAN CHILD

Four-year-old arms,
Will you carry
A basket of corn
Beyond Atitlan,
To the mercado
This misty morn?

Wary black eyes,
Will you answer
The eternal "why" —
How apples grow red,
Where the bees hover,
Why flowers die?

Dusty small feet,
Will you take her
Before day is done,
Over the mountain
To the blue water,
Where sinks the sun?

— ALICE MOORE REGAN

AS THE FATHER SENT ME . . .

The Church does not send forth paid mercenaries; the Church does not organize a network of professional propagandists. The Church sends forth volunteers. She sends forth men who are free and who surely are not paid for what is required by their work in terms of labor, risk, and merit.

The Church sends forth particular men—poor and generous, free from every compulsion, and bound within by the most sacrosanct of bonds, that of unique, chaste, perennial, consecrated love.

The Church sends forth followers of Christ who give their all to Him. The Church sends forth young men filled with ardent fervor and imagination, who have had an insight into the highest definition of life: an undertaking of divine love.

The Church sends forth humble heroes who believe in the Holy Spirit and who, like Christ, are ready to give their life for the Church of Christ. . . . sends them forth to God's people; to children, to the poor, to those who suffer, to the weary, to the disciples of the Kingdom, and to the missions, to those far removed, to all. And they go forth. What beauty!

—POPE PAUL VI, 1967

THE LAST JOURNEY OF FATHER HUGO

by Arthur J. Burks

> He was deaf and going blind but he refused to admit
> that he was ill.

The Cururu was rising. So was the Tapajós into which it flowed.
So were all the rivers which flowed into the mighty Amazon.
It was late November, and the rainy season was beginning.
Soon the jungles in all directions would be wet and moldy. The
trails between villages would be drowned. The Indians would
withdraw from the lowlands to the high places. So would the
jungle Brazilians, the *caboclos,* on the banks of the rivers and
creeks. Slender paths connecting rubber trees would be hip
deep in water. The white latex would almost cease to flow.
Central Brazil would be a drowned land.

The voices of the rivers rose higher as their crests crept up,
in some streams so swiftly moving that the middle seemed to
be higher than the sides, curving slickly down to the vanishing
banks. The voice of distant rains was in the streams. Daily the
rain poured down over the forests, the rivers and creeks. Daily
it lasted longer, fell more heavily.

Father Hugo's heart, like the rivers and streams, was filling.
He was going out, and yet he had no wish to leave his "beloved
children." He was stone deaf and could no longer hear confes-

sions. He would probably be blind, also, before he died. He had no intention of dying, however. He was simply going out because he was ill. Finally, he had admitted that he needed a doctor and hospitalization. He had had malaria more times than he could remember. He had swallowed so much quinine that there was a constant ringing of quinine bells in his ears. These were the only sound he would ever hear clearly again. Sometimes they almost deluded him into the belief that he could hear once more.

Twenty-seven years before, a comparatively young man, he had traveled up the green Tapajos to the mouth of the black-water Cururu. Then it had seemed as if the river were calling him. He had traveled up the Cururu, all its winding, murmurous course to within a few hours of the first rapids, until he reached the place where he founded his mission, the Franciscan mission on the Cururu. It was founded for a single purpose: to take the Father's Word to the black-face Mundurucus. It was a mission for which Father Hugo had volunteered. He had been in his early thirties then. In his heart he had expected and desired martyrdom. But martyrdom had been denied him.

Now he was going out, all the way to Rio de Janeiro, to die. He did not know that he would never return. He did not believe it, and would not admit it to himself as he set out. Yet he took out with him, in a small bag which he guarded as jealously as he guarded his rosary, some of the soil over which generations of Mundurucus had trodden. He intended that it should be buried with him. He would not die on this journey, but one must be practical, one must always be sure — so he carried with him the bag of soil.

He was six feet tall, straight as an arrow, his hair and chest-length beard snowy white. His cheeks and hands were pale, the blue veins visible in them. Their blue matched the blue of his eyes. He wore a brown habit, and around his waist the white, knotted cincture of his Order. His feet were sandaled, his head bare. His fingers, as if worn down at the ends by too much labor, were blunted. And though he had for years been unconscious of the blood-sucking flies, *piums,* their black marks were visible on his cheeks, neck, hands and ankles.

Father Hugo had always been the kind of a Franciscan who had never been afraid to get his hands or feet or habit dirty. A Franciscan *worked.* He had worked hard for almost thirty years. And if he could have his way, he would work even harder during the next thirty years.

If one could only hear! If only one's eyes were not failing. If only one had been more careful of one's physical well-being. One squandered youth with a lavish hand. Then one was suddenly old and deaf, and one's work was done and one must say good-by to the places where the best of it had been accomplished.

Throughout the clearings, the *campos* where the Mundurucus had their *malocas,* the news of Father Hugo's departure traveled swiftly. *Malocas* were villages. The word was passed on from cabin to cabin, from mouth to mouth, through the areas where the "civilized" lived, the jungle Brazilians who, from the banks of creeks and rivers, "worked" the rubber. Father Hugo had served them all, the Indian and the civilized descendant of the Indian. They all knew and loved him.

"Father Hugo is going out," they said to one another. "He is not returning. He is soon to die."

The aging priest dropped down the familiar, winding Cururu by small boat, went aboard a motor launch on the Tapajós at the mouth of his beloved river, at the north end of Island-in-the-Mouth-of-the Cururu, where a small chapel stood. With him, to make sure that he went out as ordered, to make sure that he was well cared for, went a Sister of the Immaculate Conception. A fellow priest went as far as the Tapajós.

Many Indians journeyed to the mouth of the Cururu to bid the sick priest good-by. They wept without shame, the men, the women and the children, when he blessed them at the last, spoke a few words in Mundurucu, the language he would never need to use again, and was borne away by the motor launch. He could not hear their answers, but he could still see their tears, which he understood because they were his tears too. A priest should not be sentimental but even after so many decades it seemed one remained human after all. There was no shame in such tears. The Mundurucus were children. Not that Father Hugo did not love the "civilized." He loved all among whom his work carried him. But the Mundurucus were something special.

The Tapajós was swift. Sunken trees were meters-deep beneath the surface. Jagged rocks were well below the keel of the launch. The outward journey was to be a swift one, four days from the mouth of the Cururu to Pimental, where the last rapids poured their waters into the series of lakes which led on to Santarém and the Amazon. It was good to go out so quickly. It did not take the Indians, then, so long to fade out behind the launch. It was not easy to stand and watch them, especially if one were almost too weak to stand. He could still see them and their tears.

He would soon return, he promised. Just a little help from a good doctor, a few weeks in a hospital, and he would be as good as new. He had never really needed help before. It was disheartening that he needed help now.

He carried with him the few, simple appurtenances of his calling. Wherever he found himself when morning came, he celebrated Mass. He would never need help for that. Nothing would ever prevent him from saying his Mass.

He had taken just as little with him into the wilderness, twenty-seven years before. That was as it should be. Franciscans lived literally the words of Jesus: they took neither extra cloaks nor shoes, they carried no scrip. What they needed they produced with their hands—or went without.

The launch moored that first night at Vila Nova on the west bank of the Tapajós, past which roars the waters of the Chacorão rapids. People there had known all day that Father Hugo was going out, that they might never see him again. None remembered, or knew, even, that his name was Mense. For a lifetime he had been "Frei Hugo" to every man, woman, and child. He had baptized so many. He had married so many, and baptized their children and *their* children. He remembered every name, too, and the date of baptism or marriage — or death; for he had administered the last rites to them, also, when he had been close enough for the family to fetch him.

Rubber cutters, sturdy *caboclos* who daily tapped the wild rubber trees and were now feverishly collecting their last latex in the rain, came in from their shadowy trails to bid him good-by. This day the *estradas,* as they called their trails, could wait, the latex overflow the gourd cups into the leaves and mold. There were always *estradas* and rubber. There was one Father Hugo.

The civilized did not weep as freely and easily as the Indians. There was something about civilization that dried up people's tears or made them ashamed of weeping. But they found tears for Father Hugo. How could he refrain from being a little sentimental? He did not hesitate to show everyone the little sack of soil, to tell them why he took it out. For almost three decades he had carried the news, however slight, and the sack of Mundurucu soil was news he must share. Not, he assured them, that he expected to use the soil *this* trip, but one should always be ready, with extra soil for one's lamp.

Again there were good-bys and the launch sped on downstream to Saõ Martinho, near the mouth of the das Tropas River, which Father Hugo knew almost as well as he knew the Cururu. Many of his beloved Mundurucus lived on the banks of the das Tropas, where he had visited them in their *malocas,* to hear their confessions, celebrate Mass, perform wedding ceremonies, baptize their children, and close the eyes of their dead. It wasn't easy on the heart, this going out. There was too much to remember. One would not forget if one could, but memory could hurt when one suspected that memory was all one had left.

Father Hugo celebrated Mass at Saõ Martinho next morning, as he had celebrated Mass at Vila Nova the previous morning — as he had celebrated Mass every morning of his life since he became a priest.

Then the launch bore him down to the Mangabal, that long traverse of the Tapajós dotted with great smoothbacked boulders, some just below, some just above the surface, past the abandoned mission of the Bacabal, where Frei Pelino, the Capuchin, had served Brazilians and Indians as far back as the '70's. Father Hugo was becoming very tired. He was too tired, almost, to fear the rapids, as all his missionary life he had feared them even when, as now, the river was so high there was almost no perceptibly fast water.

But he must say Mass at Mangabal as he had at Vila Nova and Saõ Martinho and, tired though he was, there were more good-bys to be said. For there had been many journeys on this river. There was no spot on it or on any of its tributaries where Father Hugo was not known.

On the fourth day he reached Pimental and the road around the rapids to Saõ Luis where he had to wait two days for the down-river steamer to take on its load of rubber and hides and bear him further away from his adopted children.

Every morning he said Mass.

He began the Mass at Belterra, the last morning he was to celebrate it. He could not finish. He was too ill. The Sister had tried to dissuade him for several mornings, without success. But he knew now he must heed then if he were to complete his journey.

Realization came to him slowly as the steamer carried him on down the now broad Tapajós to Santarém, there to mingle its green waters with the muddy waters of the Amazon on which he would travel eastward to Belém. For months the priests on the Cururu had been trying to tell him he must stop his work. But he had refused to feel sick, be sick. He *wasn't* sick.

Now he knew he was.

His work was finished. The bells were mourning for him. He could hear them always now, not just when Mundurucu boys rang them at the chapel on the Cururu.

"*Quinine* bells!" he snorted. "I've swallowed too much quinine. That's the bells I hear, mourning in my ears!"

But it was better to think of the Cururu bells while he re-

membered. At Santarém, when full realization came, he really
began to remember, not only back to the mission on the Cururu,
but far, far beyond.

M Y   S A V I O R   W E E P S

In many lands Golgothas rise,
And oh, how red the way—and steep!
My Savior weeps from many eyes,
In many hearts His wounds are deep!

My Savior weeps from many eyes;
His many hands and feet are sore;
On many backs the welts arise—
Oh, hurt ye not my Savior more!

My Savior bleeds in many lands
As hammers beat Him to the floor;
But holding high the hero's hands,
He shows the world His wounds once more!

In many jails my Savior prays;
His bleeding palms in pain are bent;
But on a cloth, new bread He lays,
And drops of wine from heaven sent!

In many lands Golgothas rise,
And oh, how red the way—and steep!
My Savior weeps from many eyes,
In many hearts His wounds are deep.

—LOUIS J. MALOOF

CHRIST IN THE UNIVERSE

With this ambiguous earth
His dealings have been told us. These abide:
The signal to a maid, the human birth,
The lesson, and the young Man crucified.

But not a star of all
The innumerable host of stars has heard
How He administered this terrestrial ball.
Our race have kept their Lord's entrusted Word.

Of His earth-visiting feet
None knows the secret, cherished, perilous,
The terrible, shamefast, frightened, whispered, sweet,
Heart-shattering secret of His way with us.

No planet knows that this
Our wayside planet, carrying land and wave,
Love and life multiplied, and pain and bliss,
Bears, as chief treasure, one forsaken grave,

Nor, in our little day,
May his devices with the heavens be guessed,
His pilgrimage to tread the Milky Way
Or His bestowals there be manifest.

But in the eternities,
Doubtless we shall compare together, hear
A million alien Gospels, in what guise
He trod the Pleiades, the Lyre, the Bear.

O, be prepared, my soul!
To read the inconceivable, to scan
The million forms of God those stars enroll
When, in our turn, we show to them a Man.

— ALICE MEYNELL

HIPPOS, CROCS, AND SNAKES ALIVE

by James Dempsey

A Mill Hill missioner recounts some of the dangers from the fauna of the Southern Sudan.

Many people who have never been to Africa imagine that white dwellers there carry their lives in their hands whenever they venture outside the security of their compounds. They are under the impression that the dense forests which grow almost to the settler's front door are peopled with hostile savages armed with spear and poisoned dart with which to slay, and equipped with outsize cooking pots in which to cook the unfortunate wayfarer; that behind every bush and in every clump of grass crouches a lion waiting to pounce on his prey; that from every tree hang huge pythons which drop down on their victims and crush them to death in their sinuous coils, and should the traveller escape the cannibal, the lion and the python, it is only to meet his fate from the cobra or adder which, lurking in the undergrowth, wraps itself like lightning round the arm or leg of the unwary passer-by and, driving its venomous fangs into his person, inflicts on him a horrible death. And should the traveller prefer to journey by river, his passage is thereby rendered no more secure, for as he ventures forth in his flimsy canoe (he always travels in a flimsy canoe, of course!) a great hippopotamus rises to the surface, yawns in the unhappy

*From *Mission on the Nile*. London; Blackfriars, Publications.

277

man's face, bites his frail craft in two, and consigns him to the gaping jaws of a dozen or so crocodiles which, with a nice sense of anticipation, have gathered round their victim as a field of cricketers gathers round the last batsman in.

Well, no one can assert that such unhappy incidents have not happened, do not happen, and will not happen in the future. Cannibalism was once common in Africa and even today, in response to some atavistic urge, some normally well-behaved native will invite his neighbor to lunch and make him the chief course on the menu. Travellers are occasionally eaten by lions, killed by snakes, crushed by hippos or devoured by crocs. But such incidents make news by reason of their comparative rarity, and the district in which one takes place buzzes for weeks with talk of the occurrence. They are not taken as matters of course, to be deplored indeed, but things to which one becomes accustomed, as are for example the lists of casualties on the broad highways of England. Undoubtedly one travels with much less hazard and in less peril of one's life across the crocodile-infested Nile, even in a flimsy canoe, than one does across a wide, well-paved and well-lighted street in England.

However, although in Africa, or, to narrow that huge continent down to one particular country, the Sudan, and the Sudan down to the Upper Nile Province, one does not need to exercise one's agility anything like so often to escape sudden death, as one has at home, there are occasions when one's nimbleness of movement saves oneself or one's companion from an unpleasant encounter with hippo, croc, or snake, or when one can but stand by, thrilled with horror, and helpless to assist another in danger from one of these creatures.

Such an instance occurred one evening during my first year at Detwok. It was a Sunday, and after tea the other Father at the mission and myself had strolled down to the river to sit on the embankment for a while, to smoke a pipe and enjoy the cool of the evening after the heat of the day. The Sisters, too, had come down to snatch an hour of leisure by the river, and there was the usual crowd of Shilluk, who spend most of the day during the hot season on the river bank. For some days past a hippopotamus had been in the vicinity, disporting itself in the usual hippo manner, suddenly popping up to the surface to breathe, blowing a cloud of spray through its nostrils, surveying the scene out of its small piglike eyes, and then lowering its huge bulk to the river bed again.

On this Sunday afternoon it had ventured much closer inshore than usual, and its great head appearing above the water had proved too tempting a target for the idlers on the beach who had greeted its every appearance with a shower of clods of cotton soil. The hippo apparently had tired of being used as an Aunt Sally by every Shilluk in the neighborhood and had withdrawn out of range and when we appeared was doing his usual noisy breathing exercises in midstream.

We sat there for some time, admiring the changing colors of the water reflecting the setting sun, watching the flocks of egrets coming in to roost on the trees across the river, and also idly noticing the mission boat slowly crawling across the water, bearing a dozen or so of the schoolboys coming from a fishing expedition. As the boat reached the middle of the river, the hippo surfaced close by. Whether he, seeing the occupants of the boat, associated them with his late tormentors and was determined to show his resentment of the rough treatment he had received, or whether what followed was sheer mischance, is a matter of conjecture, but the hippo, submerging again, got his body under the boat and with a jerk threw it and its shrieking occupants right out of the water. By the mercy of God, none of the boys was thrown out of the boat, and the boat itself, landing again on the water with a resounding smack, although rocking violently did not overturn. But the hippo was not finished yet. He reappeared close to the stern and one boy, striving to recover his balance among the struggling mass of boys, thrust his arm right into the cavern of the beast's mouth. Before he closed his great teeth on the lad's arm, however, the heavy rudder bar, swinging wildly round under the motion of the rocking boat, caught him a blow on the snout, and this evidently so surprised him that, literally open-mouthed, he backed away and disappeared, to leave the boys to recover their scattered wits as well as their equilibrium, then to continue in frantic haste their journey to our side of the river. We on the bank were horrified spectators of the whole scene, which was over in a matter of minutes.

It was indeed truly miraculous that it was not accompanied by tragedy, for had the boat overturned, I do not think that one of the boys would have survived. The river there is very deep with a strong, swift current where the waters divide themselves around a large island. The island too is a favourite lurking place for crocodiles, so that those who escaped being carried away by the current might possibly have found a worse fate awaiting them. It was a very subdued and chastened boat's crew that made its way to the chapel that evening to thank God for its deliverance.

However, the hippo is, as a rule, a most inoffensive animal, wanting nothing else but to be left in peace to enjoy its riverside garden, by night. We on our part were quite content to respect this sensible attitude of strict nonbelligerency on both sides, until one hippo, a lady, accompanied by a bouncing baby boy weighing several hundredweight, began to invade our garden in search of sustenance. The first intimation we received that we had guests for supper was when the reverend postman, returning from the boat in the small hours of the morning, was compelled to move far more rapidly than was his wont by the sight of two or three tons of hippo not far behind him. The cries of her neglected baby recalled the mother to her sense of duty and she gave up the chase to resume her interrupted meal.

One night's browsing was sufficient to reduce our lovely garden to a wilderness; a tank would not have done so much damage. That at least would not have eaten anything, but our lady visitor first of all cleaned up a whole season's planting of sweet potatoes in the large vegetable patch and then, crossing a narrow khor to a smaller fruit and vegetable garden, proceeded to knock the trees down, trample on the growing plants, and lie down in the vegetable plots, evidently trying each one in turn for comfort. Her nocturnal visitations went on for over a week, though after a second visit to the garden she evidently decided that that wasn't worth bothering about any longer. Still it was decidedly dangerous to venture down to the river at night in case one found her taking a moonlight stroll. We sent to Kodok requesting assistance and were kindly given permission to shoot the brute, but since the only firearm that the mission then possessed was an ancient shotgun, and for that to be effective against the hippo, the barrel would have to be poked down her ear, we hastily declined the privilege and asked instead that a policeman armed with a heavy caliber rifle be sent to rid us of our unwelcome guest. She, however, must have sensed our marked coldness toward her, and realizing no doubt that she had overstayed her welcome, left the neighborhood just as the policeman arrived, and troubled us no more.

I am happy and extremely thankful that I have no tragedies due to crocodiles to report at Detwok. The mission at Tonga is not so fortunate, for there two schoolboys were taken inside six months. The first of these was seized at night, when the poor little lad was fishing at the water's edge. As his terrified brother, who was with him, afterwards recounted, his line had snarled on some drifting grass and as he ventured out to free it, he was taken and carried away. The second was taken at midday out of a group of boys who were bathing in the river. One boy will remember with horror all his life feeling the scaly side of the brute brush past him as it crept along the river bed toward its selected victim. It is some satisfaction to know that the two Fathers at Tonga, ranging the river in search of the killer, found it, still holding its prey, under the river bank, and shot it. The body of the boy was recovered and decently buried.

The nearest we had to a tragedy was the instance of a man who was seized while fishing but who managed to free himself. On another occasion, a woman from Detwok, getting water from the river, actually bounced her water pot on the snout of a croc that was lying just submerged in the shallows and apparently waiting for a victim. The lady's leap carried her well out of range of snapping jaws, and she raced up the path shrieking as though the whole saurian breed was at her heels. But for one of the Sisters, who happened to be coming down the path and stopped the terrified woman, there is no saying how far she would have continued in her headlong flight before her scattered senses returned to assure her that no crocodile could possibly chase her all the way home.

An example of the great size that a crocodile can attain and the enormous strength it can develop is shown by the following. During the dry season, when there is no water and poor grazing on our side of the river, the Shilluk in the Detwok area transfer their cattle to the Dinka side, where there is a large lake which keeps the grass fresh and green and provides the cattle with drinking water in abundance. One morning a cow that had strayed from the herd wandered down to the river to drink. As she was drinking, a crocodile seized her and dragged her under. It reappeared in a moment or two holding the bellowing animal firmly round the middle, in its jaws, much as a dog might carry a bone. Several Shilluk had come down to the river and were just about to cross it to the cattle camp when the incident took place. The owner of the cow was among them and, since a Shilluk will recognize his own cow anywhere and under any circumstances, he was almost beside himself with grief and rage, and rushed to the garden where one of the Fathers chanced to be and asked for the loan of the mission boat to try to rescue his cow. He and two others piled into the boat and paddled across to intercept the croc which was swimming strongly upstream, still carrying the cow. As the boat approached the brute, one of the men lunged with his spear at its eye, whereupon the croc released the cow and submerged. The men managed to tow the animal, a full-grown heifer, to the bank, but the poor animal had been so badly lacerated by the croc's teeth that a few moments after the owner had got it ashore it collapsed and died.

I suppose that anyone who has lived in Africa for any length of time will have some story to tell of an encounter with a snake in which he considers himself fortunate to have escaped without being bitten. My own was an occasion when out goose shooting; I fell and found myself on all fours over a large cobra coiled up in the grass and escaped, I believe, owing to a truly marvelous backward somersault. Other Fathers in the Prefecture have had similar narrow escapes. One going out hunting when on holiday at our Mission at Yoynyang, at the last moment discarded an old pair of pumps in favor of knee-high mosquito boots, considering that they would afford him better protection against thorns and sharp-edged grasses. He had not gone far when a puff adder, a most deadly snake, wrapped itself round his leg. That last minute nudge from his guardian angel undoubtedly saved his life.

Another Father, on holiday at Yoynyang, obtained there some young saplings that he intended to plant in his own mission. The trees had been dug up with a good base of soil round the roots and the Father carried them one by one across the compound in order to wrap the roots in sacking. As he put one down, he found that he had been hugging, if not a viper to his bosom, certainly an adder, for there was one coiled around the stem of the tree unnoticed against the black soil. Why the Father was not bitten is, humanly speaking, a mystery, for the puff adder strikes on any provocation and with lightning-like swiftness. The priest's guardian angel must have interposed himself between him and the snake, and so he lived to give thanks for his escape.

The snake, apart from the more or less harmless grass snake, most commonly met with in our part of the country is the spitting cobra. It is jet black in color, and a large specimen may attain a length of about six feet. When alarmed or angered it rises up out of its coils and spreads its hood menacingly. It has the unpleasant faculty of being able to spit its venom with great force, and one of our Fathers who measured the distance of one such poisonous ejection found it to be over fourteen feet. If the poison lands on an unbroken surface of skin it seems to do no harm, but were it to alight on an open cut or sore, then presumably the effects would be as serious as if the victim were bitten and would require prompt first aid if his life were to be saved.

One of the Fathers of Detwok will remember his encounter with a spitting cobra. He had made an unsuccessful attempt to kill it, and the reptile reared up and spat its poison in his face. The fact that he wore spectacles probably saved him from blindness; a little did enter in the corner of his eye, but since the in-

cident took place close to the convent he was able to get immediate aid from the Sisters. As it was, his eye was bloodshot and
inflamed for a long time afterwards. Some of the poison landed
on the priest's white cassock, and the cloth became discolored
and rotted away as though burned with acid.

A boy ran to my room one afternoon to tell me that there were
many snakes in the Sisters' compound. I took a stout stick and
a shot gun and went across to the enclosure behind the convent
to find the Sisters and many of the children hopping excitedly
around a large heap of brushwood that had been gathered for
the cooking fires. The Reverend Mother told me, with what I
thought to be mild exaggeration, that the wood was full of snakes,
but on peering through the mass of branches I revised my opinion, for the wood did indeed seem to be alive with writhing coils
and flickering tongues. I singled out one large fellow lying along
a branch and poking the gun through the tangle of wood blew
him to pieces. As I did so, a six-footer slithered out of the
thicket and, covering ground at incredible speed, disappeared
down a hole near a store room. It was quite a large hole, on the
site of an old well that had been filled in.

Some time previously the earth had subsided to a depth of
about two feet, and the Sisters, instead of having the hole
filled up, had merely placed a piece of tin over it. I pushed
this aside and received the shock of my life, for from a little
tunnel at the side of the hole seven or eight heads popped out
as though inquiring into the meaning of the intrusion. I could
not get the muzzle of the shotgun into the tunnel, so, collecting
a number of bottles and breaking them, I blocked up the tunnel
to prevent the occupants escaping, while a workman filled up
the hole with bricks and earth. The brushwood was carefully
pulled to pieces but no more snakes were found. The impression that both Mother and I got of the place being alive
with snakes was caused by the convolutions of the two large
cobras that were raising a family in the hole and had come out
for fresh air and exercise among the branches of the brushwood.

On another occasion an urgent message from the Sisters sent
me across to the convent late one evening. A large snake, it

appeared, had made its home in the woodshed, which also served as a roosting place for the Sisters' hens, and was playing havoc among the fowls. A Brother and myself had the task of emptying the room, a long narrow passage under the staircase leading to the chapel, which was piled high with bundles of wood, by the light of a storm lamp, in order to get at and kill the pest. Blinded by sweat, bitten incessantly by clouds of mosquitoes and impeded by fluttering and squawking hens that insisted on returning to their lodging as often as we threw them out, we gradually cleared the place of most of the wood. At last we got a glimpse of the snake, slithering in and out among the pieces of wood left. The Brother took a hasty shot at it with the .22 rifle he had brought, but missed it, and the reptile disappeared toward the bottom of the pile. We had to continue to throw the wood out, but we worked very cautiously now, since we had no desire to find our hands full of very lively and very angry snake. Eventually we saw it again, when we had cleared nearly all the wood, four feet of cobra lying along the floor close to the wall. I managed to get a telling clout at it with a stick, and then an extraordinary thing happened. The serpent opened its jaws to an incredible angle, nearly 180 degrees, and one — two — three — four large duck eggs that it had recently swallowed were disgorged. The eggs were quite intact, the shells not even cracked. A couple more blows with the stick put an end to one more nuisance and the indignant hens were able to return to roost in peace.

Natives frequently come to the Sisters for first aid for snake bites. The remedy which has always proved effective for both snake and scorpion bites is to slash the flesh around the affected place and then bathe it in a strong solution of permanganate of potash and very hot water. This is repeated two or three times a day, and after three or four days, or in bad cases a week or longer, the poison is counteracted and the limb becomes normal again.

During my years at Detwok there has been only one fatality from snake bite and that was due to our not being able to give the poor victim assistance in time. Very late one night I was awakened by a voice outside my window calling for help. Slipping on a cassock, I went out and found a man lying on the ground and moaning. He had been fishing at the river bank when he had trodden on a snake and had been bitten in the heel. It had taken the poor fellow about two hours to crawl from the river to the house. He was unable to walk and so I had practically to carry him to the dispensary. I called a Sister and we did what we could for the man, but it was far too late for effective help. I had him carried to a hut for the remainder of the night, but in the morning he was dead.

And so our rather humdrum existence is enlivened now and again by an encounter with a beast, a brute, or a reptile. It adds a little excitement to an otherwise uneventful life and provides one with yet another story with which to bore one's fellow priests at the next meeting with them. They listen with admirable patience considering that one such narrative is very like another, and considering, too, that they are simply bursting with impatience to find a listener to the graphic account of their own latest meeting and narrow escape from hippo, croc, or snake.

RECOGNITION

When Christ went up to Calvary,
  His crown upon His head,
Each tree unto its fellow tree
  In awful silence said:
"Behold the Gardener is He
Of Eden and Gesthsemane!"

—JOHN BANNISTER TABB

THE DEATH OF
CHARLES DE FOUCAULD

by R. V. C. Bodley

A French Vicomte who became a hermit in the Sahara
wastes left his mark upon Africa.

A little earlier in the year, Si Mohammed Labed, paramount
chief of the Senussi, had captured and occupied Ghat, the
capital of Fezzan on the borders of Libya about 250 miles from
Tamanrasset. The defeated Franco-Italian garrison had abandoned quantities of modern arms at Ghat, and this formidable
religious leader intended to launch attacks on the French and
their supporters, who included Moussa and his few loyal
Tuareg of the Hoggar.

Ouksem ag Chikkat had already gone over to the enemies of
France, but this other small group of veiled warriors had ignored all persuasions and threats from Senussi headquarters.
Si Mohammed Labed was baffled by this illogical devotion
to the French cause, especially when it seemed lost in Europe,
but there were rumors that it was due to a white Marabout
who lived alone at Tamanrasset and had some kind of mysterious hold over Moussa and his Tuareg. Si Mohammed Labed
decided that the removal of this infidel hermit was essential
to the success of his projects. The capture of this man might
also be a source of prestige and profit if he could hold him as a

hostage. He accordingly gave instructions that the white holy man be captured and brought to Ghat. The execution of this mission he entrusted to a Targui chief, El Keraan, an enemy of Moussa, with authorization to use whatever methods he thought best and to employ as many men as he considered necessary, and with the promise of financial as well as honorary rewards.

On December 1, 1916, Foucauld followed the usual routine of the hermitage — visiting sick "parishioners," correspondence, and religious devotions. As the day drew to a close, Paul returned to his hut in the village where he preferred to sleep and sup, free from the rather rigorous conditions his master followed. Foucauld watched him go, and for a few minutes paced restlessly up and down the well-worn path outside his fortress home. Then, with a shrug, he went inside. Locking and barring the doors he retired to the chapel to pray and meditate and read. From now until sunrise, when Paul came back, he would be safe from outside interruptions.

The walls of the fort were six feet thick and twenty feet high, with loopholes running along the top and bastions jutting out at each corner. There was only one door and this was protected by a shield of mud bricks, so that anyone who opened it would be safe from a distant sniper. The door was so small and narrow that a man could not pass through the entrance erect and had to walk in a crouching position along a low passage to another door which led into the interior courtyard of the fort. In the middle of this courtyard was a reliable well and around it were storerooms, living rooms, and the chapel. There was plenty of food and arms and ammunition. Unless an enemy came with artillery, the place could withstand an indefinite siege.

Thus, had Foucauld been more on the alert for what, as an intelligence officer, he should have known might be afoot in that part of the Sahara, or if he had been less trusting in the loyalty of all of his "parishioners," he might have outlived his less worthy contemporary, Marshal Pétain, who did not die until 1951. Unfortunately for himself, as well as for France, he was not only trusting but complacent.

The sun was setting over the black pinnacles of the Djebel Debnat, the Enchanted Mountains of the Hoggar, when El Keraan and his thirty men rode into Tamanrasset. They had come a long way from their base and were eager to accomplish their mission and get back with their captive for the reward before any French column had been alerted. But when they saw the fort on the high ground a few hundred yards away they recognized that, even with their modern Italian rifles, any attempt to capture their victim by force would be a waste of time. A ruse of some kind must be devised.

Some Targui dissidents who had joined the Senussi suggested that a freed Negro slave of Tamanrasset, El Madani, might be made use of. He was on friendly terms with the hermit and knew his habits. El Madani was summoned from his hut and, after a good deal of argument and threats, accepted the treacherous mission. Whether he did this through fear or cupidity, or merely because he felt that it might be wiser to be on the strongest side, has not been established.

El Madani led the raiders, now numbering forty or so, to the fortress, where they concealed themselves in the trench which surrounded it. He then went and knocked at the door, using a signal known to Foucauld. After a few minutes, the unbarring of the inner door was heard, followed by footsteps coming to the outer door. The priest's voice asked:

"Who's there?"

"Your slave, El Madani. I have the mail for you."

Now, not only was it quite normal for the carriers to leave the mail in the village if they were in a hurry, and El Madani a likely person to be entrusted with it, but this also happened to be mail day. The opening of the door was, therefore, as natural a gesture as when Paul came to work in the morning. Nevertheless Foucauld showed a certain caution. Drawing back the bolts, he did no more than thrust out his hand to receive the letters. This was enough. Fingers like steel claws gripped his wrist and jerked him outside like a fish on a hook. Other men seized him and bound his arms behind his back and flung him into the trench.

After the first instinctive gesture of self-defense, Foucauld ceased to make any resistance. He neither struggled nor spoke. All he did was to scrutinize El Madani with a certain expression of curiosity mingled with compassion. Madani tried to avoid the burning black eyes which seemed to bore into him, but they followed him relentlessly. He slunk away and, according to his own account, had no further part in the rapidly unfolding drama.

While Foucauld lay crumpled in the ditch, most of the bandits poured into the fort, breaking down the doors and shouting with delight as they discovered what to them was fabulous treasure. Three dozen magazine rifles, boxes of cartridges, sacks of barley and flour, tinned foods, tea and sugar in quantities they had never seen, rolls of cloth and calico and linen. It was fantastic! Such commodities were not to be bought anywhere in the Sahara.

Fortunately Foucauld's papers and diaries and manuscripts meant nothing to them. They were tossed about in the search for gold which the raiders felt certain must be hidden in this Aladdin's treasure house, but they were not damaged.

Meanwhile two raiders, probably on a hint from El Madani, had gone down to Paul Embarek's hut. Binding him up, they brought him to the fort and pushed him into the trench beside Foucauld, where he lay whimpering and begging for mercy. A Targui youth, Sermi ag Thora, mounted guard over the prisoners with a cocked rifle.

By this time night had fallen. The raiders, somewhat calmed down after the excitement of ransacking the fort, began to wonder what to do next. Some of them attempted ineffectively to force Foucauld to pronounce the *Chachada*, which amounts to recanting any faith in favor of Islam. Others, more practically minded, tried to cross-examine their prisoner about French troops in the neighborhood and when he expected a convoy. Foucauld took no notice of the questions. He seemed to have detached himself from worldly matters and with closed eyes continued to pray. When El Keraan told him that his life depended on his speaking, he replied: *"Baghi n'mout* — This is the hour of my death."

The other raiders, knowing that they would forfeit their reward if they killed the white Marabout, suggested that he might give information about the troops as well as about the gold under torture. Before any decision about this could be made, the sentries who had been placed on the edge of the dried-up watercourse came doubling back to the fort. They had seen the outline of two Meharists moving on their camels up the *oued*.

The Senussi and Targui bandits immediately lined the trench with their rifles ready. Foucauld became alert. His officer's instinct had taken control of the priest's. He must warn these soldiers who he realized were the real mail carriers, but he was tied so tightly that his only chance of saving the men would be by shouting. As he was struggling to raise himself into a position against the wall so that his voice would carry to the Meharists, their silhouettes appeared against the now starry sky. Instantly twenty rifles cracked, the silhouettes vanished. The camels and their riders, riddled with bullets, rolled down into the stony river bed.

At that moment young Sermi ag Thora lost his head. Perhaps he feared that the Meharists were coming in force to rescue his captive. Placing the muzzle of his carbine against Foucauld's temple, he pulled the trigger. The priest's body shuddered and stiffened, then went limp. With what might have been a sigh of relief, it gradually collapsed and slid gently to the bottom of the trench. The eyes were open and stared sightlessly at the stars which flashed down from the black tropical sky.

The Sahara had claimed her lover, and for eternity — claimed him the way he would have wished. For among the papers later found in the fort was the following note in Foucauld's handwriting:

Consider that you must die a martyr, shorn of everything, stretched on the ground, naked and unrecognizable, covered with blood and wounds, violently and painfully killed and, furthermore, hope that this may take place today. In order that this favor may be granted, be faithful at all times to watch and bear your cross. Reckon always that your life must lead to this end, and recollect, accordingly, how unimportant are most things of this world. Reflect often on this death so that you will be ready for it and be able to judge everything at its true value.

For the raiders there were no pious thoughts. Their hostage was dead and recriminations would do no good. With Moslem resignation to the inevitable, they had to think of a way out of their quandary. Might it be a good idea to take the white Marabout's body back to Ghat and trust to getting some of the reward? Or would Si Mohammed Labed be better pleased if the corpse of the infidel were left to be eaten by jackals and hyenas?

While these arguments were going on, the Targui contingent of the raiding party, which had no interest in rewards and little in Moslem fanaticism, had cut up the Meharists' camels, lit a brush fire, and were roasting great lumps of flesh. With the oil and tea and sugar and other supplies from the fort, there was the making of a feast usually associated with the wedding of some wealthy chieftain. The Senussi warriors sniffed the grilling meat and, leaving their problems in the hands of Allah, joined the banquet.

It was a wild spectacle with the red flames fed with desert scrub flaring fiercely and lighting up these warriors, armed and exultant, as they devoured the sizzling steaks and drank the mint-flavored, sugary tea. It had some of the extravagance and picturesqueness of another banqueting scene nearly fifty years before, when the Vicomte Charles de Foucauld entertained on the frozen surface of the Moselle for a lovely lady with violet eyes. . . The uniforms were more somber tonight and it was not so cold as a French winter. Nor was there the fine crockery and the spindle-legged glasses of sparkling champagne as at the Pont-á-Mousson skating party of 1880. But the guests were all military men and their host was supplying the food and the drinks.

He was not feasting but he was there, bodily in the trench and spiritually nearby, smiling compassionately at these later warrior bandits gorging themselves. Like the extravagant Foucauld parties, the banquet kept going until dawn. Then only did these gentlemen of the sword and the tent leave the smoldering fires and pile all they could onto their camels, ready to move. They were now in too good spirits to be concerned with the disposal of the body of their victim. Unfortunately, though, just before they got on their way the mail carrier, coming from Motylinski to collect Foucauld's out-going letters, rode up to the fort. Before he could sense what was going on he was shot dead, and his body left on the desert with the other murdered Meharists. Someone suggested killing Paul, but no one was interested enough to dismount. The raid had been successful, there was food to keep everyone on full rations for some time to come, and enough rifles and ammunition to arm a powerful striking force which could bother the French and Italians for quite a while. This ought to satisfy Si Mohammed Labed and make up for not having produced the white Marabout.

As the sun rose, the column sped away in a cloud of rosy dust and disappeared into the Enchanted Mountains of the Hoggar highlands.

Then only did the Tuareg of Tamanrasset dare to leave their huts and investigate what had been going on during that night of shooting and fires and feasting, to see what had happened to their friend whom they had not dared to defend. Consternation and grief followed the discovery of the body. No one knew quite how to act. Finally they decided to cover him with sand and heavy stones until someone in authority came to Tamanrasset. This they did, without even untying the bonds which held his arms.

Then they released Paul and covered the three Meharists in the same way as Foucauld, where they had fallen. Such was their respect for the priest and so great his prestige that no one went inside to loot the fort or even to find out what the raiders had done. Instead they bricked up the entrance and went despondently back to their homes, knowing that they had lost some-one who had become part of their lives and could never be adequately replaced.

Charles de Foucauld, Viscount, Lieutenant, and Reverend Father, never brought any Tuareg to Christianity, but he es-tablished the kind of friendships among these warrior people which no officer nor White Father nor doctor, with all their prestige and authority and experience, ever approached. Whether he fell in the service of God or of France or of both is of no real importance. What matters is that he died practicing what he be-lieved in — kindness and tolerance to all men regardless of their faiths. His greatness comes from those traits, his memory is kept alive in the wildernesses of the Sahara because of them. When the governors and generals and bishops of Algeria in their splen-did graves have outlived their grandiloquent epitaphs, Foucauld's name will remain in tradition and folklore among the wandering peoples of North Africa for whom he did so much with so little.

SONG FOR TODAY, I

I go tonight
*   where the whole world ends,*
down to the sand
and the shore of the sea,
to listen to the music
in the swell of the tide
washing itself on the
long pebble drainboard of beach,
and in the busy rustle
of water on sand,
I hear more songs
than a world can tell.

—JOHN GEITNER, M.M.

GANDHI AND THE CROSS OF CHRIST

by Anthony Elenjimittan

India's great spiritual and political leader gives an appreciation of the meaning of the cross.

Of all the precursors in India who point out the ideal of the Christian way of life, the latest, the nearest, and the most influential prophet was Mahatma Gandhi. Philosophically, Gandhi was the Indian Socrates; politically, he was the Indian Abraham Lincoln; and religiously he was the Hindu St. John pointing out the gospel of the Christian cross. In this world, creeds there are many indeed, but there is only one cross. If the cross means the crucifixion of the flesh and the resurrection of the spirit, then Gandhi was one of the foremost apostles of the Christianity that centers around "Jesus and him crucified."

In December 1946, I accepted an invitation from the American Friends Ambulance Unit in Calcutta, and went with them to do relief work in Noakhali, East Bengal, where Mahatma Gandhi was camping with his followers for the exclusive purpose of offering the olive branch of peace to the Hindus and Moslems who were then killing each other in the name of religion. Pakistan, or a separate homeland for the Moslem community, was the cry in the air when India was on the threshold of her independence. It was the outbreak of communal riots in various parts

*From the magazine *The Priest,* Huntington, Indiana.

of India that finally made the Congress and Gandhi accede to the partition of the country, that political vivisection which was the most painful birthpang of Indian independence.

I had met him thrice before; but I thought my stay and work with him in Noakhali would give me that personal experience, that experiential knowledge of the frail-looking man whom I have always considered as the greatest man I ever had the good fortune to know on this planet.

On the same day I reached the Quaker camp in Hamchadi village, I hired a cycle and went to meet Gandhi, who was then living at Srirampur, about six miles from our camp. I had to wait some two hours to be received into his room. On seeing me, Gandhi said:

"So, Anthony, you have come to see me here, instead of coming to Sevagram? Well, here also you can do useful work in bringing peace in the riot-stricken areas . . . Yes, peace! 'Blessed are the peacemakers, for they shall be called the children of God.' "

That very same evening I attended his prayer meeting. Twice daily Gandhi would conduct prayer with his disciples and the vast crowds that usually followed him wherever he went. His public prayer meetings at 4:30 A.M. and at 7 P.M. consisted in the recitation of select verses from the Gita, the Vedas, the Bible, and other religious scriptures which Indian citizens use in their respective religious communities. Then were sung beautiful religious, devotional hymns chosen from Hindu, Buddhist, and Christian sources.

But the most attractive part of his prayer meeting consisted in the ten-minute address which Gandhi used to give dealing with God, the soul, immortality, and other religious topics. His speeches were not prepared orations, but the simple, natural overflow of his deeper convictions and realizations. The center and circumference of all his whole life and his superhuman achievements — for to gain independence from the British with not a single shot fired or armed rebellion is indeed a superhuman achievement — are to be found in his living faith in the living God.

God's finger, God's breath was so transparently clear in his life.

This living faith in God gave him that indomitable willpower and that God-angle of vision which urged him to undertake the "impossible."

When after the First World War Gandhi told his countrymen that we should win complete political independence from the British, even the closest and most stalwart disciples of his, like the late Sardar Patel and the Nehru family members, said: "Oh, it is impossible!" But the impossible is now an achieved fact.

Gandhi used to repeat the Pauline dictum: "Do not be overcome by evil, but overcome evil with good."

A strong theistic faith, moral values, and ethical imponderables colored all the political activities of Gandhi. To him, even the independence of India was to be but a step in the ladder of spiritual perfection, to reach God nearer and closer.

I attended his evening prayer meetings some twenty-eight times. What impressed me most was his deliberate insistence that the only purpose of human life was God-vision *(Brahma-darsan)*, and that the royal road for man to reach God is renunciation of the self and acceptance of all the crosses that God sent in fulfilling His will on earth.

The Greek wise men said: Know thyself. The Christian mystics said: *Noverim me, noverim te!* May I know myself, may I know Thee! The Hindu sages said: *Atmanam Vidhi, Devam Vijijna* — Know thy soul, know God. Well, Gandhi achieved his superhuman powers through a profound knowledge of his own soul, with all its limitations and sinfulness, and his knowledge and love of God, made real and dynamic through his love of his fellow humans, especially the underdogs, the downtrodden, the oppressed. The outcastes and the lowest strata of the Indian society Gandhi renamed *Harijans,* which means the people of God.

To him, work was worship. The Benedictine motto: *Orare et laborare* — to pray and work, found its most dynamic echo in

Gandhi's life as we have seen it from closest quarters. It is known that Gandhi was profoundly impressed by the monks of the contemplative orders of the Catholic Church. In November 1934, Gandhi set the Trappist ideal before his Congress workers to be appreciated and followed. Gandhi then said:

"Near Durban, in South Africa, there is a Trappist monastery. The rigor observed at the time I visited the place was very great. They had nothing like privacy for themselves. They had to get up at 2:30 A.M. They had a purely vegetarian diet. They strictly observed the vow of silence. Only two or three, who had to go to the market or speak to visitors, could speak. All others had to work in silence. They were giving instruction to the Zulus. They were workers for life. They added to their learning a calling. They were carpenters, potters, shoemakers. They made all sorts of experiments. Their monastery was a model of beauty, a veritable garden, with not a particle of dust anywhere, and there was a sweet silence pervading the whole atmosphere. My idea is to have a training institution of this type; if anything, I would do better; but we are fallen from grace. We used to have this rigorous discipline in our country. But we have not progressed, while they have progressed."

Gandhi always felt that Hindu India had "fallen from grace," losing her ancient discipline and ideals. On several occasions he acknowledged that the Catholic Church progressed far ahead of the Hindus because of the disciplined army of monks and nuns and dedicated souls. When I lived with him in Hoakhali, twice, while accompanying him in his evening walks, Gandhi asked me even the minute details of the Dominican Order to which I belonged.

There are two monastic vows which were dearest and nearest to the heart of Gandhi; they were his vows of celibacy and voluntary poverty. He advised social workers to take the vows of chastity and poverty, if they were strong in soul and sturdy in body, to accept life as an adventure in the service of God and man.

Gandhi's life was his message. His life of voluntary poverty was such that many Western writers compared him to Francis of Assisi in wedding his life to Lady Poverty. I have myself seen the mud hut in which that seminaked "Father of Free India" lived and worked in Wardha. I remember how in No-akhali, Gandhi would not surrender a worn-out pencil of about two inches and accept a new one for his use from his grand-daughter, saying: "We must waste nothing."

Once a group of missionaries, in late autumn 1938, and some leading Christian statesmen from the West held a conference in Madras. Prior to their meeting, they went to Gandhi to seek his advice. He told them:

"I think that you cannot serve God and Mammon both. And my fear is that Mammon has been sent to serve India and God has remained behind, with the result that He will one day have His vengeance . . . I have always felt that when a religious organization has more money than it requires, it is in peril of losing faith in God and pinning its faith on money. You have simply to cease to depend on it.

"In South Africa when I started the Satyagraha March, there was not a copper in my pocket, and I went with a light heart. I had a caravan of 3,000 people to support. 'No fear,' I said. 'If God wills it, He will carry it forward.' Then money began to rain from India. I had to stop it, for when the money came, my miseries began. Whereas they were content with a piece of bread and sugar, they now began asking for all sorts of things."

Yes, the life of Gandhi, his outlook on life and the means and weapons he chose to fight were all a living commentary on the words of Our Lord: "Lay not up to yourselves treasures on earth, where the rust and moth consume and where thieves break through and steal." In fact, the Sermon on the Mount which Gandhi repeated formed the basis of his philosophy of life, was lived to the best of his lights and ability. Besides the ethics, morals, and ideals contained in the Sermon on the Mount, the life and sacrifice of Jesus on the cross were ever an inspiration and strength to him.

Of the number of Christian hymns used in Gandhi's Ashram, sung by him in his prayer meetings, oft-quoted and meditated upon, is the following:

"When I survey the wondrous cross
On which the Prince of Glory died,
My richest gain I count but loss,
And pour contempt on all my pride.
Forbid it, Lord, that I should boast
Save in the cross of Christ, my God.
All vain things that charm me most,
I sacrifice them to His blood . . . "

This man had the courage to live his faith, even unto Calvary. He offered his life to an assassin's bullet while he was leading his people to prayer. I had the rare privilege of knowing him, and because of this closer association I am also among those who called him "Bapu," which means Father. Paradoxically, this "Hindu" helped me most to fathom deeper the mystery of the Christian cross through his example.

SONG FOR TODAY, II

I will walk
*   among the pink*
and the mist
of the night,
among the
many-patterned images
printed on the rim of the world,
printed aginst the dying sun,
walking among silent images
while plangent soundings
well up,
rise
and fade.

—JOHN GEITNER, M.M.

FATHER OF CALIFORNIA

by Dana Thomas

> Because of the unshakable faith of Junipero Serra, Spain
> did not abandon California and the foundations of
> Christianity were laid.

Father Junipero had not always been a missionary. Indeed, until
the age of thirty-six, he had lived the quiet sheltered life of a professor of philosophy in his native Majorca. He had gained a distinguished reputation and had won many academic honors. Then
suddenly, to the dismay of his colleagues — and over their objec-
tions — he gave up his life of security and rushed off to the New
World to enroll as a missionary friar.

Never once during the hardships he later experienced serving
among the Indians of the Sierra Gorda and the Apache tribes did
he utter a word of complaint. On the trip overseas to the New
World he had made clear his attitude toward personal suffering.
When a fellow passenger had protested the shortage of drinking
water aboard ship, he had replied, "I have found a remedy for
thirst, my friend. It is to eat very little and talk less. That does
not waste the saliva."

Fray Junipero rose to the very top of his profession during his
service in New Spain. Now, at fifty-five he was *presidente* of
the missions in Lower California, an area that today is part of
Mexico.

Immediately after his conference with the Father Guardian, Fray Junipero set out for Santa Ana, where Señor Gálvez had temporarily established his lodgings with a wealthy dealer in pearls.

Gálvez was a gracefully proportioned Malagan with shrewd bold eyes. He greeted the padre warmly.

"*Ave Maria Purissima!* You Franciscans are certainly a hardy lot. Señor Presidente, I have heard stories about your missionary labors. But—begging your pardon if I am alluding to a delicate subject—I hadn't realized that you accomplished all this with a crippled leg!"

"My lameness has not prevented me from doing my duty."

The other smiled. "No, of course not. Well, here is the news briefly. We have received a report from our intelligence in St. Petersburg that Russia has crossed from Siberia over to the Aleutian Islands and is reaching out for the fur trade in North America. It is a well-known fact that the Empress Catherine is hungry for new seaports. And we fear that she may already have begun explorations down the California coast.

"To prevent California from falling into Muscovite hands, I have immediate orders to march north to garrison San Diego and Monte Rey. Incidentally, Monte Rey will provide a relief station for our galleons from Manila."

The preparations for the present expedition into New California were thorough. Cattle were slaughtered to provide the necessary meat. Many varieties of seeds from Spain were labeled carefully and packed away in the holds of ships to be planted in the wilderness. One hundred and twenty-five pounds of garlic were stored, together with quantities of red pepper and dried chocolate to be converted into a delicious, almond-flavored drink. Engineers, a surgeon, a baker, a cook, and a tortilla maker boarded the *San Carlos.* Carpenters and blacksmiths climbed aboard her sister ship, the *San Antonio,* and companies of soldiers assembled to make the journey by foot.

Father Junipero limped back and forth on his game leg, making his own preparations. From the missions in Lower California, he collected seven large church bells, pictures of the

Virgin, *purificadores,* silver vials for the sacred oil, goblets and censers for the churches to be established in New California. The trip to collect these furnishings aggravated his ulcerated ankle. When he set out for Velicatá to join the expedition, he had to be lifted bodily onto his mule.

Gaspar de Portolá, the commander of troops under whom he was scheduled to march, found him stretched out in bed. He shook his head dubiously.

"Father, I cannot take along an invalid. You will only hamper us on the trip."

But Father Junipero insisted on his right to come. He had already recruited a party of Franciscan friars to work under him in New California; in fact, they had already proceeded to San Diego with the sea units of the expedition, and he was determined to join them at any cost.

Portolá finally yielded. "I'll have a stretcher built, and you'll be carried by the Indian converts accompanying us."

The friar protested vigorously. "That is no solution. I cannot permit the Indians to carry me over the mountain trails. They will be tired enough."

"How will you come then, Father!" exclaimed Don Gaspar sharply.

The friar considered the matter from every angle. Then he summoned Jean Antonio Coronel, the veterinarian.

"Son, can you cure my leg?"

"Reverend Father, I can only heal the sores of beasts."

"Then let us suppose, in this emergency, that I am one of your charges. Give me the medicine you would use for a mule!"

Jean Antonio laughed. "*Nombre de Dios!* If it will give you pleasure, I'll do it."

He prepared an ointment of tallow and herbs and applied it to the padre's leg. Perhaps the cure was psychological—at any rate, the pain lessened considerably. Fray Junipero rested quietly that night, and the following morning he was able to ride his mule although the wound remained open.

On the 16th of May, 1769, the column under Portolá, the fourth and last to depart, set out for San Diego, five hundred miles to the north. Under a brilliant morning sky, a picked squad of *Soldatos de Cuero* led the march, carrying axes to hack a passage through the underbrush. Behind them rode the military escort in sleeveless jackets fashioned from several layers of deerskin as protection against Indian arrows. Mounted on Castilian horses, the riders wore leather aprons fastened to their saddles, unfolding to the ground to protect the thighs against the semi-tropical underbrush. Each soldier carried a flintlock carbine cased in leather, a sabre, and a lance. The pack trains followed, together with the muleteers, Fray Junipero, and the Indian converts.

Following carefully prepared maps, the column traveled over parched ravines in the direction of the Contra Costa, climbing rough mountain trails and making difficult descents. No sooner did the weary travelers gain one difficult summit, nourished by the hope they would see level plain ahead, than they were disheartened by the view of a chain of mountains just beyond. All day the sun beat down unmercifully. Camp was pitched for the night where it seemed likely that holes could be dug for water. But often the shovels merely turned up mud. Then there was only what little water remained from that carried in skin bags from the previous camp.

The extreme dryness and transparency of the air threw the landscape out of perspective and deceived the eye as to distances. On occasion they saw sheet lightning rise from the blistering ground into the sky, and a huge cactus or a *garambullo* standing monster-like against foreshortened stretches of plain. They passed through dense cottonwood, over slippery *brancas* whose banks abounded with prickly pear six feet high, and through marshland choked with tule, encountering in clearings Indian *rancherias* that had apparently been hastily abandoned at their coming. Once they came upon an Indian cemetery where the grave of a local chief was marked by a grass cape unfurled from a pole.

Indian scouts alerted their tribes to the arrival of the Spaniards. The natives swarmed in numbers around the encampment, friendly and with childlike curiosity. They wore their hair in perukes plastered with white clay. Fray Junipero welcomed them on behalf of the travelers, although, for some time now, he had been in severe pain. The long miles on muleback had exhausted him, and his ankle was once again an angry ulcer. But he superintended the feeding of the visitors, introducing them to Castilian delicacies, and in return he accepted their baskets of atole and pinale, and bags made from wildcat skins. They plagued the father with their demands. They begged him for his robe, sandals, rosary. Once they made off with his spectacles. "The Lord knows I had some time getting them back," he wrote in his journal.

On traveled the column during hot, rainless days, wending its way through pastures of wild oats and patches of sycamore, over earth so finely powdered that the mules and horses skidded as if caught in a landslide.

Finally, on the morning of July first, forty-six days out of Velicatá, the salt of the sea was in every man's nostrils. The last hill was gained, and below—beyond shining sand dunes and the kelp of San Diego Bay—rode ships flying the Spanish flag.

But when the troops reached the encampment, they sensed that something was wrong. The *commandante,* Captain Rivera y Moncada, welcomed Portolá with a mournful face. "*Amigo mio,* I have terrible news!"

The water supply on the *San Carlos,* one of the two ships that had left Velicatá for San Diego, had become contaminated. This, combined with shortage of fresh provisions, led to an outbreak of disease. By the time the *San Carlos* reached port, every man aboard, including the captain and the ship's physician, was down with scurvy or dysentery. Tents were hastily erected by the crew of the sister ship which had arrived at San Diego earlier, and the sick were carried to them.

The dysentery spread rapidly in the encampment. For fourteen terrible days those who were still able to get about dug graves. The night was filled with prayers for the dying.

It was with particular sadness that Father Junipero celebrated requiem Mass for the dead. The soldiers discharged their carbines into the air, substituting the smell of gunpowder for incense and the sound of musketry for an organ. On this location, Fray Junipero made plans for building his first mission in New California, dedicated to a medieval Spanish saint—San Diego Alcalá.

The officers now met to discuss the carrying out of José de Gálvez' second directive—the garrisoning of Monte Rey. Since the number of healthy sailors was inadequate to man both ships, it was decided to proceed overland with foot troops. The *San Antonio* was sent back to San Blas with a skeleton crew for fresh provisions and reinforcements. Father Junipero was left at San Diego to supervise the nursing of the convalescents. Portolá set out to find the bay of Monte Rey, aided by Vizcaino's map and an account of the voyage of 1602.

But a frustrating thing happened. Although Portolá came practically to the edge of the body of water he was seeking he failed to sight it. For several weeks he crossed and recrossed his tracks in the vain search, on occasions camping only a few miles from Monte Rey. Meanwhile, his troops suffered severe hardships. Sixteen soldiers succumbed to scurvy and had to be strapped to the back of mules. Provisions were low, and the men were reduced to eating wild berries. Finally, Portolá gave orders to turn back to San Diego. When he arrived, he heard alarming news. The *San Antonio* had not yet returned with provisions from San Blas, and the supplies on hand were dangerously low.

He called a conference of officers and stated the facts bluntly. "*Nombre de Dios!* There are times when the wise soldier concedes defeat. Monte Rey has not been found. I am convinced that this port has been silted up by the shifting sands in the hundred and sixty-seven years since Vizcaino sighted it. The *San Antonio* has not arrived and who knows if it will? Perhaps they have already forgotten us in San Blas. With our supplies running out, there is but one thing to do to protect the lives of the men."

He regarded the assembled officers grimly. "We must quit New California!"

Don Fernando Rivera y Moncada nodded his head in agreement. "We cannot struggle indefinitely with evil luck," he said. "This expedition has lived under a blight from the outset. Let us start back for Velicatá now, while we still have enough food for our bellies."

Portolá turned to Lieutenant Don Pedro Fages, a shy, lean man with burning black eyes. "And you, Lieutenant. How do you feel?"

"I agree. The morale of my troops will soar when they hear of this decision."

Not a dissenting voice was heard.

And then, as Don Gaspar de Portolá turned to the job of preparing for the homeward trip, an elderly man limped into his headquarters.

"Señor Commandante, we must not abandon California."

"Fray Junipero," responded Portolá with the patience of a father dealing with a child, "if we remain much longer, we'll be eating wild herbs from the fields."

"The *San Antonio* will arrive with supplies. I am sure of it!" replied the padre. He reminded Portolá that it was a hundred and sixty-seven years since Vizcaino had first sailed up the coast of California, and that if the present expedition withdrew, conceding defeat, it was likely to be years or even generations — given the dilatory attitude of officials in Madrid — before a Spaniard would be sent to New California again.

"That can mean only one thing — by default it will go to the Muscovites. The Empress Catherine will pounce on San Diego!"

Fray Junipero's voice trembled. His features grew intense. "In any event, even if you leave California, Señor Commandante, I will remain!"

Don Gaspar laughed. "Indeed, do you propose to live all by yourself in the wilderness?"

The padre was serious. "I will stay with the Indians if they are willing. And, if they choose to do away with me — *dum spiro, spero*. I came to establish missions. I shall not go back."

He continued to drive home his points. "In laying plans for the missions, I studied the maps with Señor Gálvez. I am convinced that Monte Rey exists at the site designated by Vizcaino. Señor Commandante, remain here at least nine more days. I grant that the entire venture depends on the arrival of supplies. If the *San Antonio* doesn't arrive within this period, you will at least depart with a clearer conscience."

He added shrewdly: "Suppose it should be discovered after all that Monte Rey exists exactly where Vizcaino placed it. Will His Majesty in Madrid be quick to forget — or forgive — the error?"

Portolá bit his lip in vexation. The thrust had gone home. "Very well, Father. You may have your nine days. We will remain for you to say a novena. In the meantime, I'll send Rivera with an advance column to Velicatá and continue my packing."

Father Junipero walked among the troops, speaking with men of every rank, inspiring them with the flame of his own zeal. And he formulated plans of his own in case the worst happened. He paid a visit to Captain Gila of the *San Carlos* and persuaded him to remain, if necessary, after Portolá departed with his troops.

"I know the supplies will come. We can go ourselves by sea and search for Monte Rey."

Each morning he walked to the headland and looked out over the water for the *San Antonio*. As the final day of Portolá's stay in California approached without any sign of the ship, the priest prayed with utmost fervency. The will power that had turned this least physically qualified of missionaries into the controlling force of the crusade in New Spain was now being put to a severe test. On his knees, he recalled how he had given up his professorship in Majorca and what it had cost him to make this decision. And he remembered, too, the time he had held a burning taper to his flesh until the smell horrified his congregation in order to demonstrate how a man, if called upon, could endure pain. His was an uncompromising spirit.

On the ninth morning, he went down to the headland as usual and remained all day, watching the horizon. And then, just before twilight, he saw the faint outlines of a ship. But the vessel continued to move northward, oblivious of the men who had rushed in large numbers down to the water's edge. With the coming of evening it was lost to sight altogether.

During the night the encampment at San Diego was torn with discussion. Had the captain blundered past the port? Would he discover his mistake and return? Instead of the *San Antonio* might it have been a ship of another nation?

When the sun rose again, there was no sign of the vessel, and all that anxiously spent day the horizon was empty. Father Junipero alone remained confident. He pleaded with Portolá to postpone his departure for a few days. The distraught *commandante* had no longer the will to resist. His very career now depended on his avoiding an historic error.

He shrugged his shoulders. "Four, five more days, then."

And then, on November 24—the fifth day after the sighting of the ship—a cry from watchers thrilled the encampment. "*Jesus Maria!* She is returning!"

Under a brilliant noon sky the *San Antonio* rode into port and fired a salute. Her hold was loaded with provisions. On deck was a full complement of soldiers, sailors, artisans. Her mail pouches carried letters from José de Gálvez and the Viceroy himself. Juan Perez, the skipper, explained to Portolá why he had at first bypassed San Diego. Gálvez, confident that the expedition had reached Monte Rey, had ordered him to sail there directly. But when he was two hundred and fifty miles from port, his water supply ran short, and he landed at Point Conception to refill his casks. Here, Indians informed him that there were no white men north of this area. Accordingly, Perez turned and made sail for San Diego.

"It would have been serious indeed," he declared to Portolá, "if you had quit California. You would have had some explaining to do to His Excellency!"

It took no further urging now for the *commandante* to set out for Monte Rey. On his previous trip he had erected three crosses on the headlands to direct future explorers. His second cross had been planted on the heights of the very bay he had been seeking. This time he arrived at the water's edge. Eight days later, Fray Junipero, together with artisans and sailors, debarked from the *San Antonio*, which had been guided into the harbor at Monte Rey by a bonfire. The padre fell on his knees and chanted the *Veni Creator Spiritus*.

Determining to make Monte Rey the headquarters for his missionary activities, Fray Junipero hung a silver-throated bell on a stout branch of a tree, the first step in the establishment of a mission.

"Why do you do this?" asked a soldier. "There is no church as yet, and we have seen no Indians here."

"I hear them coming," answered the Father optimistically.

OUR LADY OF THE WORLD

With graceful mien and prayerful gaze,
*   Her sari draped in folds of blue,*
She teaches all her Son to praise.
Our Lady of the East.

She raises copper hands to bless
*   Her children of the plains.*
In blanket white or buckskin dress.
Our Lady of the Sioux.

From minaret to voodoo drum,
*   On desert waste and jungle green,*
She brings the joys of Christendom.
Our Lady of the South.

Her heart aflame in love for souls,
*   A Queen in silk or cotton,*
She pleads, gives hope, always consoles.
Our Lady of the World.

—DELLA GODAY

THE KING OF THE SEDANG

by Pierre Dourisboure and Christian Simonnet

A strange confidence man tries to build an empire in Vietnam.

But Baron de Mayréna had not come to be amused nor to amuse. And so he set off on a series of difficult expeditions, still accompanied by the indispensable Father Guerlach, to roam throughout the region and to conclude treaties with the principal chieftains. Gradually, however, the content of these treaties changed. It became less and less a question of a French protectorate, and more and more of a kingdom designed to federate all the tribes, taking the name of the largest among them, the Sedang.

This new kingdom needed a flag. Like a magician pulling a rabbit out of a hat, Mayréna extracted from his bags some superb azure-blue flags bearing a white cross adorned with arrows, with a red star in the center of the cross. Every chieftain who paid homage received one, and there were quite a few. This new kingdom needed a motto. Mayréna was very witty and cleverly manipulated puns. The motto of the kingdom of the Sedang would therefore be: "Never yielding, always helping." Above all, this new kingdom needed a king. Mayréna found him as easily as he had found flags and motto: he would be Marie I, and Marie I was Baron de Mayréna. (Why "Marie" when one

*From *Vietnam: Mission on the Grand Plateaus.* Copyright Maryknoll Publications.

has so much beard, for heaven's sake? Well, that was his affair, and it was a mere detail.) The Fathers were asked to sign as witnesses both the treaties and the constitutions that accompanied them. They were somewhat puzzled.

"But you shouldn't worry about it! It's a bit tricky, I admit. But in no case must I appear to be committing France. And then, won't it be advantageous to be as much at home as possible?"

Clearly, that also made sense. Besides, there were some excellent things in these constitutions: ban on declaring war between villages without the king's authorization. Ban on human sacrifice. Ban on the slave traffic with neighboring countries. The Catholic religion was the official religion of the kingdom, but religious freedom was guaranteed to all. The great war cry, in battle, would be: "God! France! Sedang!" All of this was obviously excellent—but everything did not run absolutely smoothly in the machinery of this intriguing system.

There was . . .

First of all, there was the one the Fathers scowlingly called "Queen Marie"; she was the little Annamese companion of Marie I, and it is clear that this union was not resplendent by its legitimacy. Marie I, whom nothing embarrassed, had indeed annulled a previous marriage contracted in France with the daughter of a colonel, from which union two children had been born. This annulment had been promulgated by "Royal Decree No. 37," but what did the Holy Office think of Royal Decree No. 37? To be sure, churchmen have long since learned to be patient on this point with the great of this world. Charlemagne, Louis XIV, who had their weaknesses, God knows, were nevertheless strong supporters of the Church—sometimes rather encumbering, no doubt—and then, when age and time had done their work, they became very proper, and even edifying, Christians.

There were constant incidents of protocol which complicated the most banal conversations. Marie I asked the Fathers to address him as "Sire," which was logical, and the Fathers could not manage to lose the habit of calling him "Monsieur," which is rather understandable. So they avoided calling one another anything; for the least matter they proceeded by means of circumlocution, to the point that it was enough to set one's teeth on edge, but one could hardly compromise the peace and future of the kingdom for a detail of protocol either!

There was the Marquis of Hénouï, and the Marquis of Hénouï was Alphonse Mercurol. For, besides Queen Marie, two Annamese interpreters, and four Chinese merchants, experts in gold-bearing soils, there was also a European in the retinue of the Baron de Mayréna. This Mercurol had had a few difficulties with the administration in Cochin-China over a matter of trafficking in arms, with Baron de Mayréna, naturally. Now, his faithfulness had been rewarded by the title conferred on him by Marie I—just as Marie I had named Father Irigoyen Grand Chaplain and, without delay, had written to the Pope to ask for a prelature for his new dignitary, at which the good Father was completely dumbfounded.

The Marquis de Hénouï was a former butcher's boy, who had recently been released after serving in the Marines. He had the awkward habit of getting drunk more often than was proper, which was, indeed, normal for an old colonial trooper and was not incompatible with the dignity of a marquis. The troublesome thing was that, when he was roaring drunk, he had the annoying habit of repeating like a leit motiv (among other stupidities) that Marie I had often told him that he would no doubt entrust him some day with a confidential mission: "liquidating" Father Guerlach. That too was nerve-wracking, but it was not proper, either, to attach too much importance to the lucubrations of a drunkard. The worst part of it was that he kept coming back to it constantly.

There was all the rest of the retinue (the court!) of Marie I. Its maintenance was very expensive—for the mission, of course; and since the four Chinese merchants and all the soldiers, deathly sick, spent their time stretched out on mats, Guerlach finally suggested that it would perhaps be preferable to send all these people to Saigon, and that the caravan could be entrusted to the leadership of the Marquis de Hénouï, for instance.

Guerlach had his way, and the Marquis de Hénouï, a new Du Guesclin,* did not have to be asked twice to lead this Grand Company, teeth chattering with fever and legs trembling, to Cochin-China.

Enroute, however, the Marquis de Hénouï had bartered all the expedition's supplies for a goose feather in which a few tiny gold nuggets could be seen. Arriving in Qui Nhon at the head of this half-starved retinue, whose condition loudly proclaimed the harshness of the epic which the mountain country had witnessed, Alphonse Mercurol revealed to the amazed world the creation of the Kingdom of the Sedang, the metamorphosis of the Baron de Mayréna into King Marie, his own elevation to the marquisate of Hénouï, the enthusiasm of the chieftains—and of the Fathers—the richness of the river sands, from which one raised one's boots all shining with fiery metal. The proof? What everyone could see in the goose feather! Thus spoke the Marquis de Hénouï, and then, still at the head of his twenty-odd poor exhausted devils, he departed for Saigon, whence he was never to return to ask about his marquisate.

In the early part of September 1888, what remained of the glorious expedition of April 21 reentered Qui Nhon, and headed slowly for the Bishop's house, somewhat on the outskirts of the town. The splendid man who had left four months earlier with such a brilliant company was an explorer. The man who was returning today, alone, his face etched with fatigue and fever, his forehead heavy with worry, was a king. He was alone, tragically alone. Queen Marie herself had been carried off by a deadly attack a few weeks before. But one felt a consuming respect in the presence of this man marked by suffering, but also by destiny. Did Louis XIV ever seem so great as in adversity? This is what Bishop Van Camelbeke must have thought as he listened to his guest explain the details of the fabulous expedition. Now, Marie I would proceed for several months to conduct a campaign of another type, for he needed

---

* A fourteenth-century French hero of the struggle against the English. One of his exploits was to lead the so-called "Grand Companies" out of France and into Spain.

official recognition of his kingdom, and money. Nothing would stop him, he confided to the Bishop. He would go to Hanoi, to Paris, if necessary, and even to Berlin, he would later specify!

Somewhat rested, Marie I officially confirmed by means of telegrams, letters, and reports addressed to everyone who was legally entitled (President of the French Republic, Governor General of Indochina, Minister of Foreign Affairs) all the marvels which Mercurol had proclaimed. He had barred the way to Siam and its Prussian agents. A good prince, he declared himself ready to conclude an alliance with France provided the latter was good enough to appear gentle and deferential; otherwise, he reserved the right to upset the alliances. Very much impressed, Resident Lemire sent a letter of congratulations to the monarch (still dug in at the Bishop's house), and a report to the Governor General urgently advising him to deal gently with this partner of stature. But Hanoi turned a deaf ear. Now the big game was on. But since the king has left his kingdom, and it is this kingdom which is our theater of operations, we shall sum up on the run and in a single sentence the end of the prestigious career of this hero.

Marie I alerted public opinion by means of the press, went up to Tonkin, ordered a thousand uniforms for his troops from a Chinese tailor from whom he borrowed money instead of paying him; went on to Hong Kong, presented to the Procurator General of the Foreign Missions a draft (phony) for two hundred thousand francs signed Van Camelbeke, was received by the French Consul, the Governor, and the bankers, distributed (against substantial loans) noble titles and decorations (Sedang Order of St. Margaret and Sedang Order of Merit); embarked for Europe, arrived in Paris where he was given a triumphant reception on the boulevards, contracted a third marriage with a (rich) widow who had been made a "noble damsel" for the occasion, sold a few Sedang duchies to some bankers; went to Ostend where he coined several Grand Chamberlain positions, issued postage stamps (listed by the catalogs of the period), left Marie-Rose (his third wife) in a hotel with the chest of royal jewels (empty) to pay the bill, was refloated in the nick of time by a large Belgian industrialist who was made prince and Minister of Finance for this exploit; shipped out incognito for the Far East in January 1890 with a retinue of five honorable Belgians, one of them the nephew of Minister Frère-Orban,* quickly set aside the incognito and became the real master of the ship after God and before the captain, named some consuls and recruited colored domestics at the ports of call; went ashore in Singapore while all the countries of Southeast Asia were panicking and sealing their frontiers, took a fourth wife (Malaysian), embraced Islam, and recruited three marabouts to preach the Koran to the Sedang in the face of the missioners who had repudiated him; mobilized some Indian and Malay soldiers (to which the government of the Malacca Straits was opposed), leased a cutter and sailed with his following to the isle of Sirabua, whence he sent his Belgian companions for provisions to Singapore (none ever returned); remained alone with Queen Aïsa, who soon ran off (carrying the music box with her); reached the island of Tioman (still off the Malay coast), where he was immediately joined by a sailing-ship captain in trouble with the owner, immediately made said captain minister of the Sedang navy, hunted wild pig to subsist, and died suddenly on November 11, 1890, under circumstances more suspicious than mysterious.

A fabulous man all the same, this Baron de Mayréna. It was just unfortunate that everything about him was phony: from his name (in reality, he was simply Charles David) to his death. For how did he die? Some years later, his companion, Captain Harold Scott, now a peaceable and honest pilot in the port of Haiphong, had a painting done by a Chinese artist to commemorate the historic Scott-Mayréna duel in which the King of the Sedang had met his death from a pistol shot. But the English official who examined the body before burial found no trace of any bullet. In his very detailed report, Mr. Owen opined that the death of Charles David had to be attributed to the bite of a black snake (the *tadong liar* of the Malays); still, he admitted that he had seen no trace of a bite from any creature whatsoever.

* A well-known Belgian political figure of the time.

And so the poor remains of Charles David rest, without a cross, in the small Malay cemetery on an islet isolated by the fury of the monsoons, while the character of Mayréna the charmer seems to be sublimated in the very ambiguity of his death.

One last point, however. Mayréna always had an obsession about poison. At the time of his return to Qui Nhon, it was noted that he would only drink from a rhinoceros horn which, as everyone knows, is supposed to have the power of neutralizing poisons. Whom did he fear then? The savage chieftains? Mercurol? The Fathers? Later on, in Paris, he stated that the Minister of Colonies had tried to have him poisoned! Now the report of the English official is quite according to form: the body of Mayréna bore not the slightest trace of any wound or bite. Was he poisoned then?

If so, by whom?

But that is another story.

YOU ANSWER . . .

A dog has looked at you,
    you answer for its glance.
A child has clutched your hand,
    you answer for its touch.
A host of men move about you,
    you answer for their need.

— MARTIN BUBER

MADONNA OF THE PALMS

Madonna of the whispering palms,
  the sighing waves
    and silent sands,
      listen to my plea.

I would not have you encumbered
      by stiff and starched, voluminous
      skirts of velvet and silk,
      trimmed with dainty lace,
      and glistening with the cold fires
      of fancy-colored gems,
      as now you stand on altars,
      fair with the features
      of the fairest in distant lands.
      Your pale beauty is as alien
      as paper flowers fading in your shrines;
      and alien, too, the Infant in your arms.

I would have you dusky of features
      like mine, and almond-eyed;
      midnight-black in your tresses,
      long-flowing and sweet-scented.
      I would have you in your striped
      many-colored tapis, *and sheer white*
      camisa *of* jusi *or* piña; *a red*
      pañuelo *around your neck,*
      setting off the garland
      of ilang-ilang *and* sampaguitas
      fragrant on your breast; and a dark-eyed
      Santo Niño *smiling in your arms.*

Madonna of the dancing palms,
  the laughing waves
    and singing sands,
      thus would I have you!

—IGNACIO FRANCISCO

INSTRUCTION TO MISSIONERS

A document from the Holy See to China missioners
given in 1659 is still relevant today.

By firmness of character, affability, gentleness, humility, and
every example of virtue, apostolic men should demonstrate by
action the Christian faith they profess by word. They must be
trained to live by the standard of evangelical charity.

By their natural dispositions and manners, they should be
capable of accommodating themselves to others. They should
be neither disagreeable to those who live with them nor offen-
sive or unpleasant to outsiders, but with the Apostle Paul they
should be all things to all men.

Do not in any way be a burden to the people for the material
things you need. Be mindful of the poverty of the apostles, who
by working with their own hands secured the things necessary
to themselves and those with them. For this they are all the
more your pattern for imitation, that, content with the food
and clothing available, you abstain from seeming to seek
personal gain by demanding alms or scraping for money or gifts.

Even if a gift is forced on one of you despite your attempt to
refuse it, then distribute it among the poor while the very ones
who gave it look on. Be assured that nothing so arouses admiration as contempt for temporal goods in apostolic poverty.
It surpasses all human and earthly things by far and lays up
treasures in heaven.

In no way persuade people to change their rites, customs, and
manner of life, unless these practices are flagrantly opposed

to the spirit of religion and good morals. What could be more absurd than to bring France, Spain, or Italy, or another part of Europe into China? Do not bring with you your homeland customs but only the Faith, which never aims to spurn or harm the rites and customs of any land, provided they are not evil. Indeed, our Faith wishes the good things in every land to be preserved.

Since it is almost a part of human nature to hold in greater love and esteem what is one's own, and particularly to favor what belongs to one's own country over that of others, nothing creates ill feeling and hatred more than attempts of outsiders to change the customs of a people's fatherland. This is especially true of those age-old ways to which they and their fathers have been attached as long as memory records. When the outsider seeks to substitute customs of his own nation in place of those he desires to destroy, it is particularly irritating. Therefore, never seek to impose practices on the people among whom you labor. Rather conform yourself with great diligence to their ways.

Admire and praise those things which merit praise. Regarding what does not merit praise . . . it will be a matter of your prudence at least to pronounce no judgment on them and certainly not to condemn them rashly or spontaneously.

When conspicuous evil exists, it should be censured more by silence and gesture than by words. When, then, souls have been disposed to receive the truth, an opportunity should be sought to draw them from the wrong gradually and imperceptibly.

If any king, prince, magistrate, or official, by God's inspiration, should have a benevolent attitude toward you or a kindly inclination to the Christian religion, be grateful. But do not ask for privileges, exemptions, or unusual juridical standing. Do not fail in any way to recognize the authority that they exercise.

Preach to the people obedience to their rulers, even when they are at variance with you. Privately, as well as publicly, earnestly pray from your heart for the health and prosperity of those who govern. Do not disparage the actions even of

those persecuting you. Accuse them not of severity, or repre-
hend anything in them, but await from the Lord in patience
and in silence the day of consolation.

Nor should you or yours adhere continually to the side of
anyone, or be obligated to anyone, particularly those in power,
in such fashion that you seem to be serving one man and not
the interests of the whole province. Therefore, do not allow
yourself to be shackled by excessive though insidious benefits,
which not only militate against the common good but even
impede your liberty of speaking and reprehending the vices
of the very benefactor himself.

THE TOWER

Above all, what is most needed is a spirituality of mission welling up
from a vision of the world marching toward its common goal. Something of this is beautifully and prophetically described in the very
ancient Shepherd of Hermas. The Shepherd sees a tower quarried from
twelve mountains and he is told that these mountains represent the
twelve nations of the world to whom the Apostles had preached. He
asks how is it that while mountains are different shapes and colors, yet
when built up into the tower they are all one color, and the Lord replies: "The reason is that all the nations that dwell beneath the sky
when once they heard the Gospel and believed were called in the name
of the Son of God. In receiving the seal, they took on one mind and one
spirit, in the unity of one faith and spirit of love.
. . . In this way the tower came to be built of one color and shone like
the sun."

— EUGENE BURKE, C.S.P.

MESSAGE FOR MISSION SUNDAY, 1968

As the paths of the world have opened up new possibilities of communication among peoples, the Church has felt in herself the "urgency of charity" to travel those paths—often, in fact, to be the first to walk them. She has felt this through her very nature, which is missionary. St. Paul's cry, "Woe to me if I preach not the Gospel" (I Cor. 9:16), has echoed in the Church's heart, and has reminded her of her original vocation. The history of the missions during the past few centuries shows this, an epic, as it is, full of risks, adventures, heroism, and martyrdom. Missionary endeavor has, one might say, exploded, braving superhuman difficulties, putting to the task the most rudimentary means, and men with the folly of courage and love. Faith has become what it ought to be—dynamic, irresistible, even rash. The joy of spreading the Gospel has repaid every effort, every sacrifice. Then came the council, to clarify the theological basis of this phenomenon, to remind the People of God of their native duty to expand, and to give criteria, norms, and exhortations to pursue with greater vigor and system the great work of the evangelization of peoples to whom the name of Christ has not yet been announced, and in whom the Church has not yet struck roots of autonomous life. . .

— POPE PAUL VI

A MASS IN ABYSSINIA

by Evelyn Waugh

A famous English writer describes his encounter with Eastern Christian worship, and draws some interesting conclusions.

We returned to our tent for breakfast. Beer and anchovies seemed rather discouraging after our chilly night, but there was no alternative except tinned loganberries and *foie gras*. The guard came in, finished the beer, and ate some bread and honey. He showed great interest in our belongings, fingering everything in turn — the tin-opener, electric torch, a pocket-knife, a pair of hairbrushes. I let him play with the sword-stick I happened to have brought with me; he in exchange showed me his rifle and bandolier. About half the cartridges were empty shells; the weapon was in very poor condition. It could not possibly have been used with any accuracy, and probably not with safety. I asked whether he had ever killed anything with it; he shook his head, and produced a large, rather blunt dagger, which he stabbed into the earth.

Presently the chauffeur came to assure us that he had spent a very comfortable night and felt fairly confident that he would be able to extricate the car from its position on the path, where it blocked all approach to the monastery and was causing a good deal of trouble to the herdsmen in charge of the community's cattle. We told him to remain at hand to act as interpreter, and soon a priest came to conduct us to the churches. There were two of these; the main building, where we had already been, and a small shrine, containing a cross which had fallen from heaven. The professor thought this might be a piece of the true cross brought there from Alexandria after the Arab invasion, and displayed great veneration; we were not allowed to see it, but as a special concession we were shown the shawl in which it was wrapped.

In the main church we paid a fee of seven dollars to have the frescoes unveiled. They had lately been repainted in brilliant colours and the priest was justly proud of the renovation. On one wall were portraits of Ras Kassa, Menelik, and the late Empress. It was clear that these heads had been copied from photographs, with the curious result that they stood out solidly, in carefully articulated light and shade and great fidelity of detail, against a composition of purely conventional pre-Renaissance design. Another wall was filled with rider saints. The professor made a plan of it and took down their names. We were then shown some brass processional crosses and some illuminated missals, none of any great antiquity. It was, in fact, a curious feature of Debra Lebanos that, although the community had been the centre of Abyssinian spiritual life since the conversion of the country, and had been settled on this spot for several centuries, they seem to have preserved no single object from the past. It may be that their treasures have all been pillaged in the continual invasions and disorders of Abyssinian history, or that they have been sold from time to time in moments of financial need, or perhaps simply that they did not choose to show them to strangers.

One thing, however, we did see of the greatest interest. That was the sanctuary. We might not, of course, enter it, but the priest drew back the curtain for us and allowed a short glimpse of the dark interior. In the centre stood the tabor, which is both altar-stone and tabernacle, a wooden cupboard built like a miniature church in three tiers, square at the base, from which rose an octagonal story surmounted by a circular dome. Round the tabor, in deep dust—for the sanctuary is rarely, if ever, swept out—lay an astonishing confusion of litter. There was not time to take in everything, but, in the brief inspection, I noticed a wicker chair, some heaps of clothes, two or three umbrellas, a suitcase of imitation leather, some newspapers, and a teapot and slop-pail of enamelled tin.

It was about ten o'clock when we left the church; there was a Mass at one o'clock, which we were both anxious to attend, which would not be over until half-past two or three. We were thus undecided about our movements. We might spend another night there and start back early next day for Addis Ababa; we might go and see Fiche, Kassa's capital fifteen miles away, and spend a night in the car there, or we might start immediately after Mass and try to get to Addis that night. The chauffeur favoured the last plan and was hopeful of his ability, now that he knew the way, of doing the journey in five or six hours. We had not provisions to last us in any comfort for two days, and I was reluctant to fall back on Abyssinian food. Together we persuaded the professor to attempt the journey; if the worse came to the worst we could spend the night on the plain; a prospect to which the chauffeur added romance with gloomy stories of wild beasts and brigands. As the sun mounted, it became intensely hot. We lay in the tent smoking and dozing until the *abuna* came to conduct us to Mass.

I will not attempt any description of the ritual; the liturgy was quite unintelligible to me, and, oddly enough, to the professor also. No doubt the canon of the Mass would have been in part familiar, but this was said in the sanctuary behind closed doors. We stood in the outer ambulatory. A carpet was placed for us to stand on and we were given praying-sticks, with the aid of which we stood throughout the two hours of service. There were twenty or thirty monks round us and some women and babies from the *tukals*. Communion was administered to the babies, but to no one else. Many of the monks were crippled or deformed in some way; presumably they were pilgrims who had originally come to the spring in the hope of a cure,

and had become absorbed into the life of the place. There seemed
to be very little system of testing vocations in the community.
The priests and deacons wore long, white-and-gold cloaks
and turbans, and had bare feet. Now and then they emerged
from the sanctuary, and once they walked round in procession.
The singing was monotonous and more or less continuous,
accompanied by a drum and sistrums. For anyone accustomed
to the Western rite it was difficult to think of this as a Christian
service, for it bore that secret and confused character associated
with the non-Christian sects of the East.

I had sometimes thought it an odd thing that Western Christianity, alone of all the religions of the world, exposes its mysteries to every observer, but I was so accustomed to this
openness that I had never before questioned whether it was
an essential and natural feature of the Christian system. Indeed,
so saturated are we in this spirit that many people regard the
growth of the Church as a process of elaboration—even of
obfuscation; they visualise the Church of the first century as
a little cluster of pious people reading the Gospels together,
praying and admonishing each other with a simplicity to which
the high ceremonies and subtle theology of later years would
have been bewildering and unrecognisable. At Debra Lebanos
I suddenly saw the classic basilica and open altar as a great
positive achievement, a triumph of light over darkness consciously accomplished, and I saw theology as the science of
simplification by which nebulous and elusive ideas are formalised
and made intelligible and exact. I saw the Church of the first
century as a dark and hidden thing, as dark and hidden as the
seed germinating in the womb; legionaries off duty slipping
furtively out of barracks, greeting each other by signs and pass-
words in a locked upper room in the side street of some Mediter-
ranean seaport; slaves at dawn creeping from the grey twilight
into the candle-lit, smoky chapels of the catacombs. The priests
hid their office, practising trades; their identity was known
only to initiates; they were criminals against the law of their
country. And the pure nucleus of the truth lay in the minds
of the people, encumbered with superstitions, gross survivals

of the paganism in which they had been brought up; hazy and obscene nonsense seeping through from the other esoteric cults of the Near East, magical infections from the conquered barbarian. And I began to see how these obscure sanctuaries had grown, with the clarity of the Western reason, into the great open altars of Catholic Europe, where Mass is said in a flood of light, high in the sight of all, while tourists can clatter round with their Baedekers, incurious of the mystery.

TWO MISSIONERS IN VIETNAM, 1890

Two figures were to dominate the new era. Vialleton was a man of the "calm father" type. He would direct the mission with wisdom and moderation for nearly thirty years. He would also be the one to begin to teach the savages to read and write. Guerlach was the very model of the "apostle-knight," a breed very representative of the nineteenth-century missioner. He had even been born on July 14 and, what is more, in Metz! Vialleton had set up his command post once and for all in his hammock. Guerlach was always in the saddle.

You have recognized them—the famous pair who periodically appear, except for a few nuances, in so many ages and in so many circumstances: Don Quixote and Sancho Panza, whose collaboration is often explosive, but nearly always effective. The proof of this is that during those thirty years rich in color and fertile in adventures, the number of Christian savages would increase tenfold.

—CHRISTIAN SIMONNET

CRY OF THE SQUATTER CHILD

I've seen the splendid buildings rising high into the sky
  And I've wondered is it there that people go to when they die?
For the Christians talk of heaven
  And the Buddhists tell us man will step by step rise higher.
And I wonder does it mean that one day I'll join the blessed,
  Live away from dirt and pest,
Have a shelter from the wind, and know a proper place to rest?
  Is it there that folk have money and can buy the things we make?
Is it there that we can know the taste of pork, and fruit, and cake?

I wonder if they know the way we people here must be?
  I wonder if they know of floods, of winds, of poverty?
I wonder if they wake at night and see the glare that is not light
  But fire, our dread enemy
Who eats away the little things we have,
  Who takes the roof above our heads,
And makes us cold and starved and ill,
  And leaves our mothers crying 'til
We wish we'd never lived at all.

I wonder if the people there
  Are told to quit . . .
They know not where?
  And as we cry and wonder why
They come with chopper, saw, and tool,
  And force us out.
And then we have no other way.
  Our huts are smashed, our mothers cry
We starve and shiver — and yet nearby
  The others buy their New Year fare,
And sounds of joy are in the air.

— E. ELLIOT

THE NIGHT OF SORROW

by Albert J. Nevins

> One of the great epics of New World history was the escape of the besieged Spaniards from Mexico City during the conquest of that country.

It has been over two weeks since I last recorded anything here and there is so much to put down that I doubt if I can do it in one sitting. As my last entry told of the attack on Montezuma, I shall first recount what happened to that noble lord before I tell of the terrible tragedy that befell us.

Cortes had the Mexican lord carried to the royal quarters and placed on his bed. Our captain bandaged Montezuma's head and cared for him as if the injured man were his own father. When Montezuma recovered his senses, he tore the bandages from his head and refused food. He said that he had suffered his last humiliation. Then he turned his face to the wall, and remained that way until he died. A great sadness filled our palace at his death, because all of us had come to love this man of dignity, even though we knew he would send us to be sacrificed if he had it in his power.

Montezuma was a holy man in his own way, and if he had been a Christian, few would have equalled him in the fervor of faith. He was a man of great power who commanded many people and ruled a vast land. He was a man of bravery whose conquests rivaled those of the great Khan. His sense of nobility could equal that of any monarch. But he was torn between the divine and the temporal. He could have destroyed us at any time and protected his throne, but he was not sure whether or not Cortes represented the power of Quetzalcoatl, the founder of his country, and whether acting against the Spanish leader would be to oppose the will of his gods. And so, unable to decide, he became a prisoner of those who had come to conquer him and his people.

After Montezuma's death, Cortes ordered that the king's litter should be brought and the body placed upon it. Then he commanded some chiefs who had been serving Montezuma and some priests whom we had captured to carry their lord away so that he might be buried like the great king he was. All fighting stopped as the litter was borne into the street, and we could hear the shrieks and cries of those who had been his subjects. Yet, as soon as the litter went past, they renewed their attacks upon us with even more bitterness, shouting to us that we would suffer for the death of their king and that none of us would escape with our lives.

By this time, our situation in Mexico City was truly desperate. We had no food or water, our gunpowder was practically exhausted, and our soldiers were on the verge of collapse. The followers of Narvaez, being unused to warfare, were often as much hindrance as a help. Despite repeated sallies, we could not sweep the enemy back. We would venture forth, be attacked, attack our attackers, set some houses on fire, and then be driven back to our headquarters. For an entire week, we had been under constant siege, and the wall of humanity that swarmed about us prevented any escape. Several times we had been dislodged from our palace, but each time fought our way back.

On the afternoon of the first day of July, Captain Cortes summoned all of his small band to the main hall of the palace. He came and spoke to us.

"Comrades, I don't have to tell you of the bad plight that

we are in," he said. "We have not a grain of corn and our water is gone. We are pressed on every side. If we remain here, we are lost, even though we kill twenty-five thousand Mexicans for every one of us who dies. We have done great harm to our enemy and the stink of death hangs over this city as thick as the smoke from the houses we have burned. But no matter how valiantly we fight, it is never enough. We have several choices left to us. We can remain here, dying one by one, until we are overrun. We can surrender and have our hearts torn out on the altars of sacrifice and our bodies thrown to wild animals."

"No! No!" The cry went up from many throats.

"That is the spirit of true Spaniards!" continued Cortes, showing his approval of the cries. "You know that we have no choice but to fight our way out. The Mexicans have kept the Tacuba causeway open so that they might bring up troops and supplies, and, although they have destroyed all the bridges, I have had a portable bridge built. If we are going to escape, now is the time, while that causeway remains. Tonight will be the moment of decision. It is now raining, and if the rain continues, it will make the Mexicans less cautious and provide a cover for us. Once we are on the mainland, we will be free of this trap and will be able to defend ourselves."

Cortes then ordered the treasure room to be opened. He had the gold belonging to His Majesty loaded on seven horses that had been wounded and that were useless for fighting. He also ordered some of the Tlaxcalans who were with us to carry as much gold as they could. When this was done, Cortes mounted his platform.

"I want the notaries to bear witness that I have taken all the gold that I can," Cortes declared. "There is still seven hundred thousand pesos worth remaining with no way for me to protect it. But I do not wish those Mexican infidels to get it. Therefore, you soldiers can take whatever you desire."

There was a mad dash to the treasure room—soldier fighting soldier to get through the door. Men tried to take more than they could hold, and cursed bitterly when they couldn't carry it away.

I was standing next to Galan and, when he started for the treasure room, I caught him by the arm.

"Wait!" I called. "Don't take any gold."

"Why not, Diego? Are you mad?"

"Try and get some jewels," I replied. "The gold is heavy and will hinder us. Tonight we are going to be fighting for our lives. Don't weight yourself down."

When we finally forced our way into the treasure room, we discovered that other experienced soldiers had the same idea that we did. A few of our soldiers and the Narvaez men were the ones who were carrying away the ingots. Galan and I each managed to get a handful of jewels — rubies, emeralds, and jade, and these fitted nicely in our pockets without any great drag. It was a wise move to take jewels and leave the gold, for many were to die that night when they fell into the lake and were pulled down and drowned by the weight of their gold.

After darkness had come, we assembled once again in the main hall and, in the dim light of smoking torches, Captain Cortes gave us our last instructions. Gonzalo was to command the forward troops, laying the bridge and clearing the way. As I was in Gonzalo's squadron, it meant that I would be one of the first across. Those Tlaxcalans who were not loaded with gold were to go with us, to carry and lay the bridge. Cortes was to come next, with a few soldiers, the gold, the injured soldiers, and Doña Marina and others. Juan Velasquez, my kinsman, and Pedro de Alvarado were to bring up the rear with their troops, holding the enemy back until all were safely across.

At midnight, we received the command to form ranks. Galan and I had been sitting together, speaking of old times, when the order came. We parted, I to get Blanco and join Gonzalo, Galan to fall in with Pedro de Alvarado.

"Good luck, Diego!" Galan said. "I'll see you in Tacuba."

"Go with God, Galan!"

We marched silently out of the palace and into the deserted

street. A light drizzle was falling and there was some mist hanging over the lake. We reached the mound of the causeway, Gonzalo and myself in the lead, and moved out on it. So far so good! We came to the first opening and had the Tlaxcalans set the bridge in place. Just then, a woman's scream came from a house standing in the lake and shattered the silence.

"The *tueles!* The *tueles* are escaping!"

It was as if a signal was given for hell itself to break loose. Out of the mists came swarms of canoes. From the windows of houses came a rain of arrows. Behind us, we heard cries and knew that the enemy was pouring onto the entrance of the causeway. The Mexicans had allowed us to get on the causeway and then sprung their trap. I galloped over the bridge and rode down the first Indians who were climbing up from their canoes, sending them sprawling back into the lake. Behind us came the soldiers of the advance guard, and then Cortes with the baggage. Our portable bridge was abandoned. When we reached the next opening, where a bridge had been removed, Gonzalo spurred his horse and jumped across. I followed on Blanco. On the opposite side, Gonzalo wheeled around and went back to the opening.

"Throw in the artillery and the baggage!" he shouted to the Tlaxcalans. "Fill it up!" Then he turned to me. "We've got to keep the road ahead of us free."

We rode through Mexicans who had gained the causeway, scattering them like leaves before a strong wind. Back and forth we charged, clearing the way for our soldiers and allies, who were now streaming across the filled-in opening. There was one more gap ahead of us, and we galloped there as our troops came running behind. Once again, Gonzalo spurred Motilla across the canal. I gave Blanco the signal and he rose into the air. As he did, I felt him shudder underneath me. I reached down to pat his chest and my hand felt blood, and then an arrow that was deeply imbedded.

Blanco hit the side of the causeway with a crash. My poor horse was already dead, carried over by his own momentum. I rolled clear, losing my lance, and saw Blanco slip off the edge of the causeway and disappear in the murky waters. Before I could get to my feet, a squad of Mexicans fell upon me. I rolled and twisted, fighting for my very life. I felt my helmet ripped from my head. Gonzalo had wheeled around by this time, and came charging back. He scattered the Indians, knocking them into the water. I gained my feet, cut and bleeding from a number of wounds, none serious. The whole action takes longer to describe than it did to experience.

I pulled my sword as our first troops came to the opening. Again horses and baggage went into the water. The bodies of Indians and Spaniards slipped into the opening. Narvaez men, still clutching their yellow metal, sank into the lake and were drowned. The breech was soon filled enough for men to wade across. Gonzalo rode back and forth, urging them on. I walked along the causeway, sword in hand, but there was no one to fight. The Indians had never expected us to get this far and the Tacuba end of the causeway was for the moment deserted and undefended. A riderless horse came dashing by and I caught the reins and swung myself up into the saddle. Those who had survived this far choked the causeway, as they made for the mainland. I found Gonzalo and Captain Cortes on the outskirts of Tacuba.

"Diego, we're going back!" Cortes said as I rode up. "Our rear guard is under fearful pressure from those who are pursuing from the city. We must help!"

We galloped back to the causeway, picking up another horseman or two on the way. We hurried as fast as we could, but the road was now slippery from blood and mud. As we came to the opening where the bridge had been removed, we saw some of our soldiers holding off a multitude of Indians. We could not leap across the opening for fear of crashing into our own men or having our horses slip in the treacherous mud, and Cortes told us that to attempt to walk our mounts over the bodies that filled the opening would be fatal because we would certainly fall. All we could do was watch.

There were four Spaniards and eight Tlaxcalans on the other side, under the command of Pedro de Alvarado, who had been trying to fight off the enemy the same way for the length of the causeway. Alvarado had started out on a horse, but it must have been killed beneath him, for he was now afoot. He had also lost his shield. One by one, he ordered the Tlaxcalans to leave the battle and wade across the opening, each stumbling and slipping as the pile of bodies beneath the surface shifted, due to the weight. Then the Spanish soldiers came across, one by one, until only Pedro was left. Never have I seen a man fight as he did that night. And if it was indecision that caused the temple massacre, he more than made up for it as he held off our attackers and allowed as many of our comrades as possible to escape across the causeway. Nearer and nearer he came to the opening, thrusting with his lance, cutting and slashing at those who pressed in on him. Then suddenly, he let out a great roar, swung his lance at his pursuers as one would a sword and, without breaking his motion, plunged the lance into a dead horse in the opening and vaulted to our side of the causeway, his body covered with mud and blood, his armor clattering as he landed. It was a feat that one might read about in history but never expect to see. Once he had crossed, the Indians gave up the pursuit and went back along the causeway, looking for any Spaniard who might not be dead and who could be dragged away to be sacrificed to their blood-hungry war god. Alvarado stood gazing back across the opening as if in a stupor.

"What is it, Pedro?" Cortes asked kindly.

"They are gone—all gone."

"Yes, the Mexicans are gone. We are safe for a moment."

"Not the Mexicans. The Spaniards." He turned to us, and we saw that tears were streaming down his face. "They are all gone. Eighty of them. Juan Velasquez. Lares. Morla. Saucedo. They are no more."

"Francisco de Saucedo. He was one of the first to die when the Mexicans poured out of the city and fell upon us."

"Come! We must get back to Tacuba and the others before the Mexicans re-form," Cortes said softly. "Mount behind me, Pedro."

Cortes pulled Alvarado up behind him and we turned our horses and rode off the causeway. I did not want to look back. Galan dead. I couldn't believe it. I didn't want to believe it. Galan, Galan, what lament can I write for a lost warrior? Your trail to gold and fame ended in a mist of carnage and defeat. Galan, my friend, my brother, whom I shall never see more on this earth.

Dawn was breaking when we reached Tacuba, where our soldiers had gathered. Mexicans were already coming out to attack us anew, yet it was imperative that we halt to care for our wounds, for there was not one of us who had escaped without a bloody memento to show for it. I had received a dart in my foot, cuts on my hands and arms, scratches on my face. Cortes ordered us to ascend a hill overlooking Tacuba and occupy several pyramids there. He also commanded the captains who were still alive to check among the men and determine the casualties.

After we reached the pyramids and set up our defenses, the captains went among their men and made their report to Cortes. Only 440 soldiers and 23 horses had escaped. A little more than a week earlier, when we had marched so bravely into Mexico City, Cortes had been in command of fourteen hundred men and over a hundred horses. When our captain general heard this news and saw the pitiful remnants left him, he went off by himself, knelt down under a tree and wept bitterly. There were many tears that night of sorrow, because there were few of us who had not suffered a personal loss, a friend or relative. My own heart was heavier than all the gold that lay at the bottom of the lake. Blanco, the irreplaceable. Juan Velasquez, my kinsman. Galan, my friend.

And now a new torture began. The sun came up, dispelling the mists. It was a July sun, the warmest of the year. We were hungry and sick, but we had to endure the terrible heat of the whitewashed pyramids that became like an oven. The more seriously wounded cried for water and then begged for it, but there was none to give them. One horse had been badly wounded and Captain Cortes ordered that it should be killed and eaten.

The meat helped a little to appease our hunger. The Mexicans, meanwhile, had surrounded us and sent a constant rain of stones and arrows upon us.

Darkness finally came. Captain Cortes decided that we would move out at midnight and go north around the lake. When I asked him, he told me that I could keep the horse that I had caught, since I had lost my own in his service and the one I had found belonged to a follower of Narvaez who had died on the causeway. Horsemen were assigned to the front and sides of our column. The wounded were put in the center. Several of the badly wounded were lifted astride injured horses that were no good for fighting. The rest staggered along as best they could, helped by a staff or a comrade.

We had hardly left the pyramids when the Mexicans renewed their attack, pressing us from every side. We who were on horses would no sooner drive them away than they were back at us, calling for our deaths and promising none of us would leave their country alive. When morning came, they were still at us. Thus we continued all day, fighting on every side. When dusk began to fall, we had hardly gone six leagues. We found another temple and took refuge there. Two of our soldiers had been killed during the day, and another horse. Again we had horse meat for supper and nothing else. You can't imagine our exhaustion or our suffering! Fortunately, the enemy did not attack during the night and we were able to get some sleep.

The next morning, we started out without a sign of the enemy. We had gone about a league and were thanking God for our good fortune, when Gonzalo, who had been scouting ahead, came galloping back to Cortes. He reported that the fields in front were black with Mexicans, waiting to fall upon us. Cortes called a halt, swung around and looked down on his exhausted men, weak from hunger, wounds, and the bitterness of life.

"The Mexican dogs are waiting for us ahead," he cried. "Every day they grow stronger and more numerous, while we grow weaker. If we are going to escape their roasting pots, now must be the time. If we wait any longer, we shall be too weak to lift a sword or draw a bow. This could be our last day, but it will be a day we shall meet with honor. Those who are too badly wounded to fight should go to the rear but, wounds or no wounds, all of you will have to defend yourself. Captain Sandoval, you will arrange three squads of five horsemen each. Do not use swords but lances, and aim them like battering rams for the faces of the enemy. Pick out the chiefs by their plumes and gold headdresses and destroy them so that we can leave the enemy leaderless. And you, brave soldiers, advance in the confidence of God! Aim for the stomachs and strike home so hard that you will avenge our dead brothers. God and the Virgin Mary! Up Santiago!"

Never did such a tattered army move into battle. Yet God gave us strength, for we fought as tigers. We who were on horseback charged back and forth, breaking up squadrons of the enemy, relieving our soldiers when they were hard pressed, killing the chiefs and captains wherever we saw them.

Gonzalo kept urging us on, shouting, "This is the day we are going to win. At them! Santiago!"

For several hours the battle raged, and how our wounded and exhausted men managed to stand up can only be explained by the fact that Saint James himself must have supported their arms. The turn in the battle came when Cortes spotted the place from where the Mexican force was being directed. He saw the captain general of the Mexicans, clad in golden armor, with a feathered crest of many colors, issuing orders to his captains.

"Over there!" shouted Cortes. "Break through!"

We galloped across the field, sending Mexicans flying, and smashed into the enemy headquarters. Captains went sprawling in every direction. Juan de Salamanca, a follower of Narvaez, pierced the Mexican captain general with his lance. It was this act that swung the tide of battle. Disorganized and without a leader to give commands, the enemy began to flee. We who were on horseback broke up the Mexican squads and hurried them along, while our soldiers fell to their knees, thanking God for a great miracle.

I saw one Indian dash behind a clump of bushes and I set out after him. When I was almost upon him, he turned and defiantly stood there, waiting for me to run him down, for he had no weapon and could make no defense. Yet he was not afraid to die. But I did nothing. I reined in my horse, raised my lance, wheeled about and trotted back to our soldiers without saying a word. The brave Mexican was Don Carlos. I grieved for him, as he must be grieving for his lost father and uncle.

The battle of Otumba, for that was where it took place, ended the attack of the Mexicans. We passed out of their country the next day without further incident. Our only worry now was that the Tlaxcalans might take the opportunity to throw off our rule, but when we came to the gate of Tlaxcala, ragged and beaten, old blind Xicotenga was there to greet us, along with other chiefs. Tears streamed down his face as he embraced Cortes.

"Oh, Malinche, our hearts grieve for the loss of your brothers and our sons," Xicotenga said in greeting. "We warned you of the Mexicans, and now that of which we warned you has happened. Do not think you were defeated, for you won a great victory escaping from that city! I wanted to go to your assistance with thirty thousand warriors but I could not leave, as we are still assembling them. Now you are here. You are home. Come, rest and have food."

Tell me, Beatriz and anyone else who may read these words, has there ever been loyalty and goodness shown such as that?

Now we are resting, well fed, contented, and recovering from our wounds. Cortes has promised that he will retake Mexico City and level it. I believe him, for there is nothing he cannot do. Yet none of us will ever forget that night of sadness when we fled for our lives.

FROM THE DECREE ON THE MISSIONARY ACTIVITY OF THE CHURCH

This mission is a continuing one. In the course of history it unfolds the mission of Christ Himself, who was sent to preach the gospel to the poor. Hence, prompted by the Holy Spirit, the Church must walk the same road which Christ walked: a road of poverty and obedience, of service and self-sacrifice to the death, from which death He came forth a victor by His resurrection. For thus did all the apostles walk in hope. On behalf of Christ's body, which is the Church, they supplied what was wanting of the sufferings of Christ by their own many trials and sufferings (cf. Col. 1:24). Often, too, the blood of Christians was like a seed (#5).

Christ Himself searched the hearts of men, and led them to divine light through truly human conversation. So also His disciples, profoundly penetrated by the Spirit of Christ, should know the people among whom they live, and should establish contact with them. Thus they themselves can learn by sincere and patient dialogue what treasures a bountiful God has distributed among the nations of the earth. But at the same time, let them try to illumine these treasures with the light of the gospel, to set them free, and to bring them under the dominion of God their Savior (#11).

EXPLORER OF THE MISSISSIPPI

by Dana Thomas

> The Indians reached by Father Marquette never re-
> verted to paganism. They said, "We are Indians of the
> one who prayed."

Within three weeks of his arrival in Quebec, Marquette was
sent to Three Rivers, a mission on the northern bank of the St.
Lawrence River for "on the spot" training. Two years later he
was sent to one of the furthest outposts of French influence—
the settlement at Sault Ste. Marie among the Ottawa Indians;
and the following year, to the Hurons at Chequamegon Bay to
conduct a mission entirely on his own.

His final instructions before setting out were indicative of the
grim life that awaited him. "Unless you are temperamentally
able to love the Indian like a brother, you might as well go back
to France. There will be no earthly reward for you in this life."

And then his superior general added this advice: "When you
are traveling with the Indians, never make them wait for you. If
your broad-brimmed hat annoys them, take it off and wear your
night cap. Fasten up the skirts of your cassock, so that you will
not carry water or sand into the canoe. Wear no shoes or stock-
ings. You may put them on in crossing portages. Do not volun-
teer to paddle, unless you are prepared to do so all day. Do not
lend an Indian any part of your clothing, unless you have made

up your mind to do without it for the rest of the trip. Do not ask the Indians too many questions. Take along a flint and steel to light their pipes and kindle their fires at night. Try to eat the food as the Indians cook it, bad and dirty though it is. You will get used to it. It will do no harm to play with the children, flatter the old people, speak kindly of the departed relatives. And God be with you!"

A chief stumbling block for missionaries was the Indian languages. Some of the most learned Jesuits gave up trying to learn them and returned to France in despair. But the young aristocrat from Laon was a born linguist. In the course of his career, he was to learn how to speak six Indian dialects fluently.

From the outset, Marquette encountered adventure. To reach the Hurons at Chequamegon Bay, for instance, he paddled a canoe four hundred miles over Lake Superior, through waters so treacherous at times that even today large steamers often run into trouble.

The Hurons were experiencing hard times. They were a shadow of the once mighty tribe that had ruled the Great Lakes. Reduced in numbers by war and famine, living in constant terror of the warlike Iroquois to the east, they were only too happy to welcome French missionaries and to gain the friendship of the powerful French nation.

"Greetings, Blackrobe," the sachems declared at Marquette's coming. "Never has the sun seemed so fair, or the corn so ripe, or the fishes so abundant in the streams, as today when you arrive among us."

Few white men were able to endure life in an Indian village. But Marquette entered into it without complaint. He lived in a windowless cabin so filled with acrid smoke that frequently he had to lie down and hug the floor for air. His eyes were constantly inflamed. He ate without any outward indication of revulsion the Indian meal that "tasted like the glue used for papering the walls of houses." He endured the crawling vermin, screaming children, snarling dogs, the constant quarrels of his savage neighbors. As he sat in his cabin in the dead of winter translating Christian prayers into the language of the Hurons, his ink froze and his fingers grew numb. The drinking water in his flask turned to solid ice. Sometimes, to get away from the foul air, he went into the forest and read his breviary shivering by moonlight.

He accompanied the braves on long journeys over the snow, trudging wearily under his share of equipment as the dogs led the way through the drifts. And when the warm weather came, he traveled with them many miles by canoe, suffering almost unbearable fatigue.

Marquette discovered that the Indians had no word for God in their language. But they were eager to hear about the Great White Spirit. They believed that birds, beasts, and reptiles had ears to overhear human speech, that lakes and rivers and waterfalls were living beings. Once, when the missionary asked an elderly savage about a dream he had had, the Indian replied:

"I cannot talk now. It is spring. The streams are flowing, the animals are awake. They will overhear me and do me harm. Wait until the winter when everything is asleep, and I shall tell you."

When Marquette explained about God and eternal life, one sachem asked anxiously, "But will I be able to smoke my pipe in your paradise? I cannot do without tobacco."

Marquette's chief opponents were the medicine men, whose influence was threatened by his teachings. They pointed to the breviary in which he was absorbed by the hour. "The Blackrobe is mumbling incantations to destroy our corn and bring us famine!" If the harvest were poor, or the winter unusually severe, they demanded his life.

The missionary warded off harm by matching the tricks of the medicine men with "magic" of his own. He had brought along a magnifying glass with him, and he astonished the Indians by turning a flea into a monster under the lens. He showed them a handmill which ground their corn. But their chief delight was a clock. The entire village sat for hours around him in tense silence waiting for it to strike. The Indians believed it was an animal. "What does it eat?" they asked. When the last stroke sounded for the hour, the missionary would cry, "Stop!" And to the astonishment of the audience, the clock remained still.

For two years Marquette lived among the Hurons at Che-quamegon Bay, preaching, baptizing, ministering to the sick. When, as the result of an inter-tribal quarrel, the Sioux Indians to the west went on the warpath and threatened to annihilate the Hurons, the missionary helped the Hurons to emigrate hurriedly to Michillimackinac Island in Lake Michigan, out of reach of the Sioux warriors. During the five-hundred-mile trip by canoe, he kept up their morale; and when they debarked at Michillimackinac, he shared in the labor of constructing a new village.

"I am very happy here," he wrote. He looked forward to spending the remainder of his life among these Indians, and dying in the wilderness, as Saint Francis Xavier, the man he most admired, had done.

From time to time Marquette as well as other missionaries had received reports from the Indians about the great "Messipi" River that flowed through fertile lands where the snow rarely fell and where two crops of maize were harvested yearly. The Spaniards had named it the *"Rio del Espiritu Santo,"* — the "River of the Holy Ghost" — and had estimated that it ran south of the Great Lakes. But whether it flowed into the Gulf of Mexico or into the Pacific, no European knew. The fact was that no white man had as yet explored its source. For years the nations of Europe, aware of the strategic importance of the "Messipi," had vied with one another to be the first to navigate it.

In June, 1672, France took a decisive step. A minister of Louis XIV wrote to Jean Talon, director of financial policies in New France, authorizing him to launch a new exploration. If this were successful, it would unlock the American west to French commerce and make possible the erection of a barrier of colonies that would seal the English off on the Atlantic coast. "His Majesty desires you to give this your immediate atten-tion," wrote the minister from Versailles.

Jean Talon recommended to Count de Frontenac, governor of New France, that Louis de Joliet be the leader of the expe-dition. Joliet was the son of a wagon maker, in the service of a fur company. Tall, blue-eyed, bronzed by many suns in the wilderness, a hunter, trader, and explorer, Joliet had traveled widely among the savages and was an expert in Indian dialects. He was a flesh-and-blood realization of Natty Bumppo, the hero of Cooper's *Leatherstocking Tales*.

The authorities decided to appoint a second man to head the expedition—a spiritual leader with the ability to gain the good will of the Indians encountered on the way. When Father Dablon, superior general of the Jesuits in New France, was asked to recommend a missionary, he answered without hesitation, "The best man for the job is Père Marquette."

The preparations for the trip were extensive. Nothing was left to chance. All the information about the great river compiled since the days of De Soto was evaluated. Half-breed trappers who had spent years in the western country, Indians resting at the mission en route to their tribes were called in and questioned at length. The leaders traced a huge map estimating the course of the river, based on the various reports. For this journey that would carry them several thousand miles through unexplored country, they took along five French Canadian woodsmen and two canoes. The canoes were light but strong, built of birchbark and ribs of spruce and cedar splint covered with yellow pine pitch. Four men could carry them over the portage paths. In smooth water they could be paddled at five miles an hour. Into these canoes the men packed rifles, ammunition, extra clothing, sails to take advantage of favorable winds, equipment for the making of maps, gifts for the Indians to be met on the way. They stocked up on smoked meat and Indian corn as their basic foods.

On every side they received warnings. The Indians were especially gloomy in their prophecies. "Even if you succeed in reaching the river," one chief declared, "we have heard that the heat that rises from its banks will shrivel your flesh. The river is filled with monsters who will overturn your canoes. And if you escape these dangers, you will be put to death by hostile tribes."

On the 17th of May, 1673, when the ice had broken up at Michillimackinac, the party was ready to set out. Blackrobes and trappers, Huron and Ottawa Indians lined the shore of Lake Michigan. Joliet, nattily dressed in a blanket coat and vivid blue sash, and Marquette, in his black robe and wide-brimmed hat, said their goodbyes and joined the Canadian woodsmen who were already kneeling by the paddles. Just before they rounded Point Barbe, each man gave a glance backward, and Joliet tipped his puddingbag cap to the onlookers.

They passed the frowning stone of the Point. Then they were swept up by the current that surged through the Strait of Mackinac and spun along the northern shore of Lake Michigan, entering a body of water from whose slimy bed rose vapors that fused with the odor of a salt spring into such a stench that the French called it "Putrid Bay." Sudden squalls of wind churned the waters. The air held a lingering nip. Paddling as they knelt on birchbark rushes, they proceeded into Green Bay through the "Door of Death," so called because of the crosswinds and currents that had sent many craft to the bottom of its waters.

The shores of Green Bay bristled with tamarack and pine whose pungency sweetened the air. From time to time they sponged their faces in the cool, invigorating waters at their elbow. In passing through the Fox River, they entered water so shallow that the canoes scraped on the bedrock and the men continually had to carry their craft into deeper water, wounding their feet as they walked. At points, the river narrowed into creeks choked with wild vegetation, making the passage tremendously difficult. At one stage they came on a series of rapids that could not be navigated.

"We will need guides to lead us overland," declared Joliet. "Otherwise we cannot get through."

Fortunately, a tribe of friendly Indians, the Mascoutens, who were well known to the Jesuits, lived in the area. The canoes were beached, and the travelers made their way to the Indian village for guides.

The chiefs were delighted to see the white men. They presented them with three guides and with reed mats to serve as beds for the rest of the voyage. The canoes were unloaded of all their equipment. Then, while several of the party carried the craft over their heads, the rest strapped the food and equipment on their shoulders, and the Indians led the way over the portage path that skirted the rapids. The canoes were put into the water that had dropped a hundred and seventy feet from the head of the falls. The Indians were sent home, and the paddling was continued.

Daily, Father Marquette and his colleague made notations in their journals on the foliage and vegetation, the animals and insects they saw along the banks. They took soundings of the river, consulted their maps, and speculated as to what awaited them.

On June 17th, one month out of Michillimackinac, the seven canoeists passed at last into the "Messipi." The travelers recognized the river instantly by its broad, sweeping current, the great distance between its banks — a mile at this point. They had never before seen anything like it.

"Who can doubt this is the river!" exclaimed Joliet, his face flushed with excitement as he stood up and waved his cap in a salute to nature for providing such a miracle.

Marquette's joy — "a joy which I have no words to express" — was conveyed in a more quiet manner. He knelt in prayer and thanked God that he had been spared to witness this occasion.

Eight days after entering the "Messipi," they came for the first time upon footprints on the shore. These led inward through the brush, evidently to an Indian village. Since it was their purpose to investigate the tribes that inhabited the valley, the explorers beached their canoes.

Marquette said to the five Canadian trappers, "We have come on an errand of peace and this must be instantly evident to whomever we meet. Therefore, you men will stay behind. Monsieur Joliet and I will go forward alone."

The Canadians, protesting that this was foolhardy, asked to go along with their rifles. But Joliet agreed with the priest. "Be on guard against any surprise and keep your powder ready."

The two leaders followed the footsteps for a distance of five miles and came upon a settlement of Indian huts. They drew close enough to hear the Indians conversing. And then they announced their presence.

Several savages stepped from the huts and scrutinized the strangers in silence. Other Indians quickly made their appearance and stood quietly in groups regarding the Frenchmen with noncommittal expressions. Finally, four elderly braves were deputized to greet the Frenchmen. Two of them carried pipes of red sandstone adorned with plumage. When they were a few yards away, they halted. Then one addressed Marquette.

"What do you desire, Blackrobe? From where have you come with your friend?"

Marquette was instantly relieved. He recognized the language as belonging to the Illinois tribe, branches of which the Jesuits had already had dealings with.

"My friend and I have come on an errand to explore the mouth of the Father of Rivers. We have presents for your people."

The Indians invited the Frenchmen to proceed with them to the village. Townspeople of all ages swarmed around them. Some ran a few yards ahead, then turned around and walked slowly back toward them to get a better look. This was done without a word being uttered. Even the dogs were banished—a mark of the Indians' great respect for the visitors. The Frenchmen were brought to a centrally located cabin, at the entrance to which stood a wrinkled old sachem, entirely naked, his hands outstretched to the sun as through screening his eyes from it. Around him were gathered the dignitaries of the village, eager to hear Marquette's remarks.

"I bear a message from the great pale Manitou," Marquette explained. "He has made men white and red and yellow. And He has commanded all of them to love one another."

The old sachem replied. "That sounds well. Enter our cabins in peace."

Joliet sent back word to his Canadians to bring up the presents. And the company sat down to the traditional feast. The first dish was a platter of Indian meal, boiled in water and seasoned with grease. The Indians, like all nutritionally starved people, had an inordinate fondness for grease. They even forced hunks of it into the mouths of infants. The hosts insisted on stuffing mouthfuls of meal down the white men's throats with their own dirty fingers. This was the prescribed etiquette for feeding guests.

The next course served was fish. Blowing on choice morsels to cool them off, the savages put them into the Frenchmen's mouths as one would give food to a bird. For the third course, the hosts brought forward a freshly killed dog. Dogs were highly valued by Indians, and it was the highest compliment to serve them at a feast. However, when the guests balked at eating this, the dish was withdrawn and an ox was substituted, the fattest portions of which were crammed into the guests until they were on the verge of gagging.

Marquette and Joliet passed the night in a sachem's cabin preparatory to resuming their trip at dawn. The priest had a talk with the chief, an agile-minded savage. "I have seen your cross, Blackrobe, when I have visited my cousins on the Wisconsin among whom your people have come. Will you plant a cross here in the center of town? We will decorate it with red and white skins and bows and arrows. And we will pray before it and ask the Great White Spirit to ward off famine. When, Blackrobe, will you return to teach us your prayers?"

The priest, touched by the old fellow's earnestness, promised he would revisit them or send a fellow missionary as soon as he had completed his trip.

The chief nodded his head. "That is well. Let me give you a pipe of peace to take down the river." He handed the priest his own calumet. Its stem was two feet long, decorated with eagle's feathers.

"Blackrobe, wherever you go, even your enemies will shrink from harming you when you show this pipe."

And then he added, half jokingly, yet fully meaning to flatter, "There is a warrior who guards the path to heaven. His name is Oscotarach, the Head Piercer. And he removes the brains from the heads of all men before they pass into eternal life. But you,

Blackrobe, are the cleverest man I have ever met. I am sure you will find a way to slip into heaven with all your wits about you!"

Once again the Frenchmen embarked in their canoes and continued down the "Messipi." They came upon large herds of buffalo, an animal none of them had ever seen before. Marquette sketched the buffalo in his journal. The bottom lands seemed to be crowded with them. In many cases they were hidden by the cottonwoods and elms, betraying their presence only by bellowing. One of the Canadians shot a buffalo so tremendous that it required the strength of all seven men to remove the body.

One afternoon when, according to their calculations, they had traveled over a thousand miles down the "Messipi," they encountered the trouble they had feared since the start. While passing a heavily wooded bank, they heard a war cry. A party of Indians slipped down to the water's edge armed with bows and arrows. So sudden was the meeting, it was impossible for the canoeists to turn back; and such gesture of timidity would result in a volley of arrows. The Frenchmen stopped paddling and sat rigid, their rifles across their laps. The Indians jumped into canoes and paddled out in a large semicircle as if to envelop them. Several plunged into the water from the shore and started to swim toward the French. A club was hurled through the air and barely missed Marquette's head.

Joliet motioned his men to hold their fire. While the Canadians were crack shots, they were so outnumbered by the savages they would be overwhelmed. Father Marquette rose to his feet. All his skill and courage in dealing with the Indians was now brought into play; the lives of his friends depended upon him. He held out his peace pipe and motioned for the Indians to come forward. Several of the older savages on shore entered a canoe, putting down their weapons. They paddled a short distance and then signaled the whites to draw near.

That night the white men stretched themselves out on their mats, anxiously awaiting the dawn. Not one of them slept. In the cabin of the chief, just a hundred yards away, a council of braves was held. "Let us put these strangers to death," argued several of the younger men. "The Great Sun Spirit has guided them into our midst for our own gain. We can well use their rifles and food."

"They are my guests," answered the chief, gravely, "I would willingly kill them in combat. . . . "

Then he shook his head decisively. "They are my guests."

As the sky grew gray with morning, he summoned the whites to his cabin. "You are not safe here. There are those who seek your life. Times are hard with us, and even good men are sometimes urged to evil. You must leave before we are tempted further."

And then, as a sign of friendship, he picked up his calumet and began to dance. He lifted the peace pipe toward the ceiling, offering a smoke to the deities who ruled his life, and then dipped it earthward with a graceful gesture. Sometimes he spread its feathers as if he wished it to fly, or he pushed it toward the faces of the Frenchmen, only to withdraw it quickly. The dance was in the spirit of a ballet. At its conclusion, he repeated softly, persuasively, "Leave us. Go home!"

The Frenchmen retired to their cabin and held earnest council. "We know for a fact we are now at 33'40°, and we have not reached the sea," declared Joliet. "We have established beyond a doubt that the 'Messipi' does not empty into the California ocean — or into the Atlantic by way of Virginia. Its mouth can only be the Gulf of Mexico. This is the information we were sent to obtain. Let us start back before the season becomes more advanced."

The Canadians agreed with him. "If we continue further downstream," one pointed out, "we are likely to be murdered by the Indians or fall into the hands of the Spaniards who control the Gulf. In either case, our journals and maps will never reach France."

Father Marquette concurred. "We've carried out our basic mission. Now I'm anxious to get back to my teaching."

At the end of September, before the first snowfall, the seven men stumbled into this mission. St. Xavier's was thrown into a fever of excitement. Missionaries and Indians gathered around the travelers as if they had returned from the dead. The four-month voyage had seemed like an eternity to those at home. And, indeed, there was cause for rejoicing. One of the most remarkable explorations on record had been accomplished by the Jesuit Father, the fur trader, and their five assistants. In four months they had paddled two thousand, seven hundred and sixty-seven miles by canoe to open up the heart of the continent to colonization and give the world its first authentic knowledge of the American West.

Both Marquette and Joliet spent the winter months at St. Xavier, completing their journals, drawing their maps, and preparing reports to their superiors. With the coming of spring, Joliet set out by canoe for Montreal to present his report to Count de Frontenac. When he was eight miles from the city a sudden wind capsized his canoe in the St. Lawrence River. Two of the three boatmen and a young Indian were drowned in the undertow. Joliet clung to a rock for four hours until a fisherman pulled him ashore.

The loss of Joliet's records in the rapids assured Marquette of an even more important place in history than before; for the journal that he submitted to Father Dablon, the superior general, was the only surviving account of the voyage. But the Jesuit Father was not interested in his position in history. Once more he gave himself up, mind and body, to his teaching. Nor had he forgotten his promise to return to the Illinois. Of all the Indians he had met, they had stirred his sympathies most deeply. And so in October, 1674, nineteen months after returning to St. Francis Xavier's, and although he was still far from well, he set out for Illinois country, traveling with a party of Indians.

The weather was bitter. Along the shore of Lake Michigan, they encountered furious snowstorms; blocks of ice threatened their passage. Marquette suffered an attack of dysentery and was put ashore at the mouth of the Chicago River, which was frozen more than a foot deep.

In a wasteland of sand dunes and bog where, a hundred and fifty years later, the city of Chicago would be founded, the Indians erected a cabin of bark and skins. And here the missionary spent the winter. Among his other claims to notice, Marquette was Chicago's pioneer settler.

During the winter, friendly Indians brought him food and medicine. And a fur trapper, spending the season in a camp forty-five miles away, sent him corn and dried blueberries. Then, when the streams had quickened into life again, the missionary continued on his trip to the Illinois. He arrived at Kaskaskia in April.

Easter was in the air. He preached on the Resurrection before an altar of skin and saplings as the tribal elders sat around him and a thousand braves stood in an outer circle, while the women and children listened intently from the background. All dogs were banished.

"The Great White Spirit has a special place in His heart for this land of prairies, pine forests, and the Mighty Messipi. Let us not exclude Him from *our* hearts!"

He told them that he was very tired and would shortly be going to his rest. "But another missionary will be sent you to carry on my teachings."

His health was broken; the dysentery continued to sap his strength. He felt that he had not much longer to live, and so he started back by canoe with two Indians for the Mission of St. Ignace, to receive the last sacrament from a fellow priest. As the redskins skirted the eastern shore of Lake Michigan, he was unable to assist with the paddling. He lay prostrate. And when it was evident that he would not last out the trip, the Indians beached the canoe and carried him ashore into a wood of oaks. Here his grave was dug.

"I thank God," he murmured, "that I have been permitted to die like Francis Xavier in the wilderness." He was only thirty-eight.

FROM THE ENCYCLICAL ON
THE DEVELOPMENT OF PEOPLES

Racism is not the exclusive lot of young nations, where sometimes it hides beneath the rivalries of clans and political parties, with heavy losses for justice and at the risk of civil war. During the colonial period it often flared up between the colonists and the indigenous population, and stood in the way of mutually profitable understanding, often giving rise to bitterness in the wake of genuine injustices. It is still an obstacle to collaboration among disadvantaged nations and a cause of division and hatred within countries whenever individuals and families see the inviolable rights of the human person held in scorn, as they themselves are unjustly subjected to a regime of discrimination because of their race or their color.

— POPE PAUL VI

TO SET MEN FREE

The first-century apostle presented to the world the powerful figure of the liberating Person of Christ, a man who had come to free men from the great barriers that held them imprisoned, the barrier of sin between men and God, as well as the barriers between men caused by differences of sex, race, or inequality in the sharing of this world's goods.

—JOSEPH A. GRASSI, M.M.

PEACE ON EARTH

by J. Murray Abraham

I HEAR A GENTLE POPE'S GENTLE WORDS
   OF TRUTH
  I SEE the harsh reality
  in a harsh, harsh world.

"EVERY HUMAN BEING HAS THE RIGHT
   TO LIFE"
  I SEE twins born in Singell,
  tiny, brown, Nepali twins,
  cradled in the coarse, cracked, grimy hands
   of a coolie woman,
  laid on a blanket crawling with filth,
  laid on a mud floor, clammy and cold, doomed to death,
  they lie there panting their first, precious breath.

"EVERY HUMAN BEING HAS THE RIGHT TO
   PHYSICAL INTEGRITY"
  I SEE beggars swarming around me like flies
  in station after station across sweating India,
  clutching at my arm, grovelling before me
  twisted limbs, sightless eyes, rotting bodies,
   stinking sores.
  My heart aches; my stomach is sick!

"EVERY HUMAN BEING HAS THE RIGHT TO
   THE MEANS NECESSARY AND SUFFICIENT
   FOR A DECENT EXISTENCE"
  I SEE streets in Manila, Madras, Chittagong, Alexandria,

littered with human garbage, male and female,
the about-to-die and the just-now-born,
the homeless, the fondless, clotheless,
   healthless, hopeless,
listlessly lying down to live or die
   with sacred cows and flea-infested curs.

"EVERY HUMAN BEING HAS THE RIGHT TO CLOTHING"

I SEE a grey-haired blind man
feeling his way up a mountain path toward me,
his bamboo stick clicking against the stones;
bare, calloused feet moving carefully, cautiously.
He stands before me
clothed in nothing but reeking rags.
My mind groans with shame:
"Not even a pig in all its muck and misery is clothed
   like one of these."

"EVERY HUMAN BEING HAS THE RIGHT TO SHELTER"

I SEE Sahila's shack, tin-mud prison cell,
fifteen feet by eight of dark, damp, deafening squalor,
the squalling, the bickering, the haunting laughter of
   six children under eight.

"EVERY HUMAN BEING HAS THE RIGHT TO REST"

I SEE filling half that shack and more,
their common bed of planks, rice sacks, two blankets;
bed of rest for puzzled father, pregnant mother,
   puny children.

"EVERY HUMAN BEING HAS THE RIGHT TO MEDICAL CARE"

I SEE Tibetan refugees exhausted by the roadside,
men gaunt with walking, with dysentery, with despair,
babies swollen with worms, with malnutrition,
children scabby with sores from exposure, hunger, dirt.

"EVERY HUMAN BEING HAS THE RIGHT TO SOCIAL SERVICES"

I SEE that vast, foul, fetid sea of suffering: Calcutta,
slum-dwellers in the millions;
social workers, a handful trying to empty
that stinking ocean of misery with leaking thimbles.

"CONSEQUENTLY, EVERY HUMAN BEING HAS THE RIGHT TO SECURITY IN SICKNESS"

I SEE Maleenie, desperate mother, desperate wife,
frantically pleading, pleading frantically:
"He has been sick, he could not work
(nothing to eat in the home).
He could not work, he has been sick
(nothing to eat in the house)."

"EVERY HUMAN BEING HAS THE RIGHT TO SECURITY IN OLD AGE"

I SEE Kalu-ko-babu, squatting on the rock pile,
faint with fever, sunken-cheeked,
like a corpse, grotesquely, indecently moving.
Seventy is he? Eighty?
What happens when the gnarled fingers are too feeble
to hold the chisel and chip the stones?
Young and strong you live on the edge
of the hell of hunger.
But where do you live, where do you live
when you are weak and old?

"EVERY HUMAN BEING HAS THE RIGHT TO SECURITY IN WIDOWHOOD"

I SEE a widow, young and fair and frail;
a child clinging to her,
alone,
she owns nothing!
her only security: the strength of her back,
the strength of her love
to carry and to care for her helpless,
heavy, sweet burden.

"EVERY HUMAN BEING HAS THE RIGHT TO SECURITY IN UNEMPLOYMENT"

I SEE a crowd at our building site —
men, women, boys, girls —
pleading for life,
begging, beseeching, crying for work,
just that — work, any work,
work at twenty cents a back-breaking,
    hand-blistering day.
But work! Rare privilege, work!

"EVERY HUMAN BEING HAS THE RIGHT TO SECURITY WHENEVER HE IS DEPRIVED OF THE MEANS OF SUBSISTENCE AS A RESULT OF CIRCUMSTANCES BEYOND HIS CONTROL"

I SEE a crowd of coolies, standing in the cement shed,
watching the monsoon rain with blank, bitter eyes,
rain — hour after hour after hour,
every hour of rain, an hour less pay, an hour more hunger.
It is raining pain.

"EVERY HUMAN BEING HAS THE RIGHT . . ."

I SEE — but I do not see!
Show me, gentle shepherd John (now that you know),
show me how it can be.
Are those not human, then?
These multitudes in Algeria, India, China, Indonesia?
Are they some strange animals then?
These things with arms and legs and eyes
    and hearts like mine?
But not human; for see — no human rights!
They laugh as I laugh, they cry as I cry,
    they love as I love;
but they live — not as I live!
Eye has not seen, ear has not heard in the Western world
the sights I have seen, the sounds I have heard
    in the East.
O God! the sights I have seen! the sounds I have heard!

And in the West—
the sights I have seen? the sounds I have heard?

MERRY CHRISTMAS!
I SEE stores gaudy with gifts, crammed with crowds
packed with the nerve-racking noise, the clatter,
    the chatter, the clang of cash registers,
    the clickety-clack of toys,
and underneath and above and in and through
    and around it all a song: beautiful and blasphemous
"Silent night, holy night; all is calm, all is bright."

MERRY CHRISTMAS!
I SEE windshield wipers swishing away heavy snowflakes.
My Volks crawls carefully, warily down slippery streets,
until traffic is hopelessly snarled, cars jammed everywhere.
A liquor store!

MERRY CHRISTMAS!
I SEE children tearing paper off toys—
one and two and three and four,
They stop and whine: "Aren't there any more?"
Oh yes, five and six—and up to ten.
And when you've finished, start over again!

MERRY CHRISTMAS!
I SEE the words of TIME (or is it eternity?)
    of LIFE (or is it death?)
"Four billion dollars spent . . ."
For one Christmas Day
For two hundred million overfed Americans,
more than all the help given over ten years
for four hundred million underfed Indians. O God! O God!

GENTLE JOHN, SHEPHERD JOHN,
Call us with your shepherd's voice
Lead us out of mockery, out of mean, meaningless mockery.
Lead us away from the Christmas tree.
Lead us back to the Christmas cave.

Christmas is God born poor,
homeless,
cold,
rejected.
If we have gifts to give, teach us to give to the poor,
the homeless,
the cold,
the rejected.
Christ is the starving beggar on the streets of Calcutta.
Christ is the weeping widow in the slums of Rio de Janeiro.
Christ is the child crying, crying in the hovels of Cairo.
Lead us back to Christ, gentle shepherd John.
Christ needs us.
He brought peace to us, let us now bring peace to Him.
"Pacem in Terris." Amen. Amen.

". . . in the sprawling, humming workshop of this world community, thousands of international servants are busy improving soils, purifying water, harnessing rivers, eradicating disease, feeding children, caring for refugees, diffusing knowledge, training teachers, spreading technology, surveying resources, lending capital, probing the seas, studying the weather, improving diets, setting standards, developing law and working away at a near infinitude of down-to-earth tasks, tasks for which science has given us the knowledge and technology has given us the tools, and common sense has given us the wit to perceive that interest impels us to common enterprise."

— Adlai E. Stevenson

TRAIL'S END

by John J. Considine

> Spirited away by bandits, Father Gerard Donovan was
> finally found strangled and partly eaten by wolves.

The hum of the airplane motor sounded to Father Quirk like
the orchestral dirge before the final denouement of the tragedy.
With the assistant consul at Mukden, Raymond Ludden, he
was flying from Mukden to Huai-Jen for a final identification
of the body found on the Manchukuo mountainside. That it was
Father Donovan, no one any longer entertained any doubt, but
the routine procedure had to be complied with. To the waiting
Maryknollers the matter of greatest concern was the return
of the remains.

The air journey was a brief one. Just after ten o'clock on a
Sunday morning, the machine curled down to the Huai-Jen
flying field. The authorities were waiting, with unfailing Eastern
courtesy, and a group of local officials bowed solemnly to the
two men as they alighted. It was a bleak February day with a
pale, heatless sun. They mounted the military truck which had
been sent for them and, as they rumbled off, Father Quirk felt
the great cold grip him like a vice.

At least there would now be no more uncertainty, he reflected,
and was startled at the satisfaction the thought gave him. For
months there had been that ever-present burden on his mind,
that load like lead on his spirit and on that of every other Mary-

knoller in Manchukuo. At least there was no more uncertainty. Doubt had given way forever, and this, after a long night of waiting, had its recompense. But there remained the tragic fact that with the dawn all hope of a humanly happy outcome had departed.

Yet what a privilege, what a glory, it was for Father Jerry and for all Maryknollers in Manchukuo! Here was a baptism of blood; and already, riding in that cold lorry, Father Quirk felt himself distinguished as the sharer in a rare honor.

The lorry halted, and Father Quirk and Mr. Ludden found themselves before a small house in a private compound, which the authorities had converted into a mortuary chapel. At its entrance floral pieces were massed. When the two men approached, guards came to attention. Inside, in the center of the room, stood a large Chinese coffin, its lid in place. Here, too, were flowers and more guards who came to attention.

"May we have the cover removed?" asked Mr. Ludden quietly.

Soldiers quickly complied. Father Quirk saw that the body had been wrapped carefully in a winding sheet of medicated gauze and that it rested on a bed of soft straw. A large white silk cloth covered the head and upper part of the body.

"May the silk be removed?" he heard Mr. Ludden ask, and he braced himself to face what the coffin held.

He knew in his heart what a privilege, what a glory, it was to die as Father Jerry had died. Some day men would sing praises of it. But before him starkly, cruelly, death appeared, and in the icy air of the room beads of perspiration started from Father Quirk's forehead, while every muscle of his body became tense. He felt himself swaying, "God be merciful," he gasped, and put his hand to his head as if he were numbed by a blow.

He must not show too much feeling, he told himself immediately, and resolutely pulled himself together. He was in the presence here of Orientals, who looked for self-discipline on occasions like this. Then his eyes fell again on the face before him, and all other thoughts fled. Father Jerry who in life was ever smiling, lay here with no smile. Where there had always been vigor and warmth now was only haggardness—a murky white skin pulled tightly over the bones. He who had belittled all pain while he lived could not hide its traces now, for every feature bore the terrible stamp of it, of the long, hard months of suffering.

But there was on Father Jerry's face the mark of something deeper than physical suffering. To Father Quirk came the thought of Christ on Calvary. Was it wrong to make the comparison, he wondered; was it disrespectful, with this picture before him, to imagine he heard Father Jerry calling in anguish on some Manchu mountainside, "My God, my God, why hast thou forsaken me?"

No, it was not wrong, he told himself. With Father Jerry's faith, his boundless willingness, his understanding of victory through sacrifice, God evidently had asked of him something more than hardships and pain. He had tried him by weeks and months of seeming desertion. He had called upon him to quaff deprivation to its dregs.

Father Quirk left his musing and helped Mr. Ludden with his official task. On a table by the coffin they saw what remained of Father Jerry's effects; the ragged upper half of a cassock; his Maryknoll cincture; his eyeglasses, with one bow broken; the torn fragments of his white shirt with the cuff links in place. And there were the garments his captors had given him; an old padded coat and a pair of trousers, both worn and verminous.

There were no shoes. Probably they had been taken when he was put to death. Two toes of the left foot had been frozen before death; a piece of cotton was wrapped about them. But both feet were in such a condition that it was hard to understand how they could have been used for walking.

On the table, too, was the piece of rope, the thickness of a clothesline, that had been wound double about the missioner's neck; and there was the piece of green sapling that had served as tourniquet. Over an inch deep in his neck ran the furrow made by the rope; the throat was crushed and the nape of the neck was marked by a deeper hollow where the knot had pressed.

A broken, twisted body, a few tattered clothes, a rope, and

a stick — if mere physical things counted, here was the inventory. The examination completed, Father Quirk dropped to his knees. The two Americans then silently took their leave.

The next duty was a visit to the Huai-Jen military authorities, who were waiting to give an explanation of all that had taken place. Mr. Ludden and Father Quirk were received with deference by the officers, one of whom reviewed for them, with the aid of a map, the entire case, going over the numerous steps taken by the Japanese to effect the captured priest's release.

"Finally," said the officer, "at six o'clock on the morning of February 10, the Nagashima unit of the Manchukuo Pacification Force arrested a Communist bandit named Fu-sheng, who belonged to what was called the First Anti-Japanese Communist Army of the Northeast. Fu-sheng revealed to them that the dead body of Father Donovan had been abandoned in the neighborhood of Niu-Wei-Tou-Shan. In close cooperation with the Kurosaki unit of the Japanese garrison here at Huai-Jen, the Nagashima unit began an immediate search. By ten o'clock, at a point some two hundred yards from the base of the mountain, they discovered the remains of the murdered missioner."

Mr. Ludden in the name of his Government, and Father Quirk for the Maryknollers, offered their thanks to the authorities. When the missioner expressed a desire to return to Fushun with the body, the officers explained that the road was too dangerous and they were anxious to have the visitors go back by plane. The two were waiting at the air field when a friendly young officer came up to Father Quirk and led him aside. "There, *Shen Fu,*" he said, pointing to the distant horizon, "is the mountain, sixteen *li* from the outskirts of the city, at the base of which we found the body."

"Could I not visit the spot?" asked Father Quirk eagerly.

The officer shook his head. "No, *Shen Fu,* it is too dangerous in these troubled times. But the government is marking the place with a tablet, and some day a visit will be possible."

Father Quirk stared at the barren, forbidding fastness and tried to reconstruct the last hours of Father Jerry. When found, the body was frozen as hard as stone, and so for the medical examiner it had been difficult to determine how long the priest had been dead; he was certain, however, that the end had come some time during the previous January.

Perhaps the immediate reason for his death had been Father Jerry's inability to travel farther. From the experiences of Father Burns during his months among the bandits, Father Quirk realized how difficult it was for the outlaws, hunted on every side, to secure provisions. The practice of the first weeks, when special food was purchased for the captive, had no doubt been long since abandoned, and Father Jerry had been forced to eat whatever crude and ill-cooked nourishment could be found. Growing fear of the pressing troops and growing irritation at the waning hope of any ransom might have made his guards less and less considerate of the prisoner. There were undoubtedly many days spent in warm hideouts, as the vermin in his clothing bore witness; but these periods were broken by the alerts, when, day or night, the band was forced to take to the road, their prisoner with them.

Quite possibly Father Jerry had had to submit to the indignity common to local captives, of being led by a rope around his neck, the rope attached to the saddle of one of the riders. Weakened by exposure and lack of nourishment, he had been forced to stumble along as best he could behind the horse. Father Quirk, as he stared at the mountain, could well imagine half-starved Father Jerry dragging his faltering feet over the mountainside—until there came a last and fatal fall. "Why bother any more?" perhaps had been the callous remark of his captors. "He means nothing to us. He is holding us back."

Then the decision was taken, the sapling cut. A bruise over the right temple suggested that someone had mercifully struck the captive a blow with a blunt instrument before the traditional Chinese form of strangling took place. Father Quirk felt a small satisfaction in the possibility that Father Jerry had experienced no suffering during his last moments of life. And perhaps, because of the Oriental regard for the dead, which among criminals often outstrips their respect for the living, it could well have been that the lifeless corpse of Father Jerry was carried some distance and placed by a road so that eventually it might be discovered and given proper burial.

And thus that tortured body came to rest. Quiet it lay in the winter waste, hardened by cold, buried in snow, and then uncovered by the shrill wind and the gentle sun.

But it lay in peace, for nature is never hostile. Even the wolves and dogs and small rodents which came upon it meant no disrespect. If, distracted by hunger, they stopped and gnawed at the prostrate form, as the many tooth marks gave eloquent testimony, this was in no animosity of spirit.

Only man can be truly hostile, can show hatred and cruelty and disdain.

THE FRUIT SELLER

Majid sells his fruit
  From a gay, red stall
West of the padang
  By the market wall;

He sells bright oranges
  And Chinese tangerines,
He sells red papayas
  And purple mangosteens;

And though we have money
  When we reach his stall,
When we say goodbye to him,
  We've no money left at all.

— MARGARET LEONG

JAPAN'S OLDEST PEOPLE

by Albert J. Nevins

No one knows where they came from but they go back beyond the dawn of history.

The Ainus were the original inhabitants of the islands today known as Japan. Where they came from, no one knows. Archaeologists tell us that they were in Japan at the time of the Stone Age. But anthropologists list them as one of the unsolved mysteries. Today the Ainus are a vanishing race.

The only existing Ainus are to be found on the island of Hokkaido—about 15,000 of them, of whom only about 4,000 are of pure blood. In 1915 the Ainu population was about 200,000 but war, famine, and disease rapidly reduced their number. It seems safe to predict that within another generation or two no Ainus will be left.

For many centuries the Ainus resisted the Japanese way of life. But their resistance was always sporadic, the whole tribe never uniting in a single effort. Even so, up until our own time, they managed to preserve their unique dress, their language, and their customs. However, modern civilization was their undoing. A recent survey found only two Ainus who spoke the pure Ainu language. Ainu children wear the same type of clothes as the Japanese. They speak Japanese. They farm like the Japanese. They have taken Japanese names. They marry the Japanese. The old Ainu festivals are no longer celebrated, while the Japanese ones are.

As far as anthropologists can demonstrate, the Ainus were

always in Japan. They stretch back into the neolithic era of that land. But anthropologists believe (although they cannot prove it) that the Ainus came originally from Europe, probably around Russia. How or why they migrated such a distance will never be known.

The Ainus are a white race, surrounded by a vast sea of yellow. They are true aborigines, and are said to be the most hairy people in the world. Their culture has always been primitive, yet their shell mounds, which dot Japan, go back to the Stone Age. The Ainus never had a system for writing, so their history was lost. Their language bore no relationship to the Japanese tongue other than that, during the several thousand years when the two races mingled, the Japanese accepted some Ainu words into their own vocabulary. For example, the word "Fuji," the name of Japan's most famous volcano is an Ainu word that means "volcano."

Modern Ainu history parallels that of the American Indians. Just as the white men pushed the Indians farther and farther back, so the Japanese influx into the islands pushed the Ainus back. Once the aborigines covered all the islands of Japan. Today the last remnants are to be found only on northernmost Hokkaido. Like many Indian tribes, the Ainu seem to have lost the will to survive.

What the buffalo was to the American Indian the bear was to the Ainu. What culture they had, was developed around this huge, lumbering beast. The bear was the center of their religion and the heart of their folklore. The main festival of the year was the Bear Festival, when a bear would be killed after many cruelties. The Japanese have banned this festival.

Ainu dress was ornate and cumbersome. The women wore long, heavy shell-and-bone necklaces. The heavily bearded men wore long, flowing garments, with a crown, the front of which was fashioned into a bear's head. They carried sword, spear, and bow and arrows — reminders of their hunting prowess.

Few Ainus ever became Christian. No mission was established among them, although missions were located among the Japanese on Hokkaido. They remained a people apart.

Today the few remaining Ainus make their living as tourist attractions. They put on the old dress to be seen and photographed by the travel-loving Japanese. They carve little figurines from wood which they sell as souvenirs.

It seems tragic that within a few years one of the earth's first human families will be no more. But that is the history and pattern of modern times. Simple and peace-loving people find it hard to exist in today's aggressive world.

L U L L A B Y

Now that the shadows
  Are long and deep,
Forget the warm day
  And go to sleep;

Soft rains are falling
  On the bamboo leaf.
High tides are breaking
  On the coral reef;

Over the padang
  The night winds spread,
White birds are flying
  Far overhead;

O now that the shadows
  Are long and deep,
Forget the warm day,
  And sleep, sleep, sleep.

— MARGARET LEONG

SONG FOR TODAY, III

I love Your waterways
    in lonely hills,
The silken spray
singing in the sun
among the sunburnt rocks,
    tumbling down
    in a quiet rumble,
    glazed in the sheen
    of a summer sun.
My heart is with Your hills,
among those secret waterways,
    chanting melodies
    in dizzy torrents,
    splashing white fire
    down the rocky ladders.
There go I, where liquid silver churns
among fern-deckled sluices to the widening
expanse of ocean roll;
    and outward to the awful ocean
    outward to ever and beyond,
    down to the depths and under,
    swirling and swelling
    in the wild waters welling,
    ever and ever
    and always compelling.
Then spent at length, I turn and come,
riding the rhythm of water and wind,
reveling in the flowing fountain,
to nuzzle myself on the rustling sand of the shore,
colt-like to the bosom of its mare.

—JOHN GEITNER, M.M.

THE CHALLENGE OF THE ROCK OF DEATH

by Lawrence J. Connors

Formosan aborigines guide two Maryknollers into sacred country where strange winds brought death to scoffers.

It all started late one afternoon after Mass. The sun had lost its heat, but it still suffused the sky with a brilliant orange that threw strange and mysterious shadows across Formosa's inaccessible mountains. This was my first trip to the village of Ban Tai and my first week among the aborigines. Father Bob Baudhuin, a veteran of two years in the mountains, was taking me to every village to give me the big picture of Maryknoll's work among the aborigines.

On this particular afternoon, we sat with a group of men while the women were busy preparing supper. The faces of the aborigines ranged from the wrinkled and tattooed features of Te Mu, the chief, to the darker and somewhat fierce expressions of the younger men.

It was during a lull in the conversation that Father Baudhuin pointed to a far-off peak and asked Te Mu if he had ever climbed it. Te Mu nodded in the affirmative. Father then asked the same question of the others, but none of them had ever set foot on that particular mountain. There was a kind of hesitation in their answers. Te Mu sensed our puzzlement.

"We men of the mountains do not go into that region very often," Te Mu told us. "Beyond that mountain is a great stone. It is feared by all our people. Those who walk into its presence must walk and speak with great care. It has already brought death to fifteen warriors of our village, and death to many from other villages."

I glanced at Father Baudhuin to see if my leg was being pulled, but he was all seriousness. Te Mu began to tell the story. He told how in 1931 six warriors from Ban Tai crossed to the other side of the island to take heads. Returning proud and victorious, they passed the rock. One young warrior who had four enemy heads hanging from a belt around his waist taunted the rock.

"I don't fear you," he shouted. "I am strong and brave. See! I take four heads to my home!"

Four others in the party joined in the taunting. Only one remained silent. As the men shouted, huge hailstones began to pelt them. Then a sudden and violent wind swooped down and carried the men over the edge of the cliff to their deaths. The only survivor was the man who had kept silence. There was another hunting party that dared to shoot at the rock, and another that threw leftover food at the rock. In each case, we were told, the offenders were killed by being swept off the cliff.

The next day we passed through three more villages, and made more inquiries about the rock. The aborigines all knew its story, and all feared its power. We were told that the rock had a head, arms, and legs. The aborigines called it "the first rock," and some tribes believed that mankind had sprung from it. We were told that any who approached it must use a ritual language. For example, if it is cold, you must say it is hot; or if the sun is shining, you must say it is raining. The visitor must never point at the rock or wash in its presence. As you approach the rock, you must beg it not to harm you.

The story of the rock fascinated Father Baudhuin and myself. We talked about it at night. Finally, I suggested that we go and see it for ourselves. Father Baudhuin agreed immediately.

"It won't be easy," he remarked. "It will take us about three days of rough hiking from the nearest village. Since we'll have to sleep out each night, we had better pick a time when there is little chance of rain. Say, November."

About a month later we picked up an additional member to our party. He was Captain Sid Cook, a tall Texan stationed with the U.S. military mission here; he had spent four years in a mountain patrol unit along the Austrian border. We were glad he was interested because, besides being good company, he was able to get needed equipment, such as sleeping bags and pack boards.

The date for departure was set for November 17, but at the last minute trouble developed. The aborigines did not want to go. It was one thing to talk about such a journey when it was weeks away; but as the time approached, it became more frightening. Te Mu, the chief, finally saved the day.

"If the Fathers are not afraid, I am not afraid," he said. "If they go, I go."

This brave statement bolstered the courage of the others, and seven aborigines volunteered to accompany us. They ranked in age from a boy of fifteen to Te Mu, who was over sixty-five years of age. They refused to have anything to do, however, with the captain's pack boards. They loaded supplies and equipment into their hand-woven net sacks, despite the captain's insistence that his pack boards were scientifically designed for maximum efficiency. Everyone wanted to carry the guns that the captain had brought—a double-barreled shotgun and a 7 mm. Mauser. The aborigines have their own guns, all of which are homemade flintlocks.

Thus we moved out of the village. Ahead of us lay the Rock of Death. We wondered what was in store.

About noon we reached a river and we were to recross it many times during the rest of the day as we made our way through towering mountains.

"Father we have agreed to a trip for one week," Te Mu said, "but if you take off your shoes everytime we come to a river, we'll be on the trail for a month. We're going to have to cross this same river twenty-nine times. So leave your shoes on or off."

About four-thirty in the afternoon, Te Mu gave the signal to make camp. The place chosen was a camp site for aboriginal hunters who roamed these mountains in quest of game, particularly wild boar. The site had a small lean-to, which gave little protection. That night was cold, terribly cold. Father Bob, Captain Sid, and myself dozed fitfully in our sleeping bags. But the aborigines never slept at all. They built an enormous fire and sat cross-legged around it all night. We were beginning to get a glimpse into the remarkable endurance of these mountain men. At dawn, we were all glad to be off again.

The second day was one of the toughest I have ever lived through. The aborigines were as nimble as goats, while we were as clumsy as oxen. To distract myself I began putting my feet in the same places as Te Mu. It was amazing. Without breaking his pace, his foot always found a support—a root, a stone, a hard clump of dirt. Most of the time, I never saw the foothold until I stepped on it. Captain Cook began complaining that the aborigines were not human.

"In the Alps no one ever heard of climbing a mountain straight up!" he said. "We zigzag."

"Straight up is much quicker," replied Te Mu without faltering.

At one point we came upon an aborigine's kill—seven wild boars. All that was left of each was a skull with two protruding tusks. Te Mu said the tusks made good pipes, so I took a pair. About this time, the trail ceased completely, and we had to beat our way through the thick brush, always climbing.

About three, we broke out over the timber line into a plateau of high, razor-sharp grass. We began to realize that we would never make our designated camp. We found a small shelf with a level spot and camped there. We only had a cupful of water among us, so supper was scarce that night. It was much colder than the first night, and when daybreak came we began climbing again without breakfast. The following couple of hours were up the sheer face of a cliff, the most dangerous climb of our whole trip.

About ten in the morning we reached a beautiful lake, whose surface was still frozen. I was dehydrated, so I cracked the ice and drank my fill. It was a mistake that was to cause me much distress the rest of the day. We breakfasted there.

The chief reassured us that we were not too far from our goal when we started again. After crossing a small peak, our party halted. Te Mu whispered, "There it is!" He did not dare point with his finger, but kept jutting his chin toward the opposite peak.

Looking across the valley, we saw a gigantic rock. It was a freak of nature, completely dwarfing trees of a hundred feet high. It rose out of the forest like a colossal knife, as if some giant had taken a stone razor blade and set it up. It was easy to understand how this strange monolith had become an object of superstition.

To reach the rock we would have to descend into the valley and climb the opposite mountain, but the aborigines did not wish to go any farther. They felt that seeing the rock should be enough for us. But we insisted we wanted to go to the rock. We intended to say Mass there and attach a crucifix to it. Finally, the aborigines' discussion reached a climax.

"I have no wife or children," said Pi Tu, an older man. "Besides, I owe it to my religion to go and protect the Fathers." Today, because of that statement, Pi Tu is held by his tribe as a man of great faith, a man without fear.

Pi Tu was joined by John the catechist, and with these two guides we started for the rock. As we blazed our trail, we came across two interesting finds. One was a tree with a number of knife strokes cut in its bark. Pi Tu explained that the marks had been made by a war party to indicate the strength of the group. The second was a small clearing that looked as if it had been plowed by a bulldozer. Pi Tu told us it had been done by wild boars grubbing for roots. He said it would be a good place to wait for game.

About two hours later we reached the rock. We had expected

it to be big, but it proved to be immense. It went straight up, over ten stories high. It was a sheer cliff, impossible to climb. At the base we set up an altar and wedged a crucifix into the stone. Father Baudhuin offered Mass, and our two guides received Communion.

When Mass was over, it was late afternoon. The wind was beginning to increase, and the air grew cold. Pi Tu suggested we start back. First we carved on a big hinocki tree next to the rock our names (in English and Chinese); the date; and the fact that Mass had been celebrated. We left the crucifix and hurried back to camp for our first decent meal in two days.

The trip home was quick and dangerous. Beware when an aborigine proposes a shortcut! It is always straight up or down. The only thing that can be said for descending a mountain is that you don't have to use will power. The law of gravity acts as a substitute.

We received several unexpected bonuses from the trip. Aborigines from all the villages have been questioning us about the rock and asking to see our pictures of it. The fact that we said Mass there, left a crucifix, and returned safely has been a big blow against superstition. The five days in the mountains also left me with a new and deep respect for the nimbleness, endurance, and ingenuity of our aboriginal people.

THE SON OF GOD

The fount of Mary's joy
  Revealed now lies,
For, lo, has not the Boy
  His Father's eyes?

— CHARLES L. O'DONNELL, C.S.C.

LETTERS FROM CATHAY

by John of Monte Corvino

John of Monte Corvino walked from Rome to China
to found the Church there.

I arrived in Cathay, the kingdom of the Tartar emperor, who is
called the Great Khan. With the letters of the Lord Pope I
invited him to accept the Catholic faith of our Lord Jesus Christ.
But he was too accustomed to idolatry. Nevertheless, he be-
stowed many kindnesses on Christians. I have already been
here twelve years [in 1305].

There are Nestorians here who claim the title of Christian,
even though they are far from the teachings of Christianity.
They are so strong hereabouts that they prevent Christians of
any other rite from setting up even a small oratory. One cannot
preach any Christian doctrine save the Nestorian heresy. Yet
none of the Apostles or their disciples ever came to Cathay.

The Nestorians have persecuted me incessantly either
themselves or by means of those whom they bribe with money.
They say I have not been sent by the Lord Pope. I am said to
be a magician, a foreign agent, and a deceiver of men. After a
while they even produced false witnesses who claimed another
legate had been sent [from Rome], bearing immense treasure
for the emperor. But I am supposed to have killed the real
legate in India and to have taken away the treasure. This lie
about me persisted for about five years. As a result I was

dragged to judgment several times and threatened with death. At last God so disposed that some of them confessed the truth; the emperor afterward published my innocence and the wickedness of my rivals, whom he sent into exile with their wives and children.

I was alone in this foreign land without any companion for eleven years, until Friar Arnold Alemannus of the Cologne Province arrived. He has been here for two years now. I have built a church in the city of Cambalec, which is the chief residence of the Khan. Six years ago I finished it. It has a campanile in which I have hung three bells. As I recall, I have baptized up until today about six thousand people. Were it not for the calumnies I mentioned, I would have already baptized more than thirty thousand. As it is, I perform baptisms constantly.

I likewise have bought one hundred and fifty boys, one after the other. They are the [unwanted] sons of pagan parentage, and under seven and nine years of age. They had no training before. I have baptized them and taught them about our religion in the Latin language. I wrote out the Psalter for them, with thirty hymns and two Breviaries. Already eleven boys know the Divine Office and attend choir as it is done in our friaries [back home], whether I am present or not. Many of them are copying the Psalter and other useful texts. The emperor is very pleased with their chanting. I ring the bell for all the [canonical] hours and I pray the Divine Office with a friary full of "infants and sucklings." We sing the best we can, for we do not have a copy of the Office with notes.

There was a certain king in this region, George, formerly a Nestorian, and of the family of the renowned king called Prester John. The very first year I came here he took a liking to me. He was converted to the truth of the Catholic faith through me, and I even gave him minor orders. He used to serve my Mass in his royal robes. Even though the Nestorians accused him of apostasy, he brought a large part of his subjects to the true faith. King George built a beautiful church with royal generosity in honor of the Holy Trinity and of the Lord Pope. He called it the Roman Church (to distinguish it from the heretical Christians).

Six years ago this King George died, a true Christian. He left his son and heir scarcely out of his baby clothes. Now the boy is about nine years old. The brothers of King George, because of their own Nestorian error, led back all whom the king converted, into their original heresy. I was all by myself then and could not reach that church in the country of King George, because it is twenty days' journey away. If only some co-operative helpers would come, I hope in God that the Church there might be reformed. Even now I have the right to reform it through the permission of the late King George . . .

I beg my confriars who will read this letter to bring its contents to the attention of the Lord Pope and the Cardinals and the Procurator of our Order in the Roman Curia. I beseech the Minister General of our Order to send me an Antiphonal, the Lives of the Saints, the Gradual, and a Psalter with chant notation. I have only one portable Breviary and a small Missal. If I have even one sample, the boys can copy it.

Even now I am in the process of building another church, to divide the boys into more than one group. I myself am getting old. The fact I am gray is due more to work and troubles than to old age, although I am eighty-eight years old. I am well versed in the language and script used commonly by all the Tartars. Already I have translated the whole New Testament and Psalter into the language and script of the Tartars. I had it copied in their most elegant script, from which I read and preach in open witness to the law of Christ.

I planned with the King George I have mentioned above — had he lived — to translate the entire Office from the Latin, so that he could have it chanted all over his kingdom. Even while he was alive I celebrated Mass according to the Latin Rite in the church he built, but in the language and from the script of the Tartar people — both the words of the Canon and the words of the Preface. King George's son is, in fact, named John, after me. I hope in God that he follows in his father's footsteps.

[John of Monte Corvino's second letter was written later during the same year.]

In this year of our Lord 1305, I have begun a new establishment at the very gate of the Lord Khan. There is only one street lying between us and his court—just a stone's throw from the door of his palace. Peter of Lucolongo, a faithful Christian and an important merchant from Tauris, bought the land to which I am referring and has given it to me for the love of God.

By the providence of God, I am sure there could be no more valuable and fitting location in the whole empire of the Khan to build a Catholic church. I received the property at the beginning of last August. With the help of benefactors, by the feast of St. Francis [October 4] the wall around the property was finished, plus the cells, workshops, courtyard, and the oratory, which can hold two hundred people. On account of winter I could not complete the church. Nevertheless I have lumber piled up in the friary here, so through the mercy of God, I will finish the church this summer.

I tell you it is a wonderful thing to see the new arrivals in the city who have not heard of our place. They see the new building and the red cross placed on top of it. They hear us solemnly chanting the Office in the oratory, even though we do not have any notes, and they are amazed. Sometimes when we sing, the Khan can hear our voices from his own room. This wonderful fact is broadcast far and wide among the people of the region, and will bear important fruit according as the goodness of God disposes and ordains.

LE CHEEP

by Sister Maria del Rey

> "These French Sisters! They would put the devil him-
> self to good work and make a right handy fellow out of
> him!"

It's a poor convent, indeed, that can't afford a pet. Nearly
everyone I know has some stray on which to lavish affectionate
forgiveness. It may be a canary in the superior's office; it may
be a fern in the community room; or it may be a flea-bitten dog
who haunts the kitchen door step.

In our house at Baguio in the Philippines, it was Tessie the
cat, named after the great Saint Teresa but not much like her in
virtue. Tess had her kittens regularly under the house or in the
laundry basket or on somebody's best habit. She knew our hora-
rium to the minute. She never failed to leap to the first sound of
the bell for the refectory, but chapel bells never broke her
sleep. Every one of us would have heard with joy that "that
cat!" had been done away with; but do it ourselves? Ah no,
poor Tessie wasn't as bad as all that.

In Hong Kong they have a dog who accepts you as one of the
community only after several years' residence in the house and
a lot of persuasive feeding. The Sisters construct elaborate
barricades of school desks and portable blackboards every
night to keep the all-too-zealous watchdog from making mince-
meat of every visitor, either clerical or lay.

* From *Pacific Hopscotch,* by Sister Maria del Rey. Copyright Catholic Foreign Mission Society of America, Inc.

A cute little frog used to hop around the Kyoto garden and, from a tree outside, make his daily visit to the Blessed Sacrament through the chapel window. A real contemplative he was, spending hours with eyes unblinkingly fixed on the tabernacle.

But I met the most beloved pet of any convent I know, in Seoul, Korea, when the St. Paul de Chartres Sisters introduced me to Le Cheep.

Sister Eugenia arranged the meeting. She is one of three French Sisters in a community of 170 Koreans. My high-school French does not extend much beyond, "Please pass the butter," and "Thank you," and I think Sister Eugenia could not even pass the butter in English. But my poverty in French was hardly noticeable, for *"Oui, oui"* and *"Merci"* filled any space she left in the conversation. Any space she left at all was purely by accident. And a more enthusiastic admirer of "Le Cheep" you could not imagine.

"Come," she said one afternoon, "come! Le Cheep will take us around Seoul. It is even now at the door, *ma mère*. Le Cheep is waiting for you." I didn't know who Le Cheep was, but certainly I would not keep him waiting.

There it stood — a jeep, and what a jeep! The chassis was blue, "blue for the Holy Virgin," Sister explained. The heavy wooden superstructure, a cross between a safe-deposit vault and a dog house, was bright yellow. The windows were small and awfully queer in shape. "But, *mon Dieu*," exclaimed Sister, "what could we do? The glass was left from our very beautiful stained glass window. The children (very natural!) they break so many things! Yes, the glass is from that stained glass window, broken it is now many years.

"Look well, see here the hand of the Holy Virgin. We scrub very hard the glass, but no, the hand remains. There — there on the rear window, is the eye of *La Sainte Vierge*. Good, is it not," she concluded triumphantly, "that the Mother of God regards well the back where we cannot see for ourselves?"

The chauffeur, one of those indescribable convent handymen, opened the heavy wooden door with a heave-ho and a vast show of strength. The door would have done quite well on the great meat ice-box at the Maryknoll Seminary in New York. It must have been three solid inches thick. Indeed, as I stepped high into Le Cheep, I had the strange feeling that, instead of seats, there would be great hooks to hang oneself upon and I fancied I could feel the chill of death envelop my rigid frame. But Sister Eugenia was rattling on, displaying the beauties of her beloved cheep.

"See the door," she pointed out. "Of fine wood, and double the thick. So very frequent in the street comes the army truck. 'Out my way! Out my way!' the horn noises at all. But sometimes, it is not possible for out-the-way in time. 'So,' says *Notre Mère* (oh, she is wonderful in the head, our *Notre Mère!*) 'we will double-thick the doors and walls in Le Cheep.' "

The inside, oh, the inside! The jeep had been lined with blankets and then covered with blue cotton cloth, ornamented with tiny roses and flowers. "Like the nightgown of my *grand-mère* in France!" Sister Eugenia was quick to add. "My *grand-mère*, she is dead now, but oh, so holy!"

Ceiling, wall, even the seats, were all blue cotton roses and flowers. Inside, Le Cheep was a gay little padded cell. "You see," said Sister, "very rough the roads and sometimes we must hold with both hands the seat. Even so, bop! and your head strikes the wall or ceiling. 'It is well,' says *Notre Mère*, 'that we put the stuffing over our heads and around us.' How wise is our *Notre Mère!* "

She saw me gaping at the thumbtacks of many colors which sprinkled the flowers, tacking the cotton and the blankets to the walls.

"You admire our tacks-for-the-thumb!" she was delighted. "At first we have the plain ones, silver only. It is not pretty, but we are poor religious, *ma mère*. What can we ask for in this here-below life? Must we have grandeur on earth and yet ask also for heaven? *Mais, non!* But the Good God, He is ever mindful that we poor creatures love well the beauty. Ah, He is good. He arrange to break camp a unit of those so-good American soldiers near this place. Many things they are too lazy to pack up and take away. Comes the Colonel to us. 'You want these?' he asks and throws to us many boxes of these tacks-for-the-thumb. Ay, *mon Dieu,* we are so happy! You can see for yourself, *ma mère;* I do not exaggerate. So everywhere inside Le Cheep — here red, here green, here gold, here yellow, here white. Like stars, no? So elegant! Like stars of many colors set in the blue of my *grandmère's* nightdress!"

We settled ourselves on the padded seats; the handyman let that ice-box door slam upon us, and crawled into the front seat. Sister Eugenia had one more suggestion.

"*Ma mère,* you will see our city! But let me suggest. First, you will close one eye and rest it well. The windows — yes, there is much much room for one eye. But for the other, no. It is not good for it to try to see through the hand of the Holy Virgin."

Thus I saw Seoul. I marvelled at the honored place in the community this monstrous jeep enjoyed. Would you, in a big-hearted moment, trade your Buick or your Cadillac for it? Ah no. The Sisters of St. Paul de Chartres in Seoul would as soon trade in the sainted *grandmère* herself, blue-flowered nightgown and all, for an American-model *grandmère* who wears pajamas!